Life's
Companion

Christina
Baldwin

Life's
Companion

Journal Writing as a Spiritual Quest

Illustrations by Susan Boulet

BANTAM BOOKS
NEW YORK · TORONTO · LONDON · SYDNEY · AUCKLAND

LIFE'S COMPANION: JOURNAL WRITING
AS A SPIRITUAL QUEST
A Bantam Book / January 1991
PRINTING HISTORY
Bantam New Age and the accompanying figure design as well as the statement "the search for meaning, growth and change" are trademarks of Bantam Books, a division of Bantam Doubleday Dell Publishing Group, Inc.

Library of Congress Cataloging-in-Publication Data
Baldwin, Christina.
Life's companion : journal writing as a spiritual quest / Christina Baldwin.
p.   cm.
ISBN 0-553-35202-4 (pbk.)
1. Spiritual life. 2. Diaries—Authorship. 3. Baldwin, Christina. 4. Meditation. I. Title.
BL624.B34   1990
291.4'46—dc20   90-38370
                                                                CIP

Published simultaneously in the United States and Canada

Bantam Books are published by Bantam Books, a division of Bantam Doubleday Dell Publishing Group, Inc. Its trademark, consisting of the words "Bantam Books" and the portrayal of a rooster, is Registered in U.S. Patent and Trademark Office and in other countries. Marca Registrada. Bantam Books, 1540 Broadway, New York, New York 10036.

PRINTED IN THE UNITED STATES OF AMERICA
BVG   0 9 8 7 6

THIS BOOK
IS DEDICATED
TO JOY

CONTENTS

I.   Laying the Groundwork

1. *Journeys and Journals*   3
2. *How to Write a Spiritual Journal*   17
3. *The Art of Questioning*   33
4. *Practicing Silence*   47

    Meditation: Greeting Silence   62

II.   Conditions for Travel

5. *The Evolving Self*   67
6. *Writing Your Spiritual History*   79
7. *The Role of Disorder*   91
8. *The Role of Wonder*   103

    Meditation: Sacred Moments   114

III.   Types of Guidance

9.   *The Guidance of the Body*   119
10. *Dreams: Sleep's Guidance*   135
11. *Intuition's Inner Guidance*   151

12.   Sacred Ritual   163
      Meditation: Finding an Inner Guide   174

              IV.   The Four Major Practices

13.   *Love*   179
14.   *Forgiveness*   195
15.   *Trust*   211
16.   *Acceptance*   225
      Meditation: Forgiving Yourself and Others   238

              V.   Applying the Four Practices

17.   *Paying Attention*   243
18.   *Learning to Follow*   257
19.   *Dreaming, Longing, Acting*   271
20.   *Becoming Persons of Power*   287
      Meditation: Creating a Five-Year Vision   298

              VI.   Traveling in the World

21.   *The Point of Return*   303
22.   *Finding Your People*   313
23.   *Choosing Your Stand*   327
24.   *Faith in the Process*   339
      Meditation: Child of the Universe   346

      End Piece   349
      Acknowledgments   351

Throughout this book,
I have chosen to use the term
the sacred
to mean whatever you mean
by the words you use
for spirit.

Meditations are offered to support the topics in each section. Meditation is best used if you can relax in a comfortable sitting or reclining position and have someone read the meditation quietly to you, pausing where ellipses indicate. Tapes of these meditations are also available; see page 353 for further information.

Please feel free to browse, to read this book in whatever manner suits you and your journey.

May you have good journeys and full journals.

How to Use This Book

This book is divided into six parts, each with four chapters and a meditation. The right-hand pages form a continuous narrative. The left-hand pages contain two columns, fingered together, that reflect on and expand the running text.

The outermost column on the left is a series of journal writing exercises, questions, techniques, and suggestions for enriching your writing life. The inner column consists of quotes from published and unpublished sources and from journal entries that relate to the topic at hand.

Many of the quotes used in the inner column were written before the common usage of inclusive language. I have left them in their original form, but please note: The word *man* should be read *human*, and the pronoun *he* should be read *s/he*.

Some of the journal entries are the author's; many are samples donated to the book by friends and students. All are used anonymously to reflect the private and communal nature of this form of writing. All are used with permission and with much gratitude for the willingness of these writers to let us glimpse their innermost thoughts and feelings.

Meditations are offered to support the topics in each section. Meditation is best used if you can relax in a comfortable sitting or reclining position and have someone read the meditation quietly to you, pausing where ellipses indicate. Tapes of these meditations are also available; see page 353 for further information.

Please feel free to browse, to read this book in whatever manner suits you and your journey.

May you have good journeys and full journals.

I.
Laying the
Groundwork

1. JOURNEYS
AND JOURNALS

*I have always known that at last I would take this
road, but yesterday I did not know that it would be
today.*

—*Narihara*

Here comes a journey . . . and there also comes the urge
to write it down, to bear witness to our experience, to
share our questions and the insights that come from
questioning.

The spiritual journey is the one trip we are all taking together.
You may be in a bookstore, a grocery store, at a restaurant, or
home in bed. Whatever you think you're doing, whatever else you
identify as happening, you are also somewhere in the middle of
your spiritual quest. The spiritual quest is that part of life which is
the path within the path. Spirituality is the sacred center out of
which all life comes, including Mondays and Tuesdays and rainy

Choosing a Journal

- Are you going to write by hand?
- Do you want loose-leaf paper or a bound notebook?

Look for a book that lies flat to facilitate writing.

- Lines or no lines?
- Are you going to type?

Create a file, a folder, a three-ring binder that can hold your papers.

- What do you like to write with?

Your journal is a document that you will probably want to keep a while, so you want to avoid anything that will fade or smudge.

- Treat yourself to some simple art supplies: colored pencils, markers, or pastels, whatever you like to play with.

JOURNAL ENTRY

The fancier the notebook, the more quickly I feel compelled to make a mistake: misspell a word, cross out a sentence, do something to create a healthy imperfection.

Page-one Exercises

- Start with flow writing—explained in the next chapter.
- Write a one-page autobiography.
- Plunge in with what is most compelling to you, that has led you to write.
- Make a collage of the day you begin: headlines, a photo of yourself, your horoscope, weather notes, etc.

Saturday afternoons in all their mundane and glorious detail.

The spiritual journey is what the soul is up to while we attend to daily living. The spiritual journey is the soul's life commingling with ordinary life. The fabric tears: the soul sees Monday, Monday sees the soul.

The purpose of this book is to facilitate the commingling between spiritual and ordinary life, to allow you to see both aspects more clearly and to live both aspects more fully. And the easiest, most efficient and delightful way I know to watch these levels of life commingle is to write down the details and stories of your quest as you go.

Writing makes a map, and there is something about a journey that begs to have its passage marked.

Marking passage is an ordinary process. The journey is already ongoing; it's simply a matter of acknowledging it. And the journal is an adaptable practice that can absorb as much or as little attention as you apply to it. It will fluctuate cheerfully, without complaints. The journal takes you and your journey as you are.

I first used the phrase "There comes a journey . . ." when picking up my journal again after a year of not writing. I wanted to declare a purpose, to write down the contract I was making with the universe. I had already been journeying, of course, we all are, but I wanted to state clearly my intention to accept this journey with awareness, to learn to take responsibility.

That was August 1969. I was twenty-three years old, getting ready to leave San Francisco for a year of living and traveling in Europe. The journey metaphor was an obvious choice. I wasn't sure what I was up to but recognized the moment as being significant.

I headed east to New York where I boarded a ship and steamed off into the unknown. I carried my journal with me everywhere and wrote copiously, as it is sometimes easier to do when lifted out of ordinary routine and thrust on one's own resources in strange sur-

I am afoot with my vision. . . . I tramp a perpetual journey.
—Walt Whitman
Song of the Open Road

Journey Walker

In the journal, draw the path you are currently walking:
- What does your life look like realistically, symbolically?
- Write to yourself about your life path. What do you know about where you are coming from and where you are going?

We learn to live consciously through becoming aware of inner and outer events as they are happening. Building a conscious self means becoming increasingly aware of inner events, bodily events and interpersonal events. A conscious self is able to experience in full awareness all the distinctly different components of the self, including feelings, needs, drives and values. A conscious self lives consciously.
—Gershen Kaufman/Lev Raphael
The Dynamics of Power

Journey Watcher

In the journal, draw or describe the watching part of yourself.
- Who is watching?
- Who is acting?
- What is the attitude of the watcher to the walker? (If this is not a helpful attitude, you will discover ways to change that as the journey progresses.)
- Do you remember a moment/event when you became conscious?

roundings. I wrote my way through West Germany, East Germany, Austria, Czechoslovakia, Great Britain, Norway, Sweden, The Netherlands, France, Switzerland, Spain; and I made an important discovery: my real journey had very little to do with traveling Europe, and a whole lot to do with traveling my own mind.

The spiritual journey doesn't require a grand tour. There are no bon voyage parties for the beginning of a quest. We don't even know when it began, we are simply aware one day that we are underway, that we have written a phrase such as "There comes a journey . . ."

Imagine walking down a path, participating in everything around you. You notice actions near and far, you interact with people and deal with obstacles and opportunities along the way. This is the walker: the active self.

Imagine a mirror path running parallel to the path you're walking. The mirror path reflects feelings, thoughts, attitudes, and beliefs about what is happening. This is the watcher: the reflective self.

Together these two selves create consciousness: the awareness of ourselves within our own existence. Consciousness is our second birth, the birth of our capacity to reflect and wonder. Consciousness reveals the connection between action and thought. We hear the mind think. We observe our own behavior. Consciousness is our life's companion, the company we keep inside ourselves.

Consciousness is not just the angel/devil voices of cartoon characters sitting on our shoulders, but a multitude of opinions, reflections, points of guidance, all mixed in with archaic, rote memorizations about how to be a human being, not all of them helpful.

When we take up pilgrimage, consciousness emerges as an ongoing, intimate dialogue within the self. Once awakened, we are aware of and intrigued by the processes of our own minds. Some people speak of becoming conscious as a moment of mental fusion, or a reflecting capacity—like a mirror swinging out from the mind, able to look back on itself.

Conscious people are aware of the influence and guidance available through these inner whispers. The directions for our quest most

"How does one grow up?" I asked a friend. She answered, "By thinking."

—*May Sarton*
Journal of a Solitude

Journey Writer

• Describe your writing self: how do you see the part of you who writes?
• Design a pleasant writing spot for yourself, somewhere where you feel comfortable, have privacy, can establish a ritual, put some special things around you.
• Protect the privacy of the journal notebook as carefully as you protect your most private thoughts.

I feel happy to be keeping a journal again. I've missed it, missed naming things as they appear, missed the half hour when I push all duties aside and savor the experience of being alive in this beautiful place.

—*May Sarton*
At Seventy

often come from within. The question becomes: How to keep track of what consciousness offers and sort through the mind to the spiritual layer.

So, now imagine a quiet place from which you contemplate the paths of action and reflection. From this quiet place you can observe both the walker and the watcher. You hear what the mind says. You record what the walker does and how the watcher responds. This is the writer: the self who acts and reflects on paper.

Writing bridges the inner and outer worlds and connects the paths of action and reflection. We sit down, face the receptive blankness of a piece of paper or a computer screen, pull our thoughts together, and begin to write.

Writing *is* sorting. Writing down the stream of consciousness gives us a way to respect the mind, to choose among and harness thoughts, to interact with and change the contents of who we think we are. And that is what the spiritual journey is: a major change, over time, in who we think we are, followed by a corresponding change in what we believe ourselves capable of doing.

This book helps you make these changes by offering a structure within which you make your own journey. The chapters build upon each other, leading out, leading in, creating a spiral.

My own spiral has led me in and out of formal religion, sent me reading hundreds of books, experimenting with different forms of meditation and prayer. It has been a considerable challenge to write this book about the journey, without wanting to prescribe a particular path that anyone's journey—besides my own—should take. In a recent journal-writing class the mix of backgrounds included a nun, two Mormons, an Episcopal deacon, a Zen Buddhist, and free travelers who identified themselves as having been raised Catholic, Jewish, and Lutheran but who no longer related to any of these backgrounds. This is a typical group of seekers in these times.

The twenty-four chapters presented here are puzzle pieces designed to make a picture map of the spiritual quest. Your puzzle and mine may look quite different, and yet the pieces composed

What is the purpose or meaning of life? To get your story straight. To create a safe and gentle environment for yourself, and help create one for other folks, for living what truth you can stand.

—*Rebecca Hill*
"All the Big Questions"

Starting a Journey Group

Journal writers can also be life companions.
• Gather with people who share similar values, needs, interests.
• Develop a comfortable mix of writing time, talking time, silent time.
• Commit to a certain number of meetings and then review and revise the process.
Set up a journal-writing group with simple, clear, agreed-upon guidelines. For example:
• Confidentiality applies. Whatever is said in the group, remains in the circle of the group.
• Privacy is the first right of writing; people may elect to share some entries but should not be urged to disregard their own comfort or privacy needs.
• Reading is shared for the purpose of bearing witness to each other's experience without judgment or criticism.

within them have common elements. And the mystery, which is their source and destination, is the same.

Through writing we connect our journeys to the experience of a multitude of life travelers before and all around us. We can learn tremendously from these others and their writings, and still—we have to make our own way.

We call spirituality a journey and speak in metaphors of travel, yet many of us never leave the neighborhood. The journal becomes the metaphor made real, a travelogue of the mind. There are other ways to create an identification of ourselves as pilgrims on a spiritual quest, but writing is the most tangible, and tangibility becomes an important quality on a journey that is largely metaphoric.

On days when I'm not sure what the journey is or why I'm on it, I can still be sure what the journal is and why I write. I can hold onto my journal, write in it, lament and question and celebrate. My journal goes with me nearly everywhere. When I'm home, journal and pen wait receptively on my desk. When I'm driving around town, it's on the car seat beside me, waiting for a few minutes when I can catch up with my thoughts. When I fly, it's tucked in the seat belt next to me, waiting for the tray table to be pulled down. When I'm in bed, it's under my pillow.

My journal is my life's companion. The format changes, the pens change, the contents vary, the cast of characters comes and goes. Yet this tangible object reminds me that my life is being lived on many levels; it reminds me that I need to act, watch, reflect, write, and then act more clearly. It urges me to remember to pay attention to spirit, to be led rather than lead.

I deliberately imbue whatever notebook is the journal of the moment with all these properties. I ask it to serve as a talisman of the quest, visible every day, even on days when I don't write.

Since the early 1970s, when I wandered into an adult education center, admitted I kept a journal, and asked if anybody ever taught a course about it, I have been teaching and learning from thousands of journal writers.

We are living in a renaissance of personal writing. People are

There are many thoughtful people who believe that our time is one of accelerated social and individual transformation. Fundamental world views, paradigms of reality, conceptions of human nature are being questioned and challenged. There are even suggestions from some observers that humanity as a whole species is undergoing a collective transformation. We have no precedent in our experience for this kind of evolutionary change. We are being challenged to examine our understanding of evolution itself.

—Ralph Metzner
Opening to Inner Light

A Look at Companionship

• What "companions" are you intending to take with you into the new century?

Miracles seem to rest, not so much upon faces or voices or healing power coming suddenly near to us from far off, but upon our perceptions being made finer so that for a moment our eyes can see and our ears can hear that which is about us always.

—Willa Cather

rebalancing the impersonalization endemic to modern society with an increase in personal introspection. We have enough common-knowledge psychology under our belts to know that psychology doesn't explain or heal everything and that it isn't the fulfillment of awareness, but its beginning. We are undergoing a shift in paradigms in which we are trying to develop new models for humanness and human responsibility. This is no small task. Our individual lives are placed under increasing pressure to respond adequately to both inner and outer change.

In the polarity of the times, we are asked—and are asking ourselves—to lead lives that succeed in both a worldly and spiritual sense. We are asking ourselves to integrate forces long regarded as diametrically opposed. We are trying to refashion the spiritual path, to bring it into the world of rainy afternoons and also refashion our lives to take spirituality more deeply into account in our daily affairs.

We go to work, come home tired, make supper, do laundry, watch over the children, talk to our spouses or lovers or friends. There's nothing good on TV. We try to glimpse life's meaning in trips to the grocery store, talks about the weather, thoughts about how things are at work or at home and how our lives are turning out. We feel vulnerable and perhaps disappointed. Something has shifted under us that we thought we could count on, an assumption about reality we never named, and now it isn't there. We're trying to figure something out and we don't know how to help ourselves. We are waiting for the way to be made clear, only there doesn't seem to be "a way." We are alone with ourselves as we are, and life as it is, learning to attend to what Willa Cather calls "that which is about us always." This is a perplexing situation, but confusion is the way pilgrimages and journals most often begin.

Despite the pressure of the times, the journey cannot be forced to grow like a hothouse bulb. The best any of us can do is ready ourselves with spiritual openness that we have practiced during the lulls in life, so that when the turning points come, we have a structure in place to help us decide which way to turn. We practice

. . . life has taught me that it knows better plans than we can imagine, so that I try to submerge my own desires . . . into a calm willingness to accept what comes, and to make the most of it, then wait again.

—Julia Seton
By a Thousand Fires

finding spirituality in the ordinary so that we may recognize it in the extraordinary.

What I think we are up to, we throngs of journal-writing pilgrims, is reclamation. We are searching for ways to reclaim a sense of place, a sense of empowerment, a sense of healthy relationship between our lives and times. We look for whatever can help us make sense of the moment.

We write.

2. HOW TO WRITE
A SPIRITUAL JOURNAL

*I want to write, but more than that, I want to bring
out all kinds of things that lie buried in my heart.*

—*Anne Frank*
The Diary of a Young Girl

For Christmas, the year I was twelve, my mother gave
me a pair of tickets to the touring-company production
of *The Diary of Anne Frank*. Appropriate to both the Frank
family dynamics and my own, it was my father who
escorted me to the play. Sitting in the dark, I quickly identified
with this earnest, articulate girl, confined with her family in hiding
from the Nazis while her mind and spirit soared on paper.

Like thousands of other young girls, I saw in Anne a sister-self.
It was the first time anything about art, life, writing, or individuality
struck me with full force. By the time the dreadful knocks finally

A breed apart from the diarists who write simply to collect the days or preserve impressions of foreign places are those who set out in their books to discover who they really are. These are generally very serious people, more in the way of pilgrims, with inward destinations, than mere travellers . . . —they want to use their diaries to test, and add to, their strength.

—*Thomas Mallon*
A Book of One's Own; People and Their Diaries

Rules of Journal Writing

1. Date your entries as you go.
2. Don't make any other rules.

. . . to say what you want to say, you must create another language and nourish it for years and years with what you have loved, with what you have lost, with what you will never find again.

—*George Seferis*

came on the annex door and the curtain fell, I was awash with grief.

I had loved Anne and lost her in two short hours. She was a mirror for the self I wanted to be; and so this was also the first time I had ever projected love toward myself or guessed at my own lost wandering.

I remember my father handing me his oversized man's handkerchief, helplessly patting my shoulder while I sobbed and sobbed. Other fathers and daughters, mothers, teenagers, and grown-ups passed us by, moving up the aisle to resume their lives. I could not compose myself.

I think this sudden cracking open is characteristic of the spiritual journey. We are surprised: by joy, by grief, by insight suddenly gifted to us. We are caught unawares. But that was the first time my heart broke open so clearly. I washed out a place in myself that understood the need to bear witness.

The next day, after school, I took a black, cardboard three-ring notebook down to the basement, drilled a hole at its edge with my father's drill bit, inserted blank pages, and locked it with my gym padlock. Along an interior wall, warmed by the furnace room, there was a plywood bench used only for storage. I flattened several boxes, tapped out cardboard walls in this space, brought down a blanket and pillow, rigged a small desk light. Its entrance, camouflaged by piles of musty books, was hidden from the rest of the family. I had made myself a secret annex and a journal. I started to write.

The decision to write a journal has been the most important decision I have ever made because it has led to every other important decision I've ever made. The existence of the journal provides writers with confidence and courage that we can travel as far as the mind allows, and find our way home through the act of writing.

I reread Anne Frank's diary lately, still astounded at her writing skills at thirteen, fourteen, fifteen. My first journals are superficial renditions of school activities, boy-and-girl entanglements, the barest hints at real feelings. I wanted to articulate my sense of self, life, and journey, but I had no permission even to think on this

JOURNAL ENTRY

Dear Diary,

This morning I went to church with Daddy. I love to do that. When I sit next to him I can think better. He has a soothing effect on me. He treats me like a woman, introduces me to his friends, lets me go before him out the pew or in a door.

This afternoon he and Carl worked on making the stable, it's nearly finished and gee it's going to be nice. And this evening Uncle Eddie came out to visit. He lives in California. He is nice but sort of odd. For instance, he thinks Adlai Stevenson and Eleanor Roosevelt are communists! Isn't that a good one? You can't tell him anything because he knows it all. It's been raining all day and I am downcast. Mom didn't want me to set my hair, but it's all funny from being out in the rain. So I hurried up with the dishes and then set it. I was almost finished when I ran out of hairpins and had to go to the upstairs bathroom to get some more. When Mom saw me she said, "What I say to you doesn't mean anything does it, Chrissie." For a moment I thought she was going to cry and I felt sorry for her. I don't understand why I can't set my hair. Dad came in my room and asked me to try and fulfill mother's idea a little more, but I don't want to fulfill anyone's idea but my very own.

Childhood Diary Entries

• What do you wish you'd written about at a much younger age?

• What really happened that you couldn't explain then but now have the words for?

• How are some of these issues still showing up in your journals today?

> Why Write?
> "Writing organizes my thoughts and makes me see my own experience differently."
> "Writing is both therapy and meditation for me. I learn what I'm thinking by reading what I put down."
> "I sketch first, then write a few notes about my drawings."
> —from a journal class

level, let alone write it down. I just kept doggedly at it.

The compulsion to write was there—but not much else—and in retrospect the incompleteness doesn't matter. Every journal is a seed for the next journal. Everything we learn to write is a stepping-stone for the next level of conversation we are capable of having with ourselves.

All the journal requires is the most basic writing ability and the desire to articulate the journey. Whether you've been keeping a journal for years or are just planning to start, the gift of the journal is that we will write just as we are.

The journal is a private document. It doesn't matter if you spell correctly, write fancifully, go into expansive detail, or leave only brief notations to aid recall. Whatever works, works. Whatever works will grow and change as your comfort with writing grows and changes.

I started teaching journal writing because I wanted to find out if anyone else was doing it or was interested in doing it. In my first class there were ten women, two men, all of them poets, except one man who's an antiquarian book dealer and collector of published journals. We listed major issues that we had in common: privacy, audience, self-esteem, recovery from the past, anticipation of the future. We made a map of topics to write about: memory, the inner child, dreams, fantasy, creativity, relationships, problems, sensuality and sexuality, mortality and immortality. Eventually these topics became the frame of my first book.

This group was held in 1973, just as waves of popular psychology were hitting the culture. A journal-writing group was something new. Three years later, when my first book *One to One* was published, the Library of Congress had to create a new category for it: "1. Diaries—Therapeutic use. 2. Self-Perception."

Now the therapeutic uses of writing and the connection between writing and perception seem easy enough to understand. The climate of the culture has radically changed. People think differently about themselves, what shapes their lives, and what they can do to create change. Many people started keeping journals as part of their

I wake in the middle of the night and count, dollar by dollar, what we have coming in and what money has to go out. We'll make it through the month, but Johnn doesn't get another check until Jan. 14th. I may have to borrow cash from the credit cards to make the mortgage payment. Nobody knows how long the layoffs will continue. I'm trying to find a job, and it's hard to look good when I'm in a state of panic. I've bought the children Xmas presents on holiday dollars, but won't have the money to pay off the bills when they come due in February. Dear God, I am utterly afraid. How can I celebrate Christ's birth in these conditions? I need to turn over my fear. It makes me angry, because I think it is a sign of lost faith. I can't afford to lose faith. Johnn's awake too, though he stayed in bed while I got up to write. I hear him tossing. We need a sign. You have our attention, God. Please help us get our lives back in order. I remember how Grandma used to say, "When God closes a door, He opens a window." I will feel less afraid if I consider this sleeplessness a way of keeping watch. Amen.

Timed Writing

- Choose a set time to write, 5–7 minutes serves well.
- Set a timer; watch the clock.
- Stop writing when the time is up, even in the middle of a sentence

JOURNAL ENTRY

In the next 5 minutes I will begin writing. This is page 1. Don't know what to say. Say, Hello, Billy. Hello, Billy. Maybe I should name this journal Billy—what they called me as a kid. Don't stop the pen she says, just keep writing. I'm 53 years old, been avoiding this all my life—looking in, I mean. Been too busy, running a business, being a man's man. If the guys at the hardware store saw me in this workshop they'd croak. No, it was me what almost croaked. Heart attack. Should have seen it

psychological journey. The spiritual journal doesn't mean you have to stop the kind of writing you may already be doing, only that you add a spiritual dimension. The spiritual journey comes to us all mixed in with life's dailiness, and the spiritual journal is written all mixed in with life's dailiness as well.

Spiritual writing expands the interior conversation of consciousness to include your relationship with the sacred. You are no longer alone on the quest, or on paper. You are in conversation with Something you perceive as beyond, or deep within, yourself. It is this inclusion of the sacred that spiritualizes the writing.

Sometimes we assume that spiritual experiences, at least experiences we would define as deeply integrative, only happen to saints, martyrs, and mystics. We wait to hear, and fear to hear, Joan of Arc's voices. We believe that following a burning bush is more significant than writing in a journal. We're not sure we want to go to Tibet.

The journey participates in a person's life in whatever circumstances exist. As we take up writing, the sacred responds by using writing as a vessel, a way to appear and interact in our lives. The journal becomes an open channel.

If you look at the journal entry on the facing page, and at many other entries throughout this book, from published excerpts and anonymous sharings, the writers have included the presence of the spiritual in their ordinary lives.

Four Basic Writing Exercises

Four types of writing provide the cornerstones of a journal. These exercises can be used to explore many layers and levels of writing.

TIMED ENTRIES

In timed entries, you write for a short, prescribed period of time. The purpose of timed writing is to prime the creative pump:

coming. Didn't. Don't want to miss the next big message—the one that might be fatal. So I'm learning to keep a journal. Keep track of myself. Keep aware of my thoughts and feelings. Sounds strange. It's mostly women here, but I want . . .

JOURNAL ENTRY
Each of us has a coffee cup adopted for this workshop. They sit by our hands, bright as polka dots. I wonder if that has anything to do with polka dancing, or if I'm misspelling the word. I misspell a lot of words because I just sound everything out and put the letters down phonetically. Nobody told me, growing up in Mississippi, that we said things with a lot more letters in them than were actually written. This journal has no accent. It does in my mind when I read, but the words are just standard English, the English I learned when I went up North to college. They made it very clear that dialect was not an acceptable way to read Shakespeare or poetry. This is not a term paper: this is my book. Maybe I will reclaim some of the hokey, redneck culture I come from that nobody seems to revere but me. It's beginning to dawn on me that journal writing offers some important freedoms. I could . . .

Flow Writing

• Pick a tangible object from your surroundings and use it as the opening image in your entry.
• Let your mind free-associate from one thought to the next. Write for a specific period of time, or until you have arrived at a place that feels finished.

JOURNAL ENTRY
This lounge has Grandpa's paintings on the walls. Not really, of course, but heavy oils that look like the landscapes that hung over our sofa to flatter him. He'd come out to dinner and stand there in front of

shortening writing time makes sure you have more to say than time to say it. The frustration of stopping creates the impetus to write more. You become more interested in the ideas and thoughts you want to put down and less self-conscious about the time it's taking to write. This exercise also helps develop confidence and establishes creative tension.

Creative tension is necessary for writing. The drive in the mind is to articulate. The mind doesn't much care whether you articulate by writing or talking. When you intend to write about something in your journal, don't talk it out first. Talking dissipates the creative tension and expends the impetus. Over and over again, journal writers notice that if they talk out a topic, when they finish the conversation and open their journals, the drive to write is gone.

Timed writing is also a helpful pressure for reviving journal writing when you feel as though you've written yourself out or that you are meandering without direction in your entries. A week of timed writing, especially combined with the next exercise, will sharpen your writing focus as well as help you discover a number of unnoticed time slots in which to write.

FLOW WRITING

Flow writing is practice in stream of consciousness, learning to trust that no matter where you start, words will come to you.

To start flow writing, look at an object from where you are sitting, ready to write. The object is not important, just something that attracts your attention. The examples at left all started with spontaneously chosen objects of interest. You use this object as an opening image to plunge into writing, then you allow your thoughts to free-associate and you jot them down as they occur.

You *will* find yourself supported by language. You don't need to know what you are going to say before you open the journal. You don't need to have thoughts framed or even an idea. Flow writing allows you to reach for the journal and discover what's on your mind in playful fashion.

last year's scenery as though he'd never seen it before. Haven't thought of him in a long time. Don't see him anymore—him being dead. He disappeared into senility long before he died. All the mountain paintings got worse and worse, horrid colors. His grown kids brought the ashes back here to put him in the cemetery where his family lies. Grandma is still hanging on, seems to be holding out for a card from the president when she turns 100. Or maybe living is just a habit she's afraid to give up. I hope she's not afraid. I hope her dream of the Universe is gentle. But whether it is or not, I don't know that she'd let anyone change her mind about it. God is God—has been a strict Norwegian/Lutheran God for a long time. Not to be interfered with. She used to tell me how she was afraid of thunderstorms, thought they meant God was personally angry at her. Now she lives in California—no thunder.

MONOLOGUE JOURNAL ENTRY
Early Monday morning. I think something finally clicked in my head last night. I don't feel so crazy inside. I'm not exactly a model of stability, but I have a toehold on reality after days of floating anxiety. I guess I'll go to work, stop calling in sick. Whatever is supposed to be so spiritual about disorientation, I don't get it. I don't like it. Nobody told me feeling nuts was part of the quest.

Dialogue Writing

- Open with a leading question.
- Take a breath, pause, listen, write down the first response that comes.
- Work in a rhythm of question/answer.
- This is not a contest: the voices do not have to be equally represented.
- If you get stuck and don't know where to go next, you may need to introduce an "Overvoice" that comments on how the dialogue is developing and helps you see where it needs to go.

Besides getting you over the blank-page jitters, the great gift of flow writing is that it's always a surprise. It entertains.

To keep at journal writing, you need to find it pleasurable. Free association, though we do it all the time, is not something we often admit we enjoy. Flow writing lets your mind shine.

Flow writing reveals the mind's agenda underneath the busyness of surface thought. Once, teaching a class at a senior-citizen high rise, I assigned flow writing for one week. At our next session a woman brought twenty short flow-writing entries: no matter where she had started from, the entries all ended up being about her mother, a woman long dead. We used the next exercise to bring that relationship to the surface and allow her to make peace with it.

Flow writing is the tip of the iceberg, touching on thoughts that ride deeply in your mind. You can expand the ideas that interest you further at a later time. Flow writing combined with timed writing can result in a series of quick entries or, released from time constraints, serve as the prelude to long entries.

DIALOGUE WRITING

All writing implies dialogue: a writer and a reader, a questioner and a responder. Every journal entry is made in response to some question, even if it's only a vaguely phrased "What are you thinking about?" or "What's happening?"

One of the greatest powers of journal writing is that over time it helps us notice, influence, and change the conversation the mind is having with itself. This dialogue is nearly constant. All I'm suggesting is that some of it, especially that which is directed to specific questions, is extremely helpful to write down.

In most journal writing, people don't bother to jot down the prefacing question. Therefore, journals appear to be written in monologue. When you write the questions openly, journal writing breaks into double voices: dialogue.

Dialogue writing releases insight from two angles rather than

JOURNAL ENTRY

1. Greeting and definition of the topic:

> ME: *There's something I haven't been telling you, and I want to know if you'll discuss it with me.*

2. Negotiation of terms of conversation:

> YOU: *I get this funny feeling in my gut when you start talking like this. I want a guarantee whatever this is, it isn't going to end up all my fault.*
>
> ME: *Okay, I'll look for my part, you look for yours. And the purpose of talking is to solve the problem.*
>
> YOU: *Okay.*

3. Body of conversation:

> ME: *I want you to come to synagogue with me.*
>
> YOU: *Why?*
>
> ME: *I want us there as a whole family. I want you to support the kids' religious upbringing—*
>
> YOU: *What, God the Father isn't enough?*
>
> ME: *Very funny, David! I thought you were going to let me talk about this?*
>
> YOU: *I thought you were not going to make it all my problem.*
>
> ME: *It's only two hours a week.*

Up to this point, the dialogue probably sounds like the two people would sound in actuality. Next, the writer enters the level of intuitive information not previously articulated.

> YOU: *It's only accepting five thousand years of tradition. What's it to you, really?*
>
> ME: *My father was Christian. We never celebrated anything with any singleness of mind.*
>
> YOU: *I'm Jewish. I'll be Jewish with you and the kids. I just don't like giving up my free time to something that isn't particularly meaningful to me.*
>
> ME: *I want it to be meaningful to you.*
>
> YOU: *But you can't force that issue. And it sure won't work for you to coerce me into going.*

one. Sometimes written dialogues become trialogues or quadra-logues as other voices join in the conversation.

In journal dialogues, one part of the mind asks a question, another part of the mind responds. Dialogue requires that you trust yourself to play both roles, to write in multiple voices. The easiest way to do this is to write the first impulse, the response that comes before self-censorship sets in. You don't need to identify the voices, call them A, B, C, etc. You don't need to preplan questions and answers; let them emerge while writing. Record these conversations without interfering, censoring, or applying strict rules of reality.

The purpose of dialogues is to retrieve information and insight about a situation that we may not know we have. For example, if every time you talk to your exspouse, the two of you reach an impasse, don't faithfully recite your exact words when you dialogue about this situation, but drop beneath the verbal exchange. Ask yourself and ask the other with whom you write/speak: Why do we get stuck at this point? What do you think is going on? How do you suppose we could get beyond this point? What are you willing to do? Here's what I'm willing to do. *The more specific the question, the more specific the response will be.*

Dialoguing is such an important journal-writing tool, it will show up here in many variations. Whenever you get stuck in your mono-logue, open your mind to dialogue. You will be amazed at the insight waiting for you to *ask* instead of *tell.*

Written dialogues usually have five stages:

1. greeting and definition of the topic
2. negotiation of terms of conversation
3. body of conversation
4. problem resolution
5. final contract, commitment, closure

You can dialogue with anyone or anything. Dialogue is the most versatile tool of journal writing. We can avoid looking directly at issues for a long time while writing in monologue, but dialogue gets to the heart of the matter.

4. Problem resolution is now really beginning:

> ME: *I don't want to force you; I just want some help teaching values to the children.*
>
> YOU: *We can talk about that. What if we open up the topic of values as something this family discusses at the dinner table, perhaps on Friday evenings, as part of our shabbos.*
>
> ME: *You'd be willing to do that?*

5. Final contract, commitment, and closure:

> YOU: *Yes, as long as there's no secret agenda.*
>
> ME: *You got it. We talk openly in front of the children and find out what they think too.*

Unsent Letters

• Be clear in your mind that although this is an addressed journal entry, it is not a communiqué in which you need to take the recipient's feelings into account.

• You don't need to know everything you're going to say. Allow the letter to ramble and develop in your usual style.

> *April 1902*
>
> *Dear Janey,*
>
> *I guess my diary is about finished. I am going blind—can still see to write this yet but I can't keep on to live to an avaricious old age. All hope is dead forever Janey. What have I ever done except make one blunder after another? All I have left are these little pictures of you and your father. I can't go on blind and the doctor told me yesterday that in two months I would be absolutely blind. O how I wish I had my life to live over.... Forgive all my faults and the wrong I have done you.*
>
> *—Calamity Jane*
>
> *a diary in letters to her daughter Janey*

UNSENT LETTERS

There is an audience implied in journal writing. For most of us, it is essential to the writing that we imagine that audience as only the self. However, writing implies communication. Anne Frank kept her diary addressed to an imaginary friend named Kitty who existed only in Anne's mind. People often tell me they don't keep a journal, but they keep copies of all the letters they write; or they discover that many of the letters they write someone else are really letters to the self, and they tuck them away.

Because of this strong impulse to communicate to another object/ person, letter writing is a natural part of journal keeping. Assuming that these are letters *not* meant to be sent and that they can be written in the same uncensored way as other entries, whom do you want to write? yourself as a child? as an old wo/man? your parents? grandparents? children? grandchildren? a child you never had, or lost? business associates? friends? a college lover? your fourth-grade teacher? the president? other world leaders? As you can see, the list becomes endless.

The purpose of the unsent letter is to discover what impetus motivated it—which you may not know at the beginning—and decide what you need to do next, having discovered that impetus. You may, for example, need to change some aspect of your active life. You may decide to use the unsent letter as the basis for a letter that you do send. You may discover unsent letters are excellent ways to finish business with people and events that are no longer a part of your life.

Each of these techniques, along with other exercises and ideas aimed directly at the spiritual track of journal-writing, will show up in many variations throughout this book. The purpose of the far-left column is to keep introducing specific ways the journal can serve as an interactive tool of your quest.

With these cornerstones in place, you can take your journal-writing as deeply into the spiral as you want, and you will always be able to write your way home.

3. THE ART OF QUESTIONING

Be patient toward all that is unsolved in your heart and try to love the questions themselves.... Do not now seek the answers which cannot be given you because you would not be able to live them and the point is to live everything. Live the questions now. Perhaps you will then gradually, without noticing it, live along some distant day into the answer.

> —Rainer Maria Rilke
> Letters to a Young Poet

In a book about the spiritual quest, it is the questions that count. Our quests are defined by the questions we raise and write about, whatever is most compelling to us at any given moment. At times of calm, these questions may be large and meandering: *I wonder if the Gaia theory is right, that the earth is all one organism?* At times of crisis, the questions tend to compress, focus tightly on issues of coping and survival: *How do I get through the next hour? the meeting? this temptation?*

Two Basic Questions

• What just happened here (on this level and this
and this)?
• What is it possible to learn by what happened?

> The real questions are the ones that obtrude upon your
> consciousness whether you like it or not, the ones that make your
> mind start vibrating like a jackhammer, the ones that you "come
> to terms with" only to discover that they are still there. The real
> questions refuse to be placated. They barge into your life at the
> times when it seems most important for them to stay away. They
> are the questions asked most frequently and answered most
> inadequately, the ones that reveal their true natures slowly,
> reluctantly, most often against your will.
>
> —Ingrid Bengis
> Combat in the Erogenous Zone

Childhood Rules

• What were your favorite questions when you were
a child?
• What are some of the responses you remember
getting to these questions?
• What were the understood rules about questioning
in your original family?
• What kinds of things were considered all right to
question? What weren't you supposed to question?

And sometimes we are afraid to question because we confuse it with doubt, at times when doubt cannot be indulged. Questioning is not the same as doubting, though the two words have been thrown together in judgmental ways. "Do you doubt the power and love of God!?" the evangelist thunders from the pulpit. "Nooooo!" the congregation responds. But we may, without doubting in the least, have a hundred questions that interest us about the nature of the universe and what it means in our daily lives.

When I was about five, I spent an intense Sunday afternoon with my crayons, hunched over a large piece of shelf paper on the living-room floor. My mother walked in and asked me what I was drawing. "A picture of God," I told her.

"Oh, dear . . ." She squatted down to explain. "Nobody knows what God looks like . . ."

I was not disturbed in the slightest. "They *will*," I told her, "as soon as I'm done drawing!"

A child, discovering the world for the first time, is certain that everything can be satisfactorily explained. To the child's mind, all questions are reasonable and have understandable answers, if only s/he can find a smart enough grown-up to ask.

While the spiritual mind of the child is confident it can explain the world, the spiritual mind of the adult releases its explanations and heads down the path of questioning. The presence of questions in the mind propels the quest, and the presence of questions on the page fulfills the journal. The spiritual journal cannot be written without questioning. All the great spiritual documents that guide and inspire us are based on the seeker's willingness to ask, accompanied by his/her profound awareness and interpretation of response.

Questioning is an ambivalent process for many people. We have been given opposing messages about questioning. As children, when we asked, "But, why?" we may have been told, "Because I say so . . . Because I'm bigger . . . Because I know better . . . Because I'm your father/mother and as long as you're living in my house . . ." You know how the litany goes. But that's only half of it. The same

A List of Free Questions, from the Ridiculous to the Sublime:
What's for dinner?
Who am I?
What am I supposed to be doing with my life at the turn of the century?
Who am I supposed to be doing it with?
Will I have fun?
What is the nature of spiritual fun?
Will I recognize it when it happens?
Is there a God out there, or is He/She/It all in here?
Is He/She/It laughing at all the silly questions I ask?
Are these silly questions?
Is there life on other planets?
Do they care about life on this one?
Do I care about life on this one?
What would I be willing to give up to save the world?
What are life's real essentials for me?

Assumptions Grid

In the journal, finish the following sentences:
* I used to assume . . .
* I still assume . . .
* I used to believe . . .
* I still believe . . .
* I want to believe . . .

JOURNAL ENTRY

Insight is a strange phenomenon. I never know what I'm going for until I get it. In the middle of a long series of questions I always think what I'm trying to understand is much more external than it turns out to be. The world is confusing me—I think—not that I am confusing myself. It takes me a long time to notice I am being driven by an unseen force that wants me to answer a question I don't yet know I've asked.

authority figures who wanted our compliance in certain situations urged our independence in other situations. "Think for yourself," they told us. "Question your actions, don't just do what everyone else is doing. What if all your friends jump off a cliff? Are you going to jump too?"

We made our ways through childhood trying to figure out the code: when to question, when to comply. The more liberal or relaxed the environment, the more confusing these boundaries could sometimes be. We had more room to roam mentally, which is beneficial to spiritual growth. But when rigidity erupted, it was more shocking, making us feel as if we'd committed a bigger transgression.

A friend of mine who grew up in a very strict home tells of an adolescence in which she was forbidden to date, wear lipstick, go to the movies, listen to popular music. As she began to sneak off and experiment, she knew clearly where the boundaries were and that she was deliberately overstepping them. When she got caught, she knew what the response would be and was prepared to face it. Behavior, in her parents' mode of thinking, was clearly conscribed. You were either in, or out of, line.

In my family, where both parents themselves questioned authority, religion, and social mores, the boundaries for exploring were ambiguous, and when I overstepped them, their negative reaction surprised me. Behavior was not clearly conscribed. In a household where my mother was going to séances, why couldn't I—at the height of my identification with Anne Frank—go to synagogue?

As we approach the spiritual journey, we may be uncertain what response awaits us if we open our minds and ask ourselves about the nature of existence, life and death, reality, purpose, free will, fate, the will of the sacred, etc., all topics outlined in this book, and all questions implied by the topics in this book. What will a journal based on questioning look like, and where will the written dialogues of question and response take us?

I don't know. My questioning isn't over yet, and the destination not reached. But I believe in the road itself, step by step and question by question, and that *we have been given consciousness in order to*

Posting Questions

- When you discover a question you're working on,
stick it several pages ahead of you in the journal.
- Every time you come across it, write about it a few
minutes.

> *There have been questions I never knew there were answers to.*
>
> *There have been so many answers they have all been right.*
> —Deborah Keenan
> Household Wounds

Four Cornerstone Questions

If you work with only four questions in your whole
journal, they might be:
- What's the real issue of growth here?
- What lesson is available in this?
- What am I really trying to do right now?
- What is the purpose for me in doing _____? (Or:
What is the purpose in my having experienced _____?)

> JOURNAL ENTRY
> *This has been a busy year, but I'm hanging onto my relaxation
> from the Mexico trip. Great beaches, magical snorkeling, and
> walking among the Mayan ruins somehow very calming.
> Sobering too—here was a civilization of people who disappeared.
> The people, I guess, didn't disappear, but their culture did.
> Americans need to consider such things—'tis good for our
> youthful pride. We are babies in a cultural sense and not immune
> to time, to irrelevance, to being left behind in history. Take the
> God's eye view, the ruins seemed to say. Be present to the
> moment, but don't belong to it. Belong to the long
> time, belong to vision, to journey, to purpose.*

raise questions, to be capable of having an interactive relationship with the quest.

When my friend Lynne was dying of cancer at forty-three, her suffering and death raised many questions, in her mind and in the minds of her family and friends who cared for her. These questions were different for each of us, but the process of questioning and coming to acceptance was a holy thread that bound us all together. We each went through a level of personal transformation—Lynne too, in the resolution of her quest, which she reached before dying. Our questioning gave the suffering some sense, even if there were no answers.

The poet Rilke asks us to live the questions. More than that, he says we need to *love the questions*. This is a challenge when life events bring such difficult questions to mind. In the news every day we are made aware of suffering—the sweeping suffering of nations faced with war, oppression, famine, and disease; the individual suffering of people victimized by violence, accident, losses of a hundred kinds. The questions raised by conditions of life and death are soul searching and hard to love. And they have no answers, though we may rest our anguish or seeking awhile on any explanation that helps.

The comfort that comes from questioning is this: even if there isn't an answer, there *is* response. There is a sense of the sacred reaching toward us, as we reach toward it. And the most tangible evidence of this mutuality often occurs in the journal, in dialogues and insight and the reflections of the writing process. The voice of the sacred appears gently on the page, written in our own handwriting but carrying a message of support and comfort, sometimes challenge, which we do not generate alone.

This happened to the journal writer at left who wrote herself a message (in the italicized passages) she felt had been given her to write down: pass-throughs of wisdom from the Higher Self.

As you head into the journal of questioning, there are three things you need to remember about the art of asking:

If I had my life to live over I'd like to make more mistakes next time.

I would limber up.

I would be sillier than I have been this trip.

I would take fewer things seriously.

I would take more chances.

I would climb more mountains and swim more rivers.

I would eat more ice cream and less beans.

I would perhaps have more actual trouble, but I'd have fewer imaginary ones.

You see, I'm one of those people who live sensibly and sanely hour after hour, day after day.

Oh, I've had my moments, and if I had it to do over again, I'd have more of them.

In fact, I'd try to have nothing else.

Just moments, one after another, instead of living so many years ahead of each day.

I've been one of those persons who never goes anywhere without a thermometer, a hot water bottle, a raincoat, and a parachute.

If I had it to do over again, I would travel lighter than I have.

If I had my life to live over, I would start barefoot earlier in the spring and stay that way later in the fall.

I would go to more dances.

I would ride more merry-go-rounds.

I would pick more daisies.

—*Nadine Stair, age 85*

1. ASKING IS NATURAL. WE ARE THE QUESTION-ASKING ANIMAL.

The *why*'s of childhood are evidence of an innate human curiosity. Curiosity restores us to the attitude Zen calls *beginner's mind* or *know-nothing mind*. This attitude is not ignorance, it is a sophisticated ability to see without assumption, to look freshly at the world and ourselves within it.

Curiosity is a state of heightened awareness. Culturally, this has been considered a child's activity. By the time we're grown, we're supposed to know enough not to get bogged down in life's miraculous detail. But the spiritual journey reactivates our sense of miracle and invites us to pause again, squatting over the sidewalk cracks, to ponder the lives of ants and stars.

2. LIFE SIMPLY OCCURS. WE RAISE QUESTIONS IN RESPONSE TO THESE OCCURRENCES.

A tree falling in the forest is just a tree falling in the forest until the human mind contemplates it. Questioning imbues any event or idea with the potential for spiritual significance. The map of your journal evolves from the line of questioning you pursue on the page.

You grant your life's events their meanings and place your questions in a context that builds the way you see yourself and your relationship to the universe. You construct meaning out of the flow of events and ideas and turn them into *the story of your life*.

Perhaps a friend talks excitedly about reincarnation and you, too, decide to explore it. You read books, attend a lecture, find quotes about reincarnation to put in your journal and respond to. References to reincarnation you hadn't noticed before seem to crop up in conversation, in print, even in your dreams. You ponder all these things. You raise questions. You weigh your new thoughts with your old beliefs and see what seems to fit. You enjoy your

Curious Questions

* If you had *your* life to live over, what would you do?

Curiosity requires a good grounding in the physical senses before asking heady questions.

* What does your office look like if you lie on the floor?
* How does the skin on your forearm taste?
* What sounds have you ceased to hear?
* Write for three minutes about a favorite outdoor smell.
* Right now, how do the clothes touching your body feel?

Different sets of facts are real at different vibration levels. The truth is the same for everyone; the facts are always a little different for everyone.

—Thaddeus Golas

The greatest enemy of any one of our truths may be the rest of our truths.

—William James

Nothing changes, but it can.

—James Read

I am a lie that always tells the truth.

—Jean Cocteau

Choice is an illusion. I have no choice. My only choice is to grow.

—Gayla Reger

There is nothing I can do for you and I am doing it.

—Frank O'Hara

curiosity. You ask "what if?" questions. You choose. You update, change, and adapt your beliefs. This is how you grow.

3. PARADOX IS THE USUAL STATE OF AFFAIRS.

A paradox is a statement that seems contradictory or absurd on the surface, and yet, on a deeper level, it can be true without resolution. Paradoxes exist everywhere; they are the nature of things. In the spiritual journey, we touch paradox over and over as we move through different layers of awareness regarding the same "facts." As Thaddeus Golas suggests, we look for the truth, and let the facts adjust themselves accordingly. Paradoxes in our lives create tension in the rational mind. Tension, in turn, creates momentum: It is what we don't understand and are not comfortable with that drives our journeys.

In the list of paradoxes at left, the tension is obvious. The statements don't make sense to the rational mind, and yet the intuitive mind may be able to encompass the paradox, to have an "ah-ha" response to it, even smile in pleasure at its inscrutability, and let it be. As long as our questioning resides within the wide parameters of a paradox, the paradox will carry us deeper into mystery and revelation.

Living the questions requires a willingness to live with paradoxes, to endure confusion in our rational minds that only the intuitive mind can entertain: Intuition accepts the paradox instead of changing it.

Something happens. We ask, Why? Then we go through a long sorting process in which we discover the potentials for growth in this particular instance. Through the sorting process, especially in written sorting, we map our way through the question Why. The reason becomes obvious, and then we ask, "Well, Sacred, was it really necessary for this to happen in order to teach me this?"

And the response comes: This is how you learn. Whether it is the only way to learn is irrelevant. These conditions are handed you for questioning, and you use them. An art professor who was

Paradoxical Practices

Paradoxes invite us to observe on many levels. Practice writing from differing levels of the spiral. Ask yourself, What is true here, and here . . . and here?

- What is happening?
- What are my responses/feelings to what's happening?
- How am I being objective? Subjective?
- How am I interacting with the paradox?
- How is the paradox interacting with me?

leading a painting seminar informed his students: "There will be no course work, no exam. You will paint one painting every day for the next twenty-five days. I will come in at the end of the day, look at your painting, and ask, What did you learn? What are you going to do next?" This is the same learning process we provide for ourselves.

4. PRACTICING SILENCE

Daily silence experienced in humility and fervour as an indispensable exercise in spiritual nourishment gradually creates within us a permanent state of silence. The soul discovers in such a silence unsuspected possibilities. It realises that life can be lived at different levels.

—Pierre Lacout
God Is Silence

Contact with the sacred occurs in the stillness of the heart and mind. If there is any real destination to the spiritual quest, it is this point of silence, the middle of the spiral, the center of the self. Center is the gate between the *self* (which perceives itself as distinct and separate, even if connected to the scheme of things) and *unity* (in which the self merges with the scheme of things and gives up separateness). When we become quieted enough, we can reach through the usual tumble of our thoughts and find the still point at the center of the self.

You have already experienced this: touched and been touched

I have calmed and quieted my soul . . . like a child quieted is my soul.

—*Psalms 13:1–2*

Journal Questions about Silence

In this book, the word *meditation* is generic, meaning any form of practicing silence.
* What do you think you could get out of a practice of silence?
* What is your resistance to practicing silence?
* What kind of practice would you like to experiment with?
* In what ways are you already practicing silence?
* List all the things you do, or would be willing to do, that are meditative in nature.
* Call your practice of silence whatever you want.
* Design it to best fit your needs and personality.

JOURNAL ENTRY

The creek near my house seems to flow at different speeds according to its depth. I think this is illusion, but the surface water seems to skip along, rushing debris of the season toward some larger destination. And beneath this current, a slower stream swirls trails of mud like chocolate marble cake. The top stream courses fast; the bottom stream meanders.

My mind works this way too. Top thoughts slide by in an unending tumble of free association. Bottom thoughts are ponderous, careful, barely worded. When I sit to meditate, I notice these speeds. Just slowing down enough to watch my mind at work is satisfying. But I move on through my thoughts until there is that timeless touch for which I practice when there are no thoughts at all. I cease to think. I cease to observe. I am the river, and the river is silent.

at the still point. To have been opened to unity creates a longing that serves as the impetus for most of us who travel the spiritual quest. Sitting somewhere in nature, listening to music, holding a sleeping child, we have been transfixed. There are mystical moments in each of our lives when we seem to move out of our *selves* and into something else. We lack words for this experience; we call it unity and do not know what more to say.

Most of the time we have experienced unity accidentally, felt lifted out of ourselves by a force that seems to sporadically find us and to hint of another reality. Unity is not sporadic; it is a state of the universe to which we are only sporadically open. We can initiate this receptive state, take deliberate action to open ourselves to union, by practicing silence, the most universal practice of the journey.

The only map that does the spiritual traveler any good is one that leads to the center. The journal is one way of drawing this map in which you order experience by putting it into words. Prayer or meditation is another kind of map in which you put words aside for silence. The journal of the spiritual quest is inspired by silence. Through the desire to bear witness to experience, the journal makes form, story, and meaning out of silence. There are limits to what words can convey about unity, but like a photograph that is able to transport you back to the scene, once you've been there the words of the journal are able to recreate experiences of unity in your mind.

Silence is important because it provides direction. What waits for you in silence is the insight and direction you need to determine the next step in your quest. Silence is the source of knowing what to do, or what not to do.

Popular culture does not value silence. We are encouraged to surround ourselves constantly with meaningless sound. Many people wake to the clock radio, turn on the television for morning news and talk shows, listen to the car radio or cassette player everywhere they drive, and then are subjected to Muzak and background advertising in elevators, offices, and stores. The daily average for

Noise and Distraction Study

For one day carry a notecard with you and every hour
jot down what kind of noise surrounds you; notice
when there is silence.
• What do you want in the way of silence that you
don't have?
• What do you have in the way of noise that you
don't want?
• What can you do to create a more contemplative
environment around yourself?

*The necessary thing is, after all, but this: solitude, great inner
solitude. Going into oneself and for hours meeting no one—this
one must be able to attain.*

—Rainer Maria Rilke
Letters to a Young Poet

JOURNAL ENTRY
*I'm a dreadful, cranky, angry person. I feel riddled, laced,
bulging with anger and frustration and I don't even know why.
Or I probably do, but I don't want to talk about it.
How do I make a monastic, contemplative space around myself?
My life is full of people I love, but they feel up against my skin.
I won't forgive myself for wanting silence, wanting space,
wanting only to walk by myself.*

Space for Silence

• Create a space in your house where you go to
practice silence.
• Make it comfortable, calm, and away from family
distractions.

television viewing in the United States is seven hours. To create such a statistic, a lot of homes must have the television on nearly twenty-four hours a day. If that isn't noisy enough, we can wire our bodies for sound, wearing miniaturized radios, tape and disk players with earplugs attached. When people have no silence in which to reflect, they cannot reflect.

In this cultural atmosphere, to reclaim your right to silence is an act of independence and the first necessary step in finding a spiritual center. Turn off the electronics and notice: notice the quiet interruptions of the natural world, notice the background noises of your neighborhood, notice the stillness that punctuates all sound.

Contemplative silence is necessary for the spiritual journey. A pilgrim who travels without inner stillness puts him/herself in danger. Without the centering guidance of silence, you cannot be sure how to respond on a spiritual level. Silence is rich with spontaneous offerings. You may function well for a very long time, but if you are cut off from the "still, small voice" of inner guidance, you will be more fearful about the decisions you make. Many people try to lead sane, healthy, reasonable lives without being in touch with silence. They don't understand that the resource they most need is the simple silence they're missing.

In the modern world, solitude needs not only to be attained, but carefully sustained. Most of us, when given a few minutes or hours of silence, nervously reach for the nearest distraction. We never experience the great inner solitude Rilke recommends. As spiritual travelers, we need to learn to be comfortable with contemplation and contact. Silence waits for us to discover its gifts. It is you and I who spend hours, weeks, years, putting off this meeting at the center of the self.

• Collect whatever helps you feel the presence of the sacred: meaningful images, natural objects, candles, incense, sage, a special pillow or mat.
• Create a ritual for approaching silence: a time of day, loose-fitting meditation clothes, preparations for calm.

> *You must have a room or a certain hour of the day or so where you do not know what was in the morning paper; where you do not know who your friends are; you don't know what you owe anybody, or what they owe you—but a place where you can simply experience and bring forth what you are, and what you might be.... At first you may find nothing's happening.... But if you have a sacred place and use it, take advantage of it, something will happen.*
>
> —*Joseph Campbell*
> The Power of Myth

Time Alone

• Write about a time you stayed by yourself for at least one day and night. If you've never done this—go do it.
• What did you discover about yourself in those twenty-four hours?
• Write about a time when you truly stayed "in the present" without ruminating on the past or anticipating the future.
• What stops you from living life in the present more often?

The practice of silence occurs in several stages:

1. a ritual of preparation
2. sitting down with intent
3. focusing to calm the mind
4. allowing profound silence
5. gentle return.

Preparation

The ritual of preparation that leads to silence can be practiced in any number of ways. You can experiment until you find what feels right to you. The key is repetition: to light the same candle, burn the same incense, listen to the same music. *The mind habitualizes silence and will learn to respond to your ritual by beginning to calm itself.*

Sitting with Intent

When you are ready to approach silence, assume whatever physical position will be comfortable for the duration of meditation. You may sit on a chair, sit cross-legged or in full lotus, or lie flat on a mat or carpet. What you need is a posture that keeps the spine and neck straight and aligned. This aids the flow of inner energy that accompanies stilling the mind. You also need to take your physical aptitude into account. Find a position you can tolerate without squirming. Take time to adjust and relax. You want your body at ease so you can turn your attention elsewhere. *The body, too, habitualizes to silence and will learn to respond to your sitting with intent by beginning to join the mind in calm.*

You don't have to sit in the same position all the time. Some days you may feel like sitting and some days like lying down. There are many ways to look for silence, and once you touch the center, all the ways of getting there become the same. Noticing your breath and following it into a slower pace will signal your body that this is the approach to stillness.

Silence at Home

• Develop family rituals that support each person's need for silence.
• Perhaps a blue ribbon looped over the doorknob means: Do not enter, do not talk to me.
• Give yourself and your partner permission to be alone together, to feel comfortable in each other's silence.
• Arrange times of observed silence when no one in the family or household talks.

> Meditation has several phases. It has an active moment of sitting down, visualizing, chanting, whatever means the person has; then stillness of mind; then action, going out and doing something. It may be doing what you saw in the stillness. It may be what you saw upon the screen of your mind before the stillness. The action is as much a meditation as are the sitting and the contemplation.
>
> —Dhyani Ywahoo
> Weaving the Visions

Focusing Sounds

A mantra is a spiritual phrase or name for the sacred repeated over and over.
• You can chant the word *om*, which is regarded as the sound of the universe.
• "Aum Mani Padme Hum" is a simple Tibetan mantra meaning, "The All is a precious jewel in the lotus flower which blooms in my heart."
• "Christ have mercy," is a Christian mantra.
• "Sh'ma Yisroel, Adonoi Eluhenu, Adonoi Echod," may serve as a Jewish mantra.
• Navajo prayers are mantras: "May it be happy before me. May it be happy behind me. May it be happy below me. May it be happy above me."

54

Breath is the core of sitting with intent. As you settle into position, notice your breathing and allow yourself to breathe with the diaphragm, letting your stomach muscles move gently in and out. Breathe in a rhythm of long, slow breaths, as though air were heavy, needing to be sucked into the body cavity and pushed out, not too strenuously, just with satisfying exertion.

There are many breathing techniques associated with meditation, ranging from the simple to the complex. I stay with the simple, counting my breaths on the exhale from one to five, then repeating the count, over and over, always on the exhale. This is a light form of self-hypnosis. Sometimes I imagine my diaphragm is attached to a string which pulls my chest up like a bellows, then lets it collapse, then pulls it up again. Breath is life, is silence, moving in and out of the shell of your body.

Focusing

Focusing techniques for silence are as varied as opening rituals. The purpose of focusing is to bring the mind to quiet attention: paying attention to only one thing instead of the constant distraction of thought. This is a form of mental discipline: to think one thought instead of many. If you haven't tried this lately, you may be surprised at how difficult it is. Focusing provides a center point to bring your attention back after it has wandered. And your thoughts will wander! Even the minds of practiced yogis wander.

You have prepared yourself. You are sitting with intent. You are breathing quietly, and you have chosen to count your breaths on the exhale, one to five and repeat, one to five. All this seems simple enough. You calmly say to yourself, "Onnne . . . twooooo . . . I wonder if Miriam's going to call today, and what happened after David left the party last Saturday night . . . uh-oh, where was I? Onnnne . . . twoooo . . . thr—my foot itches. It may be going to sleep. Can it be good for my circulation to be in this position? What if I'm so stiff I can't get up and the laundry needs folding. There's a kid outside this window but I can't tell if it's mine

The use of mantra sets up one thought, one wave, that repeats over and over again, dislodging your attachment to all other thoughts, until they are like birds gliding by. . . . Offer your thoughts as a sacrifice to the mantra. . . . Instead of doing mantra, the mantra is doing you . . . you gradually become a channel of God's will.

—Ram Dass
Journey of Awakening

JOURNAL ENTRY

Why am I so resistant to meditating on a regular basis? I feel much better when I meditate, more connected to the Universe, but I still resist.

So, I brought my awareness deep into my body and asked myself: "Are you willing to settle down?"

"Yes and no."

"What's under the no?"

I saw an image of a pig, a silly postcard pig with a napkin under its chin and a knife and fork. "I'm stubborn. I dare you to try and discipline me to meditate!"

I turned the image around, and inside the pig was a frightened little girl who fears life and God and doesn't believe she deserves good things. I asked myself, "Why won't I accept this little girl/ self?" Immediately I see a garden full of beautiful flowers, but something about the scene repulses me. I know the garden is myself too, but I don't want to accept it. Why?

"If I was a garden"—the thought comes quickly—"it would be boring." That's it! Being rooted into the earth you're stuck and can't move no matter how beautiful you look. Being centered, being grounded, seems no fun at all. I see a bee flying from flower to flower and I say, "That's what I want—to be the bee! I want to flit. I want variety. I want to move . . . but that's how I

or not—eeeee . . . fourrr . . . This is great. I wonder if this is what is meant by profound silence? I haven't been this calm since that time I got lost in the mountains . . . fiiiive . . . Now what? Oh, yes, start over. Onnnne . . . twoooo . . . This isn't so hard; my mind isn't wandering at all."

It takes many thoughts to get to one thought. Eventually you will succeed in sustaining your focusing technique without so much mental wandering. Do not be discouraged. Do not berate yourself; it just adds to the chatter. Every time you notice you are unfocused, simply return to focus without comment, discussion, or self-criticism. In this way you make spiritual choices, even within your mind. You decide to lead yourself purposefully in your quest for silence, no matter what seems to be going on at the edge of your awareness.

The Center of Silence

As you approach silence, breathing slows, heartbeat slows, you become more focused and more diffuse. You are successful, for longer periods of time, in maintaining focus instead of drifting off into thought. You are coming to center: the silence behind thought. Your entrance into this space is hardly noticeable. Thought suspends itself. Time suspends itself. You suspend your awareness of what you are doing and are able to just *be*.

To be in center, in silence, is a drifting sensation. There is nothing really to take note of: you lose track of your focusing technique because you have merged with it. No thought separates you from experiencing oneness with your breath, with a candle flame, with a mantra. As soon as you notice you are at the center, you aren't quite—you've stepped back to notice. You can't notice while in it: you can only notice you've been in it.

This description of lost time and awareness may sound vaguely familiar. You already know now to become one with what you are doing. Any time you concentrate fully you step into a kind of union with the activity itself. You've done this driving—where all thought

injured myself when I was a professional dancer. I loved to move fast but I didn't pay enough attention to the signals in my body. So now I am slowed down, but I begin to see the relationship here. The bee and the flowers talk to each other. The bee takes the pollen and is off again, but it carries the flower inside itself all the time. It touches base with the flowers for its nourishment.

That makes sense to me. That I am willing to do. I was trying to be a flower. I need to meditate as a bee meditates: short, quick check-ins with my Higher Power, ways to stay conscious of the honey, the life of the flower within me. I need the flower and the bee.

Then I see the little girl is not cowed from fear, she's just asleep. She's waiting for life to be more fun, less serious. "Even prayer," she tells me, "can be lighter."

My resistance became my teacher; once I stopped beating myself up for not doing it right, I learned what I really needed. Bees in mythology, a friend told me later, were considered the messengers of the gods.

Ways to Meditate Besides Silence

• Sit with your journal; focus on the blank page until you are given a message to write down.

• Work with clay, molding images with your eyes shut, discovering shape and form coming through your fingers.

• Draw, draw to music, draw after silence, upon waking, sketch dream images.

• Dance, jog, walk, and breathe regularly; do t'ai chi, yoga, swim laps, etc.

• Peel an orange and really taste it.

• Fold laundry, being aware of the texture of each item, making origami of the socks and underwear. Bless the wearer in your mind.

was suspended and you found yourself on a familiar path home without remembering how you got there. Or playing a sport, when you've stopped trying to follow your mind's ideas of how it should be done and simply merged with doing it. This time the activity you merge with is spiritual practice.

It takes practice to sustain profound stillness. Some days you will be better at it than others. Don't be discouraged. There are many books and courses available on meditation. Don't be punitive with yourself. *Meditation is a gift of love: it is the contact point between your ordinary self and the sacred.*

Gentle Return

After the suspended moment of silence, your mind will naturally begin to rise again toward the surface. First there is the thought, "Ohhh, I was there." Then there is resumed awareness of your focusing technique. If you left a question to be pondered in your mind, an insight may come. Observe your thoughts again, stretch out your body. Make notes to yourself; draw or write in your journal.

I usually take my journal or a pad of paper with me into my meditation space because things come to mind that I want to jot down. I like to have an open page before me as I come out of silence. Journal writing slips easily with us into and out of a meditative state. After meditating, you may find yourself several paragraphs down the page, with no conscious memory of having written. You may find doodles in the margin, messages from the quieted mind.

The real challenge of return is to sustain a core of silence that accompanies you back into the hubbub of your life. We live life best when we maintain an inner calm in all that we do. This is not easy, may not even be fully possible, yet that is the quest of the meditator: to stay connected to the connection.

The image of the river is often called upon to describe meditation, and it's an image that frequently comes to my mind when I

Every man should be made to bake bread sometime in his life. The world would be better for it. It's the closest he will ever come to knowing birth. The kitchen becomes a bedroom, the pine table an inverted four poster. The great stoneware bowl with the blue band running 'round is a surrogate womb. The finely ground wheat, the white milk, the yellow butter, the egg, oval, brown and pure are gifts given from the Mother. The yeast smells of sex and life. The mixing and kneading, the thrusting of his hands are the gentle aggression of copulation. It leaves him strangely relaxed and spent. Now he must wait for his child to grow in the dark bowl, under a towel. He must wait for its form to finalize in the dark heat of the oven. He must burn himself on taking it out, for there must be some pain. And then he must share his golden child with the world.

You do not need to leave your room. Remain sitting at your table and listen. Do not even listen, simply wait, be quite still and solitary.
The world will freely offer itself to you to be unmasked, it has no choice, it will roll in ecstasy at your feet.

—*Franz Kafka*

am bobbing along on my blue meditation pillow counting my breaths and waiting for silence.

Meditation allows us to wake up one day and realize we are being carried along in a great river. The river seems to be flowing somewhere, though we're not sure where. Maybe we try struggling back to shore, but the current doesn't allow it. After awhile we notice everyone else and everything else is in the river, too, and there doesn't seem to be a shore. We grow more comfortable. Life in the river begins to seem normal. We discover we can carry on most aspects of daily living in the river. We also discover that we are not just swept along, but can relate to the river, diving deep and surfacing, cleansing ourselves, getting caught in eddies, and figuring out how to get back into the central flow. We think we are human beings. Then we think we are fish. Finally we see: We are the river.

Meditation

To prepare to use this meditation and others throughout the book, find a quiet place where you will not be interrupted for twenty minutes or so. Ask someone to read the meditation to you or to play back a version of the meditation you have made yourself or ordered from the back of the book. The points of ellipsis (. . .) indicate a significant pause—silence maintained within the text. Pause for as long as you feel comfortable; five to ten seconds can seem a long time in meditation. Double ellipses indicate longer silence.

GREETING SILENCE

Close your eyes and relax your body. . . . Take all the time you need to get comfortable. . . . Shift muscles . . . stretch and relax. . . . Make sure your spine and neck are straight and aligned . . . not held stiffly; there is no stiffness here . . . just comfort, the beginning of calm. . . . There is no hurry now. . . . There is nothing else to do . . . or think about. . . . Just relax.

Notice your breath. . . . Let your breath enter deeply into your body. . . . Let your breath roll into you like soft, heavy clouds that fill you with silence. . . . Inhale slowly . . . deeply. . . . Exhale slowly . . . thoroughly. . . . Let your breath sink in and out. . . . Your breath is a rhythm of calm. . . . Follow your breath. . . . Exhale extraneous thought. . . . Inhale silence. . . . . . .

What is silence like? . . . Does it have color? . . . texture? . . . weight? . . . . . . You may want to sigh . . . or smile. . . . It's all right. . . . You may be aware of vibration. . . . This is the energy of silence riding in your body. . . . You may hear ringing in your ears. . . . You may notice the delicate thump of your heart. Make the movements and sounds of your body part of your silence. . . . Make your breath and your heartbeat part of your silence. . . . . . . This body is your home. . . . You are filled with the source of all knowing. . . . You are attuned to your body, and your body is attuned to the universe. . . . . . .

62

Let your awareness drift in a quiet, safe space. . . . It may no longer be the room where you are sitting. . . . You may see this space clearly in your mind's eye, or only sense it. . . . It may feel familiar. . . . This is the light that you came from. . . . . . . This is the light you are traveling toward. . . . . . . Here, in the light, everything is all right. . . . . . .

In the light, create an ideal setting for your writing. . . . Put all the things around you that protect and symbolize your journey. . . . . . . Remove anything that does not belong. . . . . . . See yourself in this space. . . . See yourself writing in your journal. . . . . . . You spin silence into words. . . . When you run out of words, you dip your mind and your pen back into silence. . . . . . .

When you are ready, open your journal to the next blank page. . . . Let the blankness of that page turn to white light that glows from your journal. . . . Bask in this light. . . . Fill yourself with journal light. . . . . . . Ask your journal to reveal to you what you need to say at this point in your spiritual journey. . . . . . .

When you have received this message, thank your journal. . . . Thank the light. . . . Set this ideal writing space in your mind. . . . You may come here anytime. . . . You are always welcome in the light. . . . . . . Slowly . . . gently . . . follow your breath back to this room. . . . Emerge out of the silence of your body. . . . There is no hurry. . . . Stretch your body. . . . Open your eyes. . . .

Take some time to draw or write, whatever you want to record from your vision.

II.
Conditions
for Travel

5. THE EVOLVING SELF

We cannot go beyond the ego . . . if we have never reached the ego. We need the human ego to assimilate, house and channel the beyond-ego, the non-ego forces that touch us and that we are so eager to touch in return.

—*Ann Belford Ulanov*
"The God You Touch," from
The Christ and the Bodhisattva

Once in a Quaker meeting, on a beautiful spring day when the fresh air blew temptingly through the silent circle of meditators, a Friend stood up to speak her piece and changed forever how I regarded myself and everyone else there. "I am not my body," she said. "I am not my work or my role. I am not my gender. I am not my nationality. I am not a human being . . . I am a spiritual being having a human experience." I wandered out after meeting, sat on the grass among the dandelions, lay down in the sunlight, and looked up at the

Who Are You?

- If you didn't already "know" who you are, how would you find out?
- Whom would you ask?
- Write imagined responses to these questions.

JOURNAL ENTRY
I called my grandma and asked her who I am. She lives in a nursing home, when she bothers to reside on this planet at all. Her mind is the most freed up space of anyone I know.
Yo, Jonnie, she said, you're a Martian, just like us. Now it's a heritage to be proud of, a good planet to call home.
But what does it mean, Grandma?
Well, it means you have the chance to see this world differently, if you'll take off your human contact lenses and look at how things really are.

- Who is the self who resides in silence?
- How does consciousness thrive beyond thought?

According to Buddhist tradition, the spiritual path is the process of cutting through our confusion, of uncovering the awakened state of mind. When the awakened state of mind is crowded by ego and its attendant paranoia, it takes on the character of an underlying instinct. So it is not a matter of building up the awakened state, but rather of burning out the confusions which obstruct it. In the process of burning out these confusions, we discover enlightenment.

—*Chögyam Trungpa*
Cutting Through Spiritual Materialism

infinite sky, wondering who I really am and how far I have come from "home."

To be human is to be both flesh and spirit, ego and unity. This duality never leaves us as long as we are alive, and yet in the course of the spiritual journey, the sense of self—who we think we are—is likely to undergo almost complete transformation. This transformation is usually generated by reflection, by the willingness to become consciously introspective and exploratory concerning the nature of the self.

I am informed, from time to time, that there are ways of experiencing consciousness other than following the introspective path. I don't fully understand what this means—whether there are people with enough innate consciousness that they do not need a second awakening to life, or if these are people staving off the moment when they, too, must dive deep into their own subconscious and make the long swim back to the surface as the rest of us do.

Saint Francis spoke exuberantly of himself as "God's fool," but he founded a highly introspective order of monks. Joseph Campbell speaks of the capacity to live at the center of the turning wheel, instead of being lashed to its spokes, going around with every revolution. From this position, Campbell challenges us "to follow our bliss," yet he certainly implies that it takes significant learning to center ourselves enough to know what bliss is and release the turnings of the ego.

Whether or not there might be another path to transcendence, the path of this book is based on the one I know, the one I have been teaching, and the responses of hundreds and thousands of journal writers.

In every religious and spiritual tradition, there seem to be fairly universal conditions of travel that create and foster the spiritual quest. However expressed, these conditions require an interior process that teaches us to disidentify with the ego and discover a fuller self. This is a long process, with many gradations of insight and occasional leaps through hoops of great awareness. If, as the Quaker woman clearly implies, the purpose of introspection is to allow us

Ego-Speak/Self-Speak Dialogues

- Write dialogues that allow each self its say.
- You don't need to identify which voice represents what part of the self; just let the conversations spill forth.

JOURNAL ENTRY

ME: *You sure seem jittery these days.*

EGO: *I'm afraid for you.*

ME: *Afraid for me or for yourself?*

EGO: *We're the same.*

ME: *No, we're not or we couldn't be talking to each other. We are part of each other, but separate too. How can I help you not be afraid?*

EGO: *Stop growing so fast.*

ME: *I don't think I can. Nor do I choose to. Life is growing us very fast. That doesn't mean you have to be scared.*

EGO: *I don't feel safe.*

ME: *What do you think safety is?*

EGO: *No surprises. Nothing threatening.*

ME: *My definition of safety is deciding to trust the surprises . . .*

The ego is the mind's belief that it is totally on its own.

—Dr. Helen Schucman
A Course in Miracles

. . . the ego neuroses that once preoccupied me haven't all gone away. What has gone is my identification with them. Now they are merely quaint and fascinating . . . a passing show. . . . More and more I am just awareness.
Life lives itself. I am involved with it all, yet I cling to none of it. It is what is. No big deal.

—Ram Dass
Journey of Awakening

to see ourselves as spiritual beings, then everything that happens to us has the potential to contribute to this changing definition of the self.

The self we most likely know best is the workaday ego persona we have created for getting through the world. This persona is a clever collection of ingrained mental and emotional patterning, social skills, learned behaviors, body language, gesture, and so forth.

Meditation teaches us that consciousness is a loose-fitting robe. Through meditation and other practices of silence, we have the opportunity to become more and more aware of the depth and breadth of what the self may be. Journal conversations, the question-and-answer processes of thought, all open up the issue of how to define the self. And the more we look at the self, the more inclusive a concept it becomes. The self contains many voices, perceptions, viewpoints, and abilities. In writing, we see ourselves functioning as a conglomerate and don't even find it odd.

Whenever I watch programs about sea life I am amazed yet again that what looks like one great thing—a coral reef, for instance—is actually an infinite number of individual units, corals, each having a life that is both its own and irrevocably connected to the communal entity. Out of many corals—one reef. It is even more amazing to think that we are like this also: out of many selves—one being. The reason it's so hard to think of ourselves this way is because the ego is doing most of the thinking.

This ego-self, which has, since childhood, been driving us forward into the world, cannot go the length of the spiritual journey. Ego is too limited, too invested in its fantasies of uniqueness and separation to carry us all the way. Eventually, some greater identity must emerge in the mind and assume leadership in reunion with the sacred.

The ego is like the wizard of Oz at the moment of exposure. It sits all puffed, powerful, and illusionary on the throne, and shouts, "Pay no attention to the man behind the curtain!" There are, in each of our minds, many selves behind many curtains, waiting for the

> *. . . it is just in the death of an ego-centered existence that a*
> *sturdy concrete ego is also needed to receive the One who*
> *comes . . .*

—*Ann Belford Ulanov*

Mythic Stories

Think about this particular time in your life and what
is happening to you.

* Write it as a mythic story.
* Personify the forces you are working with; make
your own scarecrow, witch, and wizard.
* Create the landscape of your pilgrimage.
* Check in with this story over time, expand and
change it as your sense of self and journey evolves.
* Simply begin, "Once upon a time . . ."

> ### THREE JOURNAL ENTRIES
>
> *Once upon a time there was a poor little rich girl. She was poor because
> she didn't have much money. She was rich because she had many
> talents. She was still a girl because she had not fully realized her power.
> One day she set out on a quest to give up her poverty, gain her riches
> and claim her power. . . .*
>
> *Once upon a time there was a soldier who came home from the war and
> couldn't stop fighting. He was very confused. Nobody else seemed still at
> war but him. And all the enemies he chose to battle were
> invisible. . . . After awhile he decided to become a soldier of gentleness. . . .*
>
> *Once upon a time there was a child who belonged in the world, but not
> in her family. This was very confusing. Outside, in nature, she felt at
> home. She liked to climb trees and run and explore. She stopped at mud
> puddles and anthills and loved to blow the heads off dandelions. They
> didn't mind. But inside, in her parents' house she was not at home.
> Inside felt colder than outside. The child didn't understand. It has taken
> her forty years to understand and perhaps she doesn't yet. But she
> knows enough to believe that it's more important to be at home in the
> world than in the family and that she was given the harder and wiser
> choice to make.*

moment in our journeys when we are ready to dethrone the ego and see who else is there.

Ego tries to convince us that *it* is the only one there: the primary source of identity, protection, sustenance, and survival. Like any good employee in search of ultimate job security, the ego makes itself appear indispensable. It attaches itself to behaviors and thought patterns that other aspects of the self could do as well or better, and takes credit for them. And to a degree the ego *is* indispensable, for we would not be human without it. Even the great sages, saints, and prophets still contend with ego. What makes their mental structure different from yours and mine is a shift in perception, the degree to which they understand the true nature of the self and the ego's role as one aspect of that self—not its core.

Professor Ann Belford Ulanov, quoted at the chapter opening, wisely stresses the ego's role in the spiritual process as the part of us that bears witness and translates the raw forces of spirituality into human terms. To travel the journey as a human being, we must remain fully human. Spiritual growth is a process of expansion. We remain ego *and* spirit; body *and* soul. This is the dichotomy and paradox we live in. Ulanov says that we need to retain the ego, to have a self that is ready to meet the universe at the moment of longed-for reunion. Like a coupling on train cars, the journey propels us down the track toward spirit, and when we have readied ourselves to touch the sacred, there needs to be an entity the sacred can touch in return.

In the journal, especially in dialogues, we are able to observe these many voices and sort through the confusions that cover awakened mind. The journal is invaluable in this process because it gives us something tangible to read and reflect upon while sorting, and allows us to look at the manipulations of thought we have recorded and to devise new ways of managing the mind. Writing down your many voices need not be a power struggle for lead singer, but an enjoyment of the richness of your inner experience and a commitment to discern and follow inner guidance as it becomes clear.

s = self, o = orphan/child-self

S: Well, Orphan, remember when we had this insight and you made the leap out of the past into my arms? Here it is months later and you seem to still be feeling orphaned. What's going on?

O: I don't know. I don't know how to talk about it. I just feel bad still. Sad. Mad.

S: Are you staying in my arms? Are you letting me take care of you?

O: Yes. But that's not enough. Maybe it's not me, the child who is feeling like an orphan; maybe it's you, the grown-up. We did all that therapy. I got you out of the bargain. Who have you got?

S: I've got God/Spirit.

O: You have God/Spirit in your head, but have you made the leap into God/Spirit's hands the way you asked me to leap into yours?

S: No. I want to, but I don't know how to—I feel like I'm waiting to leap, and I can't yet. Like I'm waiting for God. Or waiting for my readiness to see that God can be there, catch me, like I caught you. How did you make the leap?

O: I saw you. I saw that I was a mere shadow compared to you. You were solid, real, a living force in the world. If I wanted a vehicle to ride out my life in, to accomplish my dreams in— you were it. I accepted my shadowness and leapt onto your realness.

S: I understand. I have to give up seeing myself as the ultimate reality and see God that way.

O: I have lost nothing—at least nothing important enough for me to even remember it—by this leap, and I have gained everything. You will lose nothing: gain everything, too. Get ready for God, and when It gestures—Leap!

As you experiment with written dialogues, you may notice the presence of an overseeing voice who comments on and helps direct the discussion's progress. Befriend this voice. Learn to identify it, dialogue with it, and discover how you may depend upon it. This voice is the self, the observer, and your connector to the sacred.

In the story of Oz, the wizard stays comfortably in the castle he's created by impressing and frightening the populace, while the pilgrim, Dorothy, goes off on the quest. Accompanied by the attributes of spiritual growth—intelligence (Scarecrow), feeling (Tin Man), and courage (Lion)—she faces the trials of her journey. When she comes back to the egotistical wizard for her reward, he drifts off without her. Dorothy cannot ride the ego back to Kansas because ego can't take her to the "home" she now longs for. She despairs, until the good witch Glinda reveals to her that she doesn't need the ego's tricks, only her own readiness. Dorothy had lost faith in herself, and in the trip through Oz she rediscovers it within. When she wakes up in Kansas, the attributes of intelligence, feeling, and courage are gathered around her and she recognizes them. She has become conscious.

We all live in Oz, and the transformation Dorothy makes is the same transformation we are all trying to make. The conditions of travel may appear different in how our stories unfold, but the mythic elements are the same. As the ego becomes our servant instead of master, we are able to see our life stories differently: to interpret events in terms of their purpose and our growth.

This may sound like a spooky process, but we experience it all the time. As you write a journal, over time you see the pattern of your pilgrimage emerging. You see your identity change through dialoguing with the voices of the mind and interacting with the events of your life.

The ego isn't comfortable with all this shifting. Since it perceives itself as the only real self, it views the shift into expanded consciousness as a kind of death. So, in the midst of everything else that's going on, you will find yourself grieving. Or the ego may throw last-ditch fears and obstacles in your way. But there's a trick

Other Self

- If you are not your ego, whom will you be?
- Write about the self you are becoming.
- Own your growth and power.
- Discuss humbleness of heart.

> *Ego is constantly attempting to acquire and apply the teachings
> of spirituality for its own benefit . . . the main point of any
> spiritual practice is to step out of the bureaucracy of ego. This
> means stepping out of ego's constant desire for a higher, more
> spiritual, more transcendental version of knowledge, religion,
> virtue, judgement, comfort or whatever it is that the particular ego
> is seeking.*
>
> —*Chögyam Trungpa*
> Cutting Through Spiritual Materialism

End of Innocence

- Write about particular kinds of innocence you have valued.
- How did you lose your innocence in these areas?
- What did it feel like to say good-bye to moral innocence, sexual innocence, family innocence?
- When you lose innocence, what do you hang onto instead?

of the mind to be noted in all this: If the ego is so sure it's the only self, then who is it yelling at? Who is it trying to control?

"Me!" you say. "The ego is trying to control me." There, you've just made the shift. *You* are standing outside the ego, being your *self*.

At first, going beyond the ego may feel laborious, like trying to walk naturally as a child pulls at your leg screaming, "Don't go! Don't go!" *The ego's response to the idea that there is some place it cannot go is to want to go* only *as far in the journey as* it *is able.* As you venture deeper into your journal, into silence, into spiritual experience, the ego may keep interrupting to tell you that you should stop, now, and be content, or that it's dangerous to continue.

You may not have thought about it in exactly these terms, but you're familiar with the ego's voice. Ego runs distractions through your prayers and meditations. Ego tells you what a wonderful pilgrim you are and encourages self-satisfaction. In moments when hard choices need to be made, the ego usually sides with comfort and the status quo. It acts the devil's advocate and discourages you from taking risks beyond its grasp.

But the more you persist in experiencing yourself outside your ego, the calmer your ego will become. It will eventually grasp and admit the possibility of self beyond its own perceptions. The paradox is that you are already beyond the ego's grasp, and always have been. All you need do is awaken. And—you are already awake.

6. WRITING YOUR
SPIRITUAL HISTORY

*There is this path we all think about walking down
towards our future. There is this path that we already
walked on. That's all I can think about, this path, this
road that is one perfect straight line even if it goes around
the world through heat and fog and rain and snow and
it's my life I keep thinking. It's my life.*

—Deborah Keenan
"Small History" from Happiness

Sometimes, in the kind of journeying the spiritual quest
requires, the best way to figure out where you're going
is to understand where you've been.

You have come this far through your willingness
to explore and be surprised, through willingness to accept and
incorporate new information. As a result, the quest keeps revealing
itself to you in complexity and depth. Before you get too deeply

How I Got Here

On alternate days, or as alternate entries, write quick,
one- or two-page statements starting with the phrase
* How I got here . . .
* Where I'm going . . .

> *JOURNAL ENTRY*
> *How I got here: small town, Iowa landscapes. I was the dream of
> a couple trying to find love and happiness late in life. Always the
> church as my background—pompousness, maleness, restrictions.
> My father was a Presbyterian minister. He had taken it all on,
> the form without the substance. It translated for me into Sunday
> school, Bible verses, must-go-to events and the seasons of the year
> framed by religious holidays. I am also, especially now, defined
> by the amount of education I got. Dad always said I'd be
> married and dead a long time, his phrase meaning "Get your
> education first." Conform and don't make waves. Do what's right.
> Don't drink. Don't smoke. Don't ask or talk about sex. It's a
> miracle I've discovered any sexuality in myself, but I tried most
> of it—a rebel at age 18, quietly, secretly. . . . It's all gone by far
> too fast. Marriage, children, working, all have put a signature on
> me. Reacting rather than initiating—at least as far as setting my
> own goals. Is there a plan? Who's drawing it? What does one
> need for a journey?—a vision,—someone to share it,—a way of
> processing it,—insight. I am a reading, curious woman with close
> friends, not quite fulfilled. Laughing. Wanting to think more. Love
> solitude.*

Another version of this exercise is to begin entries
with the following statements:
* I used to be a person who . . .
* I am now a person who . . .
* I want to be a person who . . .

involved in where your quest is taking you, it is important to understand how the quest has brought you this far.

Each of us comes to the quest from somewhere, from a way we first learned about the sacred, the ways our families and culture framed the notion of God. You may have been nurtured in this environment or found it restrictive. Whatever your history, it influences you. And it is part of your pilgrimage. This chapter offers you a chance to affirm the good things that came from your past and to lay the painful experiences aside.

The spiritual quest is a commitment to define your own sense of truth. In the course of your journey, you may forgive and heal old spiritual wounds; you may find and salvage still meaningful elements.

As you review the individual patterns of your spiritual history, you will learn a great deal about your original commitment to the quest and the nature of the next commitment you are getting ready to make.

Mythologists and philosophers believe that the ways we see the sacred are the masks we put on God in order to comprehend spiritual reality. Limited perception is a condition of travel we all deal with: we are trying to picture clearly that holy presence to which we are drawn, and we are limited by our human comprehension. Culturally, religiously, personally, we develop our own "mask of God."

Over the centuries, we have called this presence by many names: Spider Grandmother, Father, Tao, Buddha Consciousness, Shiva, Holy Spirit, Christ, soul, Higher Power, Inner Light, om. All images and concepts we have for presence are metaphors. We apply whatever names, images, symbols, and traditions best translate for us the energy of the universe. Our spiritual histories are the stories of this evolving perception.

If you've never told yourself these stories before, you may be surprised at the amount of recall generated. These memories may literally take over the journal for awhile, but if you follow your inclinations, these tangents will write themselves out and leave you a wealth of information.

You may view your religious experiences as helpful, irrelevant,

*I used to be a person who felt confident in the world. I was my
father's favorite son. This was an advantage I didn't even know I
had until he loaned me money for a house and didn't loan money
to my brother for a business. Now, I am a person who questions
whether confidence works unless it has been tested. Now, I am a
person being tested. My marriage is falling apart. My job going
nowhere. The dreams my father had for me appear wasted. He
had a heart attack and sometimes I think it's his disappointment
getting to him. I don't want to be so disappointed at his age. I
want to be a person who's confident again with a spiritual basis
for my confidence.*

Clustering

This writing technique, also called mapping or
webbing, helps release a wealth of material attached to
your spiritual history. Use a focus word or concept as
the center from which you can spin off freely
associated ideas. For example:

- Each word anchors memory.
- The phrase chosen to represent this memory will
bring it fully to mind.

JOURNAL ENTRY
*Me in tree: I am sitting at the top of the sycamore next to our
yard in Indiana. I don't remember climbing up here, but I am
high up, so high the wind is swaying the branch I sit upon. It is*

or highly damaging, depending on your history. You may be contentedly attending church, synagogue, temple, or mosque, or burdened with a great deal of confusion about your religious upbringing. You may have radically changed religious views or sought an individual spirituality outside religion. Journal writing will help you look differently at any of these experiences and decisions.

Religion and Spirit

For most of us, the language of communication between ourselves and the sacred is based on some kind of formal religious background. Writing your spiritual history is an invitation to review your religious background and integrate religion and spirituality until you understand the unity that sustains the quest, no matter what language you choose to speak.

If thoughts and ideas come so fast you can't keep track of them, cluster them in the margins or jot brief marginal notes and continue with your main thought. Use flow writing. You will not really lose important information; the mind gives us more than one chance to capture a thought.

Religion is the codification of raw spiritual insight and experience into story and doctrine. Religions are founded by inspired teachers who record their direct contact with the sacred and leave a body of teachings for believers to follow. Later, other insightful leaders emerge within a religious tradition and add to it. Religion is the story of how an identified group of people relates to the sacred, and how they perceive the sacred relating back to them. A body of knowledge grows, and along with knowledge, a body of story. A certain interpretation of the world and spirit is developed and passed on. Rituals, symbols, prayers, and prescribed behavior separate believers from nonbelievers.

Over time, religions permeate the cultures in which they grow. Religion impacts civil laws, civil morality, social conduct, family

*an utterly new sensation to be off the ground, caught in the wind.
I am six years old, enthralled. Part of me thinks I should be
afraid, but I'm not. The tree has a safe hold on me. I feel at one
with the tree, the wind. This is ecstasy—joining myself
seamlessly to the world. My mother comes out of the house
looking for me. I answer from the tree, but she looks very small
and faraway as though "I" am a lot higher than the tree. She
screams in fright. I laugh at her fear. When she stays frightened
I let her coax me down. But I do not forget, keep climbing trees,
trying to re-create that freedom.*

• Choose a central concept broad enough to have
smaller specific concepts associated with it, but not so
broad you get overwhelming response.

Spiritual Lifeline

• Mark several journal pages in year segments; leave
space to note experiences.
• Working with chronology, write memories.

> JOURNAL ENTRY: LIFELINE:
> *1946: on the beach, summer, I was 1 or 2, feet in warm, soupy
> sand, feeling safe, connected to life, the sea and God(?).
> 1953: first theological question. I asked my mother, "Who made
> God?" She didn't know, told me to ask minister. He didn't know
> either, said no one did, God has always been. I didn't understand
> and wasn't satisfied.
> 1958: lonely and homesick at boarding school. I made the honor
> roll, my parents didn't write.
> 1961: sailing, salt spray, s.w. wind coming over the bow as we
> slice windward on Buzzards Bay, laughing, urging the boat
> forward with will and skill.
> 1963: Kennedy's assassination. Stunned, numb, Mrs. Sweeney
> standing in front of her tv crying. I went to the chapel, prayed.
> No one else came. Dreams died with him and faith in humanity.*

and class consciousness, and governance. And, after a couple of thousand years, you and I get born into this religious/cultural/spiritual soup and try to clear our own way to direct and sacred dialogue.

Religion passes on spiritual insight in a kind of code. Religious doctrines and stories can be interpreted on many levels, and it depends on the readiness of the hearer to determine the level at which s/he listens.

All religions are practiced on multiple layers of awareness. The *exoteric layer* is the level of observance deemed suitable for the general community. The *esoteric layer* is the point of mystical contact. Ordinary worship is based on the exoteric. The "priest" leads followers through familiar observances. The gate to the esoteric, the "hidden doctrine," is alluded to, but not shown. Throughout religious history and development, the esoteric is coded within the exoteric. The esoteric can only be discovered through direct spiritual experience, either by crossing this boundary spontaneously, or being led across it through initiation. Religions sometimes blur the boundary between exoteric and esoteric practices. When observance crosses into trance, speaking in tongues, chanting, ecstatic dance, or deep contemplation, the boundaries of observance are opened to direct connection.

The presence of both exoteric and esoteric practices creates the hierarchy present in most religions. The follower is expected to enter a period of preparation and spiritual development before s/he is ready to delve into the "mystery."

It is this layer of mystery that is often given the term *spirituality*. Over and over we hear people say, "I'm not particularly religious, but I consider myself spiritual." I think what's being acknowledged is that religion—as the observance of rituals alone—has lost its appeal. But spirituality—the direct experience of the sacred—has retained its appeal.

As you write your spiritual histories, you may find events that occurred outside religion and events in which religion allowed you to touch the esoteric layer. You don't need to stop being religious, or become religious, in order to be spiritual, but you need an

*1977: Call to seminary and priesthood, cried out of sheer joy:
everything in my life up to that point suddenly made sense, had
meaning: parents' alcoholism, Air Force in Europe, inner city
work, my marriage/divorce,—fit together, made sense. I knew that
God had been there all along. Relief strength.*

*1983: long depression, being turned down for ordination,
housesitting alone, crying, aching, despairing, screaming at God,
rationalizing, grasping for grace. I just kept saying, there has to
be a reason, I'm supposed to learn something. Worst 5 months of
my life, but also full of grace. God is weird.*

*It is popularly supposed that between those who use the word
"God" and those who do not there is some great gulf. But the gulf
lies elsewhere. It lies between those who dogmatize, either positively
or negatively, and those who recognize in great humility that
something within them bears witness to realities which may be
momentous in our lives, but which lie beyond the grasping net of
our categories of thought.*

—Phillip Hewitt

Religious Inventory

• What's your first memory of being in a church or
synagogue?

• What are the first things you remember about a
member of the clergy?

• What were your parents taught and how did that
influence what they taught you?

• How did your religious attitudes change in
adolescence? youth? midlife? old age?

• What social/historic events have influenced how
you regard religion?

• What religious rituals do you observe? Why?

JOURNAL ENTRY
*If I perceive God as a Parent in the sky, then it's extremely
difficult for me to imagine that this Being has the time or*

environment that encourages you to see through observance to mystery. Without direct experience of the sacred, religion eventually becomes formalized, and you lose faith. Exoteric practice was never meant to replace esoteric experience, only to provide a map that points the believer in the right direction. Religion provides a language and tradition inside which seekers can feel safe enough to experience spiritual contact themselves without relying on a designated intervenor. The seeker makes the leap of faith, opens the mind . . .

The problem with religion, for some, is that it becomes a social institution and reflects the prejudices of the culture as much as it reflects the values of its tradition. Religion develops vested interests in how society functions and how followers contribute to the social order. Some religious administrators have ambivalent attitudes toward the institution's essential rooting in direct spiritual revelation. They aren't sure what is most important to protect and foster: revelation or stability.

On the one hand, religious hierarchy wants to keep believers in line, sustaining the "church" without challenging it. On the other hand, religion is dependent upon the personal, outside-the-norm experiences of those whose contact with the sacred allows religious understanding to grow. These risk takers become the saints, prophets, gurus, and shamans who revitalize religion through new experience and the interpretation of mystery. That doesn't mean the hierarchy has to like it, but it can't stop it either. This tension between stasis and change exists in every religion. You and I are part of that tension, making our ways through it as best we can.

Your interest in the spiritual quest is part of the explosion of spiritual longing occurring on a global scale. No hierarchy is in control of this longing, no tradition contains it. People are waking up and directing their spiritual lives. They are using every conceivable bit of information and framing to get themselves where they are drawn to go. They are driven forward by only one commonality: The desire to make sacred contact and to allow that contact to alter their lives in significant ways.

inclination to oversee the daily actions of my life. But, if I perceive God as all available Energy—like light or air—then it becomes possible to imagine a more immediate and intimate relationship.

You have to go past the imagined image of [the sacred]. Such an image of one's god becomes a final obstruction, one's ultimate barrier. You hold on to your own ideology, your own little manner of thinking, and when a larger experience of God approaches, an experience greater than you are prepared to receive, you take flight from it by clinging to the image in your mind. This is known as preserving your faith. . . .
I don't have faith; I have experience. I have experience of the wonder of life.

—Joseph Campbell
The Power of Myth

Spiritual Inventory

•   What are the most meaningful spiritual experiences you ever had outside a religious setting? What has been frightening or confusing?
•   What role has nature played in your spiritual awareness?
•   Do you remember a place that you felt was "holy"?
•   Did you, or do you now, have a place you identify as the source of peace and unity for you? Describe this place—real or imagined.
•   What role have other people played?

My son called to me that God was inside his red fire engine. He wanted to show me. I did move as fast as I could, spilling like water through the kitchen door into a summer day, but God had left by the time I got there. My son smiled, told me I'd missed him by seconds.

—Deborah Keenan

When you step beyond the exoteric, you are on your own . . . but that's all right. That's the step that every pilgrim takes into what Campbell calls "the larger experience of God."

Writing your spiritual history gives you the opportunity to declare spiritual independence. You may choose to stay within a religious structure and use it to support and acknowledge your own path, or you may acknowledge the path beyond that structure and the freedom it has brought you. You bear witness to your spiritual experiences in whatever context they occur. You grant yourself the time to sort and take with you everything that was, is, or can be made good. And to make peace with, forgive, and leave behind everything that was harmful to or limiting of spiritual growth.

You will need this cornerstone of tested experience because someday, if it hasn't already, the journey must lead you out of perceived order and into perceived disorder. You will step into the storm of the quest.

7. THE ROLE OF DISORDER

In the middle of the journey of our life, I came to myself within a dark wood where the straight way was lost.

—Dante
The Divine Comedy

When I was only twenty-three years old, a few weeks after I'd declared my journey on paper and was preparing to leave for Europe, an older friend whom I much admired asked me if I'd ever gone through a "dark night of the soul." It was the first time I'd heard this phrase, originated by St. John of the Cross. It is an evocation: if you've ever gone through a dark night of the soul, you know it. But while you are in the middle of it, you may not know. I thought then the notion sounded romantic. It is not. A dark night is a shattering, confusing, painful experience that is also an ordinary, to-be-expected part of the quest.

Despair is like the winter of sophomore year, you think it will never end and that nothing different is ever going to happen to you.

—Peter McDonald

Despair is the ultimate blackness that every person must endure in gaining full maturity . . . and this is not such a bad thing as we have been led to believe.

—John Brantner

Naming What's Happening

- What reasons can you see for your current disorder and despair?
- How long has this been coming?
- What hints have you been avoiding? What ways have you put off facing disorder?
- What do you know intuitively about this time in your life?
- How are you willing to facilitate the process of disorder?
- What old expectations of order are being cleared out?
- What new order is emerging?
- What assumptions seemed to bring this on?
- What assumptions are you letting go of?
- How is life different right now?
- How has your perception changed?
- What is despair teaching you to pay attention to?
- What blessings can you imagine coming out of this time?

Do not attempt to answer these questions all at once; they are set here together to provide a framework, a way of normalizing your experience.

92

The spring I turned forty, anguishing about the lack of creative direction in my writing, feeling as though everything I knew how to do was over and I didn't know what was next, a friend in my writer's group used the word despair. "You sound in despair," she said. I promptly burst into tears of relief; someone had seen my condition and given it a name. Now I could begin to interact and respond. I could use the naming as a rock to stand on.

It's a strange thing about life with gravity: we cannot leap without first pushing off from something solid. Until we admit our despair, or until someone/something helps us name it, we are in free-fall. We have no mechanism for gaining enough ground to jump. And what despair requires of us is tolerance during the free-fall, and then the courage to take a leap of faith.

John Brantner, for many years the chair of psychiatry at the University of Minnesota, was a philosopher who specialized in helping people understand despair, grief, and difference, all elements of life and spiritual experience that we tend to overlook. Even though we have been told by saints and sages that there *is* a dark night, that we *will* lose ourselves in the woods, we may still be shocked and surprised to find ourselves there. It is part of human nature to hope that spirituality will save us from this experience, that we can combine enough luck and faith not to suffer.

In Brantner's worldview, this is not only not possible, it's not desirable. He defined despair as an integral part of human maturity, an avenue of learning that should not be avoided. This seems to be true. Despair is such a nearly universal experience among people who have chosen consciousness, that you and I would do well to accept it, name it, and prepare ourselves as willingly as possible to submit to the process.

I like to read biography, to see how other lives are going along. I am especially interested in the lives of the great human role models. I want to glimpse what it takes to be a person capable of carrying that kind of stature. When I look at the records of their lives— words left in their own journals and private writings, words recorded by biographers—an implicit code emerges, a telegraphed

You gain strength, courage and confidence by every experience in which you really stop to look fear in the face. You are able to say to yourself, "I lived through this horror. I can take the next thing that comes along." You must do the thing you think you cannot do.

—*Eleanor Roosevelt*
You Learn by Living

Looking at Order

Spend a day noticing all the ways you maintain a sense of order. Write about some of these in the journal.
• What is their purpose?
• How did you develop these behaviors?
• What assumptions underlie your rituals?
• Write your own definitions of the concepts presented in this chapter. Define:
—order
—disorder
—despair
—new order
—transformation.
• When you think about "having your life in order," what does this mean to you?
• When you think of your life "falling into disorder," what does this mean?
• How are you preparing yourself to move on from despair?

Treat Yourself

Buy a new journal, find a hopeful image, a postcard, or saying, to paste to the cover.

survival. The insights that inspired these people were first endured in private anguish: they did not fit in their surroundings; they were not comfortable with their socially prescribed roles; they found they could not settle for satisfactions others seemed to enjoy; they felt alone, isolated, alienated from community and spirit; they despaired, cried out to the sacred, "What do you want of me, then?"

And slowly they made their way through. They did not shirk despair. They did not turn back. And they did not destroy themselves or abandon their dreams even at moments when all seemed lost. These people used despair as an avenue for deepening consciousness, for allowing themselves to be changed. Reading their course to maturity, we can find a map adaptable to our own course. A hopeful message: If despair comes to our own small lives, so comes the avenue for allowing it to deepen and change us.

Each of us has expectations about what life ought to throw our way. We get up in the morning with the assumption that we know approximately how the day is going to go. We hug our loved ones, drive carefully through rush hour, walk around ladders, and look both ways before crossing the street. These little rituals create a sense of order. Order is seen as one of life's favors bestowed upon us. It works most days, works for long stretches of time, but we sell a bit of our souls in exchange. We come to expect order, but we have to deal with reality.

There are times when the spiritual quest stretches our expectations to the limit, and our sense of orderliness is torn away. The harmony we fancied between ourselves and life seems irrevocably broken. We cannot think about this clearly. We are disoriented and without language to explain. And most of us can't go to a mountaintop to figure it out. Ordinary life continues to demand that we function, no matter what else is going on. We are required to go through the motions of daily chores, work, relationships. These are the times when a half hour of journal writing, first thing in the morning or last at night, may be the greatest gift we can give ourselves.

Despair is the human psyche's initial reaction to disorder. De-

*When you come to the edge of all that you know, you must
believe one of two things: There will be earth to stand on, or you
will be given wings to fly.*

*—author unknown,
but thank you.*

A Blessing a Day

Before going to sleep, pause and review the day.
• Write a brief statement, choosing one thing you've
noticed that you are willing to accept as a spiritual gift
from the day.
• End the entry with the words *Thank you.*

You may want to circle these paragraphs in your
regular journal, so you can page through and read all
your blessings, or get a special little notebook to keep
by the bed.

JOURNAL ENTRIES: BLESSINGS:
I heard a cardinal singing in the snowstorm. Thank you.

*On the way home from work, a stranger in the check-out line at
the grocery store and I got to telling jokes, really cracked each
other up. Thank you.*

*I cried in church this morning after taking communion, saying
silently, Thank you for bringing me home.*

Grief Work

• Take 10 minutes a day in private space.
• Ask yourself: What might I be grieving for?
• Grieve it.

spair is a state of shock. We have expected certain things to be true and these things no longer appear true. The mind doesn't know what messages to generate or what behaviors will help.

Disorder can be generated internally or externally. When something breaks down in our belief system about life's progress, then disorder is generated by hidden, unseen, often unconscious, forces. Psychology has defined despair as a breakdown in communication between the self and the world. When the world is not behaving according to our deepest hopes and beliefs, the mind is thrown into chaos. We don't know what to believe. We don't know what beliefs are being challenged.

The journal may be your only way of glimpsing what disorder is about. It's hard to talk to others, to say, "My expectations aren't being met and I can hardly stand the pain . . ." Your job in the journal is to articulate the individual nature of the problem, to go in search of the beliefs that seem broken, to mend them and replace them with mature beliefs. Dialogue is your strongest tool in this process, along with writing after meditation and taking time to grieve. Breaking out of old beliefs is a natural part of the spiritual journey—so is creating mature beliefs.

Listing specific questions can also be helpful in reestablishing a sense of mental order, but this is only one way of writing in your journal during crisis. The blessing-a-day exercise helps you move from negative to positive focus by acknowledging that a relationship with the sacred is still occurring daily and looking for the good in what is happening. A blessing a day is your grounding point.

Disorder is also visited upon us by outside events: the business fails, you're fired, your relationship or marriage crumbles, a child falls in with drugs despite all you do, you or loved ones are struck with injury or illness: or the state of the world finally gets to you, the thousands of children who die of dehydration, and you feel helpless to intercede, to solve problems or prevent similar disasters. These events break into the orderliness of our lives and change them—often irrevocably—without permission. Nobody asks for disaster: we cope.

Grace realized with a suddenness that sent sorrow and anger, too, to the very root of her being—that life had not stopped, just as the sun had not failed to come out that day. . . . Not one dogwood withheld its splendor, and not one bird had stopped its rowing across the sky. Not one. The world was going on. And on. And this shocked her more than her mother's death. The sameness of life after death, that is what haunts the living, she thought. It is the indifference of the earth to a life being snatched away that wraps around the mourners' hearts and intensifies their grieving.

—Emily Ellison
First Light

There are really only two things to do: one is to be still and listen, the other is to take spiritually based action. Everything else is bogus activity which only gets in the way of our real understanding.

—Joy Houghton

Renaming What's Happening

• If "despair" were not labeled in your mind with negative connotations, how might you experience it?
• If "disorder" were not labeled, how would you perceive this time in your life?
• What do you think would happen if you gave up negative assumptions and let disorder and despair carry you where they will?
• What prevents you from allowing this?
• Draw a metaphoric map for what you are exploring.
• Draw or dialogue with images from dreams and meditations.

Again, the journal may be the most receptive place to dump the responses that accompany disruption: feelings of anger, fear, disorientation. The journal holds our questioning of life and spirit while we grow large enough to encompass this latest event within an expanded sense of orderliness.

Life is neither ordered nor disordered: life just is. Disorder comes through the process of having our assumptions challenged, sometimes brutally challenged. In the gap, we learn to re-perceive life, to review our assumptions, to adjust to altered conditions for travel.

In despair, you feel as if life is not keeping its end of the bargain. The only problem is there was no bargain; you only assumed there was. You are confronted, over and over, with your own fantasy of life. Use the journal to probe what these fantasies are. Dialogue with your belief system, with the inner child, with the fantasies themselves. Dialogue with events and people involved in these events which have precipitated the crisis. Look for the lessons that may be learned from disruption. Ask for—don't demand—insight. Eventually you will be able to allow disorder to become acceptable, to make despair a friend.

A friend! All those dark nights, head laid upon the windowsill, the anguished questions and lack of comforting response; the gut-wrenching fear when you realize you are not in control of anything; the anger at being stopped in your tracks and torn apart while the rest of the crowd is still playing golf. Yes, this too is your quest.

The spiritual journey is a step-by-step process for giving up illusion. Each time illusion drops, we experience temporary disorder because we're not sure how to adjust to life as we now recognize it. *The gift of despair is that it offers us a process for making peace with what is and becoming comfortable with new perceptions.* That process of peace is a gradual understanding of what it means to surrender: from ego to spirit, from the past to the future, from despair to joy. Surrender is not an easy concept for most of us: despair is where we begin to learn it. We are challenged again and again to cope with lack of control and switch our allegiance to trust.

Shadow is a Jungian term often used to describe the part of the

JOURNAL ENTRY

In meditation I see myself crouched under my despair. I stand to face it. Despair is thick, black smoke. No light can penetrate it. I try to embrace it. I try to push it away. I decide to let despair do what it wants with me.

It becomes a black hatchet. I feel it take the mark of my hair, as if it will fall on my part, split me down the middle. I stand still. The hatchet falls, shears off my left arm—not my head. No pain, only curiosity. The hatchet becomes a feather, which turns into a black snake. It encircles me, slithers down to the ground. It swallows my severed arm, raises up beside me, a huge hooded cobra, and becomes an Egyptian sarcophagus.

I open it. Inside is my arm, turned to gold. I take it out, don't know what to do with it. I turn the arm upright like a torch. It lights the darkness—turning to dawn. I walk through the despair until I come to the edge of it. There is a large wooden castle door. I put the arm—like a crossbar—across the door to bolt it shut. The golden arm holds the kingdom of despair at bay. I stand in the natural world.

A voice says to me, "You are wounded, but whole."

Fear not, for I have redeemed you; I have called you by name, you are mine. When you pass through the waters I will be with you;
and through the rivers, they shall not overwhelm you;
when you walk through fire you shall not be burned,
and the flame shall not consume you.

—Isaiah 43:2

100

self that previously has remained unknown. A woman's shadow may be a strong inner male figure, a man's may be a gentle female figure. The shadow is neither negative nor positive; it is simply unexplored. Despair stirs up the shadow in the journey and in ourselves.

We engaged the quest as a way to explore this missing element. We imagined living more fully aware lives, becoming our ideal selves. Perhaps, like me, you believed for awhile that some precipitating event would accomplish this transformation, that something would happen *to you*.

One idyllic summer between college years I read Tolkien's Middle Earth trilogy and was struck with the metaphor of transformation when the wizard Gandalf fell into the Crack of Doom and disappeared for much of the next book. When the battle between good and evil is at its height, he re-emerges as Gandalf the White, a personage who has been burned back to the bone, whose power and wisdom have been honed in the fires of earth itself. Meanwhile, we hobbit-like travelers tend to become enchanted with promises of growth and spiritual reunion and avoid asking exactly *how* this transformation is likely to occur. *Despair is the transformational event. Despair is our chance to wrestle with fire and come through.*

Journal writers show up in my seminars bearing despair that needs to be expressed and explored. A single mother is barely getting by when she's diagnosed with multiple sclerosis; a man in charge of his grandfather's business is losing money and afraid the company won't survive to support his sons and daughters; a nun finds herself in a crisis of faith; the followers of a guru don't understand how he can die of cancer like anyone else. . . . The list of disordering events is endless, specific, and universal.

In each of these instances we are offered the chance to allow an old life cycle to come to an end. We are asked to be like the phoenix, the bird of eternal regeneration. There is nothing left to do but build our nest of sandalwood in the Tree of Life and wait for the sun to set it all ablaze. We need this burning out. We know it and are still afraid.

8. THE ROLE OF WONDER

*Life is not on anyone's side. It is up to us to take up
the fardels and put ourselves on the side of life and go
wherever it leads.*

—*P. L. Travers*
Parabola, *vol. XII, no.* 3

So far, the spiritual journey looks like a pretty serious trip, but there is a reward for our willingness to learn from despair; that reward is wonder. Wonder is the light side, an up side, a playful, happy quality of the quest. It comes upon us like sunshine after rain, refreshing our hearts. We are snatched out of ourselves, transfixed in the middle of the world.

I remember taking my first train ride, traveling with my parents between Indiana and Montana the summer I was five; my brother, Carl, was three. In the corridors between the cars, the plates of the

*World, I am your slow guest, one of the common things that
move in the sun and have close, reliable friends in the earth, in the
air, in the rock.*

—*William Stafford*
Allegiances

Looking for Wonder

• Think back to moments of pain and look for the
wonder hidden in these times.
• Write down what you may not have recorded at
the time.
• If you like, make additional notes to yourself in the
margins, adding joy, wonder, insight.
• If you choose to do this, date your notations.

• If you hadn't already decided an experience was
painful, how else might you see it?
• Where is the wonder in it?
• How has your "wounding" made you whole?

*It is in affliction itself that the splendor of God's mercy shines,
from its very depths, in the heart of its inconsolable bitterness. If
still persevering in our love, we fall to the point where the soul
cannot keep back the cry "My God, why hast thou forsaken
me?", if we remain at this point without ceasing to love, we end
by touching something that is not affliction, not joy, an essence,
necessary and pure, something not of the senses, common to joy
and sorrow: the very love of God.*

—*Simone Weil*
Waiting for God

flooring jiggled over the couplings. I loved to stand there feeling the momentum of the train speeding along its track. Our parents would indulge us in this delight, let us stand, spraddle-legged, balancing on the rhythmically jostling floor, while we screamed in unison. This was wondrous space, full of sound and light and motion. They held us in the train's half-opened doors, our small bodies pressed tight against parental hips, as though we were centaurs, while upper torsos, arms, and faces flung free, suspended in the hot, roaring wind racing along the train's sides. Mouths open, words pulled off our tongues and thrown into the landscape, I can still hear the timbre of my voice shouting, "I'm flying! Let me go . . . I'm flying . . ."

Wonder is not a Pollyanna stance, not a denial of reality; wonder is an acknowledgment of the power of the mind to transform, to notice, to decide what experience shall mean. I can look back at that train ride with wonder because I felt safe. I could shout for my parents to let me go—and they didn't. Wouldn't.

We are in the same position now with the universe. For wonder to occur, we need to feel safe. We need to be able to shout unreasonable demands, including freedom to fly, and to know that the sacred will not let us go flinging off into danger. And once we have that assurance we are free to explore life in ways most of us have not explored since we were very, very young.

It takes a period of disorder, I think, to teach us wonder, to inform the heart that we are not abandoned, that we may still find in anguish, as Simone Weil notes, that we are being touched by the essence of something large and holy.

Wonder and despair are two sides of a spinning coin. When you open yourself to one, you open yourself to the other. You discover a capacity for joy that wasn't in you before. Wonder is the promise of restoration: as deeply as you dive, so may you rise. As far as you are willing to venture into shadow, so far may you venture into light.

You may have grown accustomed to writing in and about crisis. Crisis is a circumstance when the urge to write is very strong and overcomes our usual reticence about revealing ourselves. You may

*It is never external events, it is always the feeling inside me—
depression, uncertainty or whatever—that lends these events their
sad or menacing aspect. It always spreads from the inside
outwards with me, never the other way around.*

—Etty Hillesum
An Interrupted Life

JOURNAL ENTRY
*Pink around the lake in late October is hard to see at first. But it
is there and quickly falls into two categories. Nature's pink:
granite rocks piled along the shore in pastel silence; amid
blackberries, the leaves of shrubs once bright, now faded, like tiny
bowls of cream of tomato soup cooling in the weakening sun. The
bottom of an overturned canoe, once screaming red, has lost its
voice to sun and water and faded to a whispered pink. Roses
running along a chain-link fence enjoy a last look around before
their pink is buried with brown leaves. Unnatural pink: a woman
jogs past in a hot pink sweat suit. The tinny pulse of the
unshared music from her earphones beats, beats, beats as she
passes by, the white soles of her running shoes flashing like a
deer's tail. The two lifeguard towers painted bright pink look like
playhouse furniture left behind by some giant's forgetful children.
Who would have thought that pink could be a color of
melancholy?*

Wondering Questions

•   How could you respond to what's happening now
in your life with wonder? with joy?
•   What are you willing to contribute to allow more
joy into your journal and your life?
•   If life is neutral, what are you going to color it?

*The beauty of things is in the beholder's brain—the human
mind's translation of their transhuman intrinsic value.*

—Robinson Jeffers
Not Man Apart

not have noticed or recorded much about wonder, you may even ask, What's there to write about?

Most of us have developed a fairly extensive vocabulary for describing pain, as though the journal were a doctor requiring much detail to make the correct diagnosis. The roundness of the spiritual journey cannot be expressed without developing an equally extensive vocabulary for talking to ourselves and others about the nature of wonder, joy, ecstasy, love, transfiguration.

The pilgrim's wonder is a seasoned joy, comprised of little gifts noticed along the way. The pilgrim's wonder is an awareness of potential, seeing something whole, the spectrum of possibility. These are the things—small ponderables of the individual heart— that we learn to put in the journal along with paragraphs of pain and recipes for carrot cake.

It happens, I think, like this: you are going through a time of change. You are in turmoil, inner or outer. You are in pain. You don't understand why things are happening, or what they mean. You pray that you will eventually understand, eventually be able to assign some meaning to these occurrences. Meanwhile, you endure. Every morning you make yourself get up and face the day, go through the motions, cope with whatever has to be coped with.

And then you see a bird at the feeder who does not fly away when you walk by but stops and looks back at you with his beady black eyes. Or an acquaintance you had nearly forgotten calls to tell you a remark you made two years ago has changed his life. Or you are walking with a child who spots a feather in the path, pulls on your hand to notice, and suddenly your heart opens. You are swept into the moment, connected with a sense of blessing, kindness, wholeness. In the midst of your hardship, life is so sweet you can hardly bear it, like honey on the tongue.

These moments of joy seem to come out of nowhere. They are surprises. Sudden shafts of light. They bypass the intellect and land straight in your heart. You are overcome with wonder and gratitude for this insignificant little event because it was just what you needed, when you needed it. And you need to respect it, by writing the incident down.

Marvel-at Moments

- When something wonderful happens, pull over, step back, take the time to write it down while your heart is still full.
- Marvel at life. Is there not enough miracle to keep you busy writing?

JOURNAL ENTRY

I asked in meditation for an image of my wonder. I got a poppy seed—so very small, it fell into a crease in the palm of my hand. I could hardly see it. Not to lose this tiny, precious thing, I licked it up with my tongue and swallowed it. I felt it drifting inside me, sinking into the whirling darkness of my fear. There it joined the swirl, a tiny star nebula, just beginning to glow. But starborn, casting its pinprick of light, making an orbit for itself. My chest felt lighter just to know it's there. Reminds me of Jean's T-shirt, a silk-screened image of the Milky Way and an arrow pointing into the midst of it. "You are here," it says. That's what I need to remember: where I really am and who I really am and to place the details of my current life in perspective. Wonder, whirling minisculely through the blackness I have created. Let there be light . . . Amen.

Closing and Opening

- Meditate on images of closing and opening.
- As you breathe in, say silently, "opening . . ."
- As you breathe out, say silently, "Closing . . ."
- After meditation, write or draw your impressions.
- Ask yourself: What are you open to? What are you closed to?

108

Wonder is a personal code. When journal writers share entries of wonderment, they may sound ordinary to outside listeners because wonder is experienced inside a spiritual connection that is intimate and temporary. But you will not forget. Going back over your blessings a day later, rereading moments of recorded wonder, the words recall the feeling more than the event itself.

When we are in pain and turmoil for a long period of time, all we want is relief. We begin to search for anyone or anything that can help us get through. Our search sensitizes us so that our observations are much keener than at less traumatic times. Little things become symbolic of what we hope for, symbolic of our will to survive and our will to make meaningful whatever we are being required to endure.

We look for signs of an order larger than the personal disorder we're experiencing. One bleak winter, a friend whose house sits on a hill made a commitment to write about sunrises and sunsets as a way to get herself through depression. A man recovering from a broken back spent hours with binoculars, watching birds outside the nursing home windows. His journal is full of sketches and song. For pages and pages he forgets to record his pain.

When our lives are disordered, we become human beings in the raw; our nerves float so close to the skin that every passing brush with life is exaggerated. We are open to the best and worst that life dishes out. We have only two options: to close down further or open up further.

If we close down further, we die. Maybe not right away, but dying begins. Atrophy occurs in our hearts. Despair continues. If we open up further, we live. Maybe we don't notice right away that some spiritual corner has been turned, new life has begun. Regeneration. Hope. *Wonder occurs when you decide to live, to endure and assign meaning to your experience.*

You are already living, of course, already getting along through your life as best you can; but have you *decided*? Have you put yourself, as Travers says, "on the side of life"?

I don't know why things happen to people. I don't know why

New Vocabulary

* If the words won't come, grab markers, colored pencils, pastels—and draw.
* If imagery doesn't come, turn on the radio and dance.
* There are many ways to express yourself and the relationship you are having with life.
* Today, taking a walk may be your journal entry.

> *JOURNAL ENTRY*
>
> *Our assignment was to walk in the woods and find some blueprint from nature for our lives. . . . I came to a small clearing and saw three deer browsing. Before they noticed me I leaned against a tree and went motionless. They wandered closer and I saw it was a doe and two fawns. Closer yet. The doe saw me, froze and stared. Her ears came forward in keen attention. I didn't move. Even my breath came shallow. She came a few steps closer and watched me—every muscle in her alert for danger. She sniffed the air. For perhaps ten minutes she made her way around me, carefully leading her fawns. Eventually she curved within five yards of where I stood. The fawns followed her, their bodies relaxed, unconcerned. They were interested in their mother, in me, in the ground they sniffed and the twigs they nibbled. And then I knew what the pattern was: it's about trust. The fawns lay down in the snow to rest. I am 56 years old and just beginning to hear my own story. I must sit quietly, breathe still. God give me as much patience and compassion for myself as I had for the deer.*

my friend died of a brain tumor. I don't know why one person's career takes off like a skyrocket while another's equally fine work goes unrecognized. I don't know why some marriages flourish, and others don't. I only know that when these circumstances present themselves, each of us must decide to grow or not to grow. And that the decision for growth is lifelong and subtle and takes us through many twists and turns.

There is a moment of yes-saying that needs to occur, some tipping of the scale. We all go through it. The moment may not feel extraordinary as it approaches, and yet it carries importance that impacts us forever. I remember one such moment on an icy highway when the cars around me twirled on the ice. I barely avoided being in the middle of a major pileup. As I drove carefully on, I found myself shaking and shouting to no one in particular: "I want to live! I want to live!" Every life has such moments, when we cross a line of commitment that we hadn't even known was there.

Once we are determined to place ourselves in a yes-saying relationship with life, we begin to assume that things have meaning, and that if we understand the meaning, we can begin to create an overall picture of life's growth. The search for meaning—both universal and individual—is the driving, surviving force of the quest. Meaning drives us from despair to wonder, from confusion to clarity, from hesitance to confidence. And the only place to find meaning is in the importance of small things.

Out of the depth of pain you begin to experience true, spontaneous joy. Your emotional range is broadened again, the way it was when you were a child, or the way it should have been then. You begin to have hope for yourself and your life. You notice a string of little miracles that seem to carry you along, buoy you up, offer you hope whenever you are discouraged.

Wonder is essential to the quest because it gives us the courage to keep being curious, to keep asking questions. There is always the chance that the next response will be wonder filled. And so we keep going, and the further we go the more wonderful the quest becomes.

First Day

* Make a list of things you wonder about. Be creative, silly as well as serious.
* Go back to child/mind. See things with the new eyes of spiritual curiosity.
* What if this really were the first day of your life?
* Get up and write with the dawn. What do you see?
* What were you wondering the day after you were born?
* What are you wondering today?

And yes I said yes I will Yes.

—*James Joyce*
Ulysses

Driving with my niece Erin a few weeks before her fourth birthday, she asked from the backseat, "How did we meet?" I explained to her that I went to the hospital the day after she was born.

"Did you hold me?" she asked.

"Yes, I did. I was wondering who is this new person who's come into my life that I don't know yet."

"Want to know what I was wondering?"

"Of course . . ."

"I was wondering how come I'm in a baby body and everybody else is already big."

Meditation

To prepare to use this meditation and others throughout the book, find a quiet place where you will not be interrupted for twenty minutes or so. Ask someone to read the meditation to you, or to play back a version of the meditation you have made yourself or ordered from the back of the book. The points of ellipses (. . .) indicate a significant pause—silence maintained within the text. Pause for as long as you feel comfortable; five to ten seconds can seem a long time in meditation. Double ellipses indicate longer silence.

SACRED MOMENTS

Close your eyes and relax your body. . . . Take all the time you need to get comfortable. . . . Shift muscles . . . stretch and relax. . . . Make sure your spine and neck are straight and aligned . . . not held stiffly; there is no stiffness here . . . just comfort, the beginning of calm. . . . There is no hurry now. . . . There is nothing else to do . . . or think about. . . . Just relax. . . . . .

Notice your breath. . . . Let your breath enter deeply into your body. . . . Let your breath roll into you like soft, heavy clouds that fill you with silence. . . . Inhale slowly . . . deeply. . . . Exhale slowly . . . thoroughly. . . . Let your breath sink in and out. . . . Your breath is a rhythm of calm. . . . Follow your breath. . . . Exhale all extraneous thought. . . . Inhale silence. . . .

In your mind's eye, go to a room that is comfortable and relaxing . . . settle into a favorite chair or large pillows. . . . You are going to watch some movies of your life. . . . When you are ready, pull down a movie screen in front of you. . . . These movies are scenes of your sacred moments . . . times in your life when you have felt protected . . . touched . . . sheltered by a holy presence.

Accept whatever scene is given you. . . .

There are three scenes coming.

The first is a scene of beginnings, a moment when you accepted

your quest. Watch yourself in this moment. . . . What age are you?
. . . Where are you? . . . What support surrounds you? . . . What
is the form of the gift being offered in this moment? . . . What do
you know now that you wish you had been able to tell yourself
then? . . . If it feels appropriate, give yourself that information
now. . . . . . . Send blessings to the person you were. Wish yourself well. . . . . . .

The second is a scene of healing, a moment when you were
made more whole. Watch yourself in this moment. . . . What age
are you? . . . Where are you? . . . What support surrounds you?
. . . What is the form of the gift being offered in this moment? . . .
What do you wish you had accepted in this moment that you weren't
sure was yours to take? . . . If it feels appropriate, give yourself this
added gift now. . . . . . . Send blessings to the healing of this
person. Wish yourself well. . . . . . .

In the last scene you are being given a sense of new direction. . . . Watch yourself in this moment. . . . Where are you?
. . . Who else is with you? . . . What support surrounds you? . . .
What is the direction being offered? . . . What gift is offered that
makes this direction possible? . . . Send blessings to this person
setting out. . . . Wish yourself well. . . . . . .

When you are ready, return to the room with the movie screen.
Follow your breath back to this room. Emerge out of your silence.
. . . There is no hurry. . . . Stretch your body. . . . Open your
eyes. . . .

Take time to draw or write whatever you want to record from
this vision.

III.
Types of Guidance

9. THE GUIDANCE
OF THE BODY

*Here in this body are the sacred rivers: here are the sun
and moon, as well as the pilgrimage places.*

*I have not encountered another temple as blissful as
my own body.*

—*Saraha*

In 1969, a group of friends and I drove down from San
Francisco, where we were all living, to spend a weekend at a cottage in Laguna Beach owned by one friend's
mother. It happened to be a time when the Pacific
coast tossed up one of its miracles. That night's incoming tide bore
billions of microorganisms that glistened on the sand and turned
the surf an eerie luminescence.

We five friends ran along the midnight beach, laughing and
thumping the sand with our feet to watch the water spatter through

Lie back, daughter, let your head
be tipped back in the cup of my hand.
Gently, and I will hold you. Spread
your arms wide, lie out in the stream
and look high at the gulls. A dead man's
float is face down. You will dive and
swim soon enough where the tidewater
ebbs to the sea. Daughter, believe me,
when you tire of the long thrash
to your island, lie up and survive.
As you float now, where I held you
and let go, remember, when fear
cramps your heart, what I told you:
lie gently and wide to the light-year
stars, lie back and the sea will hold you.

—*Phillip Booth*
"First Lesson"

Child-Body Images

- Write about early body messages.
- Write about early sensual memories, being aware of
your body as a young child.

Two Journal Entries

My first real memory is of standing on the toilet seat watching
my dad shave. It was the old brown bathroom at my parents'
first apartment, so I had to be under two, just old enough to
stand by myself. I loved to flush the toilet, feeling the hidden rush
of water shake the old porcelain bowl. My dad used to let me
flush the toilet as much as I wanted. I got such a physical thrill
out of it, remember laughing in that utterly dedicated way that
little kids have.

My crib was placed under the window where the afternoon sun
came in and I remember waking up from naps aware of the
warmth and light. I didn't want anyone to come and disturb me,

darkness like sparklers. One by one we became quiet, more deeply entranced, took off our clothes, and waded into the surf. We swam in loose formation. The neon tide coated our bodies—every hair follicle, every crevice of skin, the space under our fingernails and between our toes.

I saw my body turn to light. I could almost see through my skin to the blood vessels running like rivers, the bones bouncing on sinew strings, pushing against the water, propelling me forward, keeping me afloat in the glowing turbulence.

A friend swam within sight, her waist-length hair alight with tiny stars. She dived around me like a dolphin, turned, and laughed. Each bubble bore a candle to the surface. Her lashes blinked brightly in front of darkened eyes.

My friend and I hated our bodies. Like most young women of the times, we were raised against a ridiculous standard of beauty we did not fit. Her legs were as heavy as tree limbs. My breasts were too small. We never discussed this; we knew the hatred was there by how we treated and referred to ourselves. But this night in the sea we were mermaids. We rolled on our backs and waved starry hands at the Milky Way. "You're beautiful!" I shouted to her. "If only you could see your hair."

"You're beautiful too," she called back. We told each other the truth and we knew it. We saw ourselves at that moment as we really were. Here in the magical tide I knew for the first time that body and spirit are one. To love the light surrounding me, I had to love the body held within the light.

All spiritual growth is experienced through the instrument of our human selves. It is finally becoming clearer to us in the West, that body and mind are one. When Saraha writes, "I have never encountered another temple as blissful as my own body," he is proclaiming the body's ability to join with the mind in plumbing the depths of the spiritual quest.

Part of the reason we have had a hard time integrating body/ mind in the journey is due to cultural and religious traditions that have been openly antiphysical. You cannot revere the body as a

would lie there a long time, perfectly content. But I also remember the cold, wet feeling of cloth diapers clinging to my butt, and that would finally get me screaming for Mom and dry clothes.

Aboriginal Journal Writing

With your journal group or other trusted friends
• Paint yourselves.
• Adorn your own and each other's bodies.
• Make plaster casts and write on and decorate them.
• Dance and drum and get a little wild.
• Meditate together.
• Make an energy circle.
• Practice silence together. Practice chanting.

> *You have to be nude a lot before you can ever be naked.*
> —Ann Marsden

Naked Journal Writing

• Find a place that combines privacy and comfortable temperature, and undress.
• Write in your journal, read, knit, put together a puzzle, dance, do yoga.
• How does it feel to hang out in your skin?
Do not run negative comments about what you observe: just observe.
• What if you'd never seen a body before?
• Look at all your moving parts.
• Look at how everything functions.
• Trace an outline of your hands in the journal; draw images of the energy emanating from them.
• On a large piece of paper, have someone trace your whole body; write and draw inside this image.

temple at the same time that you despise it. You cannot divide the body between extremes of asceticism or debauchery and expect to understand its role as a spiritual vessel. In this conflicted atmosphere we learn to live in our minds *or* our bodies, but not to live in the body/mind.

The body is the original "church." Aboriginal cultures remind us of this. They paint, adorn, tattoo, and scarify their bodies in ways that communicate their sacred traditions. They mark rites of passage by altering the body and going through prescribed physical trials and feats of endurance. We are fascinated by this primitive beautification because we sense its inherent spiritual symbolism.

We too paint, adorn, tattoo, and alter our bodies. We manufacture feats of endurance in a culture that allows us to avoid them. But we have lost the underlying spiritual reasons for making ourselves strong and beautiful. We do it to impress each other instead of to acknowledge the sacred as present in our lives. *We forget: we are made in the image of the sacred.*

Many people are reclaiming their bodies as holy vessels. There's an artist in my city who conducts day-long plaster-casting workshops. People make body molds and when they are dry adorn them with feathers and beads, are able to turn around and see their bodies as art. Informal groups of wild women and men meet in the north woods and at retreat centers where sensuality is included in the meditative routine.

The journal is a safe and private place to reclaim our physical nature, and for most of us there are words to be said, feelings to be expressed, histories to be witnessed. There is something important and healing about deciding to "come physically home." *The body cannot become part of your spiritual life until you are energetically "in" it.* And you cannot be in it until you heal the rift between body and mind.

I don't know why some bodies are "grander" than others, why some people struggle with handicaps or illness; all I know is that each body successfully shelters a human soul and gets that soul through a lifetime no matter what the physical constraints. Physical

The atoms and molecules within you dream they are people.

—Seth (Jane Roberts)

Stream-of-Body Consciousness

- Notice the running commentary you make about your body.
- How do you want to change it?
- Do you generally send your body negative or positive messages? List them.
- If you weren't obsessing about some physical flaw, what would you be doing?
- Do you use your body to prevent yourself from attaining goals? how?
- Do you use your body to help yourself attain goals? how?
- Dialogue with your body.

> JOURNAL ENTRY
> . . . had the strangest experience yesterday morning, woke up in my own womb. Dark red velvet space, paintings of my parents, grandparents, and other ancestors hanging on the walls. Very soft and comfortable, full of down pillows. Twilight, too dark to read, just enough light to see. God, I felt at home. Didn't want to come out. No wonder Amanda was born crying. I think we should get a waterbed.

> I believe that the human body is an outrageously ingenious demonstration of the power of consciousness to turn energy into matter and matter into energy.
> . . . The body is a natural transmuter. It is the Philosopher's Stone, capable of converting other forms of energy and matter into itself.

—Brugh Joy
Joy's Way

acceptance is a cornerstone of spiritual clarity. If you do not treat your body well, find someone to help you change your attitudes, habits, and behavior. There are groups designed to help people with eating disorders, sexual disorders, chronic diseases, and disabilities. If you are addicted to something, get unaddicted. Attitudes are changing swiftly; you can find support to make healthy decisions.

Our bodies are the instruments through which we experience spiritual ecstasy. Pleasure, experienced in and through the body, is a genuine aspect of the sacred. Perhaps you have read the works of an ecstatic mystic; they appear in all spiritual traditions. When a mystic writes that s/he is "enthralled in God," or "writhing in holy ecstasy," what physical condition do you think is being described? If you are not prepared to experience spiritual pleasure through your body, it can be frightening and confusing.

Esoteric traditions regard the body as an energy field held in place by consciousness. Yogic tradition believes each cell has defined intelligence, leading an independent but carefully coordinated life. The wholeness of the body's energy comes from the life force emanating from each cell working in unison to produce the form of life that we are. Chinese tradition traces the electrical circuitry of the body through the intricate pathways of acupuncture points and meridians. Medieval doctors and philosophers regarded the body as having "seven humors," related to the major organs, which needed to be in balance to support mental and physical health.

All this knowledge assumes there is something in the body that "powers" it. If the body is the vehicle of the spiritual journey, this life force is its fuel. We are imbued with energy vibrating at the frequency needed to maintain our particular life-form. We are vibrating at different frequencies and levels of intensity, and so is the world around us.

All living things give off energetic vibration. Everything receives and passes along energy. Kirlian photography has captured on film the brilliant energy shooting off our fingertips, surrounding a piece of lettuce, or emanating from objects we don't usually consider

Chakras and Journal Writing

Chakra energy is often experienced in meditation.
Keep your journal nearby to record images and
impressions.

• Concentrate on one chakra at a time. Meditate on
filling that chakra with white light.
• Draw how the chakra "looks" to you when you
begin working with it, and again after you've focused
on it awhile.
• Dialogue with a chakra that seems blocked.
• Dialogue with a chakra for guidance.

JOURNAL ENTRY

I've been experiencing these shifting, unidentified pains around my
upper chest. They first appear in one spot, then another.
Sometimes the aching subsides for long periods of time, then
returns. I have been afraid of this pain. I have prayed for it to go
away. I've taken my pain to the acupuncturist, nutritionist,
chiropractor, finally to a medical doctor who ordered a
mammogram and X rays. Nothing showed.
Last night I woke up and thought my chest was breaking apart.
There seemed to be hot sparks of energy flying off these aching
places. "What are you?!" I demanded to know.
An inner voice answered, "I am love."
"What?"
"Love."
I put my hands on my chest and cried for all the probing of these
tender places, for all the treatments and tests I'd endured. "Love?"
I asked. "You're just love?"
My spiritual heart has opened.

"alive." The energy of a hummingbird is very different from the energy of a rock, but both vibrate with their essential livingness. This vibration is registerable as light.

This electrical energy system is universal. In spiritual tradition, the energy patterns people describe and discover as part of their spiritual discipline are essentially the same. We may reach this state of vibration through different means, but once attained, the energy is experienced similarly.

One way of thinking about these energy patterns is to visualize seven major energy centers located in the body along the torso. The Sanskrit word for these centers is *chakra*. As you spiritually reclaim your body, you will become aware of these centers as energy fields where vibration seems to pool and radiate. Vibration is a natural state for us: our bodies are always vibrating, we are just more or less aware of it, more or less attuned, running more or less voltage through our cells.

Chakra knowledge is an ancient theory with several names and traditions. A standard rendition of the major centers is as follows:

7. Crown Center: about two inches in diameter at the top of the head, the body's gate to the universe; color—purple.
6. Brow Center or Third Eye: located in the center of the forehead, just above the eyebrows, the locus of intuition and psychic abilities; color—indigo.
5. Throat Center: about three inches in diameter, just above the junction of the collarbones, represents creativity and self-expression; color—sky blue.
4. Heart Center or Sacred Heart: a circle on the center of the breastbone, between the breasts, the source of compassion; color—yellow/gold.
3. Solar Plexus or Power Point: an area in the top of the stomach cavity, two inches below the ribs, the source of personal power; color—kelly green.
2. Spleen/Sex Center: two to four inches in diameter located above

Sex, Sense, and Journal Writing

- How's your libido? Why? Why not?
- How does your body reflect your mental, emotional, spiritual condition?
- How do you replenish and nurture yourself physically?
- When was the last time you let yourself turn into light?

Shielding Exercise

- When you open your own life energy, you become more permeable to other energies around you. While still in silence, imagine yourself surrounded by white light, as though you were the yolk inside an egg of light. This shell is transparent. You can see out and be seen, but it provides a barrier. Behind this barrier you are not available to indiscriminate energy. You are not vulnerable to people who want to drain your energy. You are not susceptible to the confusions or manipulations others have about their energy.
- Sit in your shell of light and surround yourself with whatever conscious thoughts you need for protection.
- Pray for guidance.
- Ask the sacred to help you determine who and what you let into your life.
- Proceed slowly, calmly.
- There is no rush.

128

the pubic bone and below the navel, the source of physical health and sexual focus; color—pink

1. Root Center: one to three inches, located on the perineum, the skin between the genitals and the anus, the source of libido, life force, the will to live; color—red/orange.

When you establish a routine of meditation or prayer, you are likely to become more aware of these energy centers in your body. Meditation may turn your body on, as though the voltage suddenly went up. Your hands, feet, or whole body, may buzz with energy. You may find yourself swaying slightly, as though keeping time with your heartbeat. Muscle groups may jerk. You may feel the vibration of your body exaggerated, or that your consciousness has a tendency to float, until you aren't quite sure you and your body are in the same place. These are natural phenomena of energy. They will last only as long as you stay receptive. You can close yourself back down by becoming afraid, analytical, or withdraw from the experience. Open your eyes: reorient yourself to your external environment and shift physical positions. *You are in charge of your level of openness to the universe.* Take in and transmit only the amount of energy you are comfortable with and that is appropriate to your situation.

These energy shifts are not especially dramatic. You can move in and out of them simply by changing the focus of your attention. Dramatic shifts, especially if manipulated by leaders in large group exercises, can be dangerous and coercive because they pull you away from the path you know intuitively is correct for you. *Energy is real; so is energy tampering.* Take as much care about what kinds of energy you expose yourself to as you do about what kinds of food you eat. Only put into your body what is good for your body; this includes the energy you allow or invite in. Use the shielding exercise, and always retain the right to leave a situation that doesn't feel comfortable.

Being spiritually/physically open creates the obligation to be responsible with your increasing energy. When body circuitry

Body as a House of Prayer

• Describe what you experience in your body when
you meditate or pray. Do not censor. Do not label or
judge sensations. Just notice.
• How are you interpreting these feelings?
• Do you have "intentions" for this energy?
• What part of you has these intentions?
• Are they spiritually clear?

> *You have an innate ability to meditate. It is not something you
> have to learn how to do. You do have to allow time for the
> experience, but, in essence, you do not have to structure the act
> itself.*
>
> *. . . To experience at will the naturally induced states of higher
> consciousness, to shift from the self to the Self by nothing more
> than the lowering of the eyelids, to experience the melting of one
> solid definition into the soft, amorphous, undefined, to begin to
> claim one's inheritance as a conscious universal entity—all can
> be accomplished through the art of meditation.*
>
> —Brugh Joy
> Joy's Way

Sorting Attractions

• If you feel a spiritual attraction toward another
person, write about it.
• Let yourself write whatever you need to write.
• Write your fantasies, hopes, delusions, desires,
questions, ambivalence, forewarnings.
• Write dialogues between yourself and the other
person.
• Ask for guidance.
• Write dialogues between yourself and spiritual
guidance.
• Expect to be confused; use the journal until you are
clear.

opens, the mind tries to label and understand what is happening. What is happening is that you are transmitting more life force; however, that may not be the message in your head. Since the culture is obsessed with eroticism, attachment, power, and attraction, it is not unusual for our egos to assume that the energy we're feeling should be defined as erotic, focused, powerful, and attractive.

Sexual arousal and spiritual awakening are both experienced in the chakras. When the energy center at the base of the spine opens in prayer or meditation, it creates sensations that *we have been taught* to identify as sexual. You are not sexually aroused, you are simply energized. If you shift your attention to your hands, you'll notice they have the same intense level of buzzing as your pelvis. You don't say, "My hands are aroused," or "My third eye is aroused." You say, "Energy is flowing in my hands, in my heart, in my third eye, and in my pelvis . . ." The energy of the universe is unconditional love. You are experiencing a kind of psychic passion generated by increased transmission of energy. People who sustain this energy level seem to "glow" a little more than the rest of us. If they do this from a spiritual framework, they diffuse energy toward other people and focus energy on the sacred. This is the enthrallment mystics speak of.

The difference between sexual and spiritual energy occurs in intent and focus.

Sexual energy is specific. Sexual energy seeks release through intense focus. It becomes more and more acutely focused until released through orgasm. It desires response, polarity, to be met with equal passion. *Spiritual energy is diffuse.* Spiritual energy seeks release through diffusion of focus. It wants to flow without discrimination, to exist as light everywhere, uncontained, shining through the body, sent in blessing to the earth, the air, to other people, without coercion or need for response.

If you become sexually focused, you can become spiritually diffused by shifting your attention (to your heart, your hands, your head . . .), then releasing the energy. You will feel it flowing away, going back to its source in the universe.

As we experiment with living in an opened energy system, we

I can tell the difference between sexual and spiritual energy, even though they emanate from the same place in my body. Sexual energy wants orgasm and then is satisfied. Orgasm passes through spiritual energy like a blip on a radar screen. It is not particularly satisfying, and it's somehow not relevant.

Having a lot of energy in my body is a strange sensation, both pleasurable and slightly uncomfortable. I try to convert spiritual energy to sexual energy sometimes because I know what to do with sexual energy, I know how to dissipate it.

But there is some essential difference I recognize from the start of the sensation. I would have gotten myself in a lot less trouble over the years if I'd been willing to admit I knew this difference and then honored it. The reason I don't is that when I'm full of spiritual energy, I feel like spirit wants me to do something that I'm not very good at—passing on unconditional love. I feel hokey sending "love energy" out of my body into the room—like, I'm not a saint. I don't want to be a saint. I want to play softball and go dancing, have a couple of beers . . . and I guess I want to be a spiritual conduit too because I keep meditating. The cats come in and make a purring circle next to me. They're picking up something. Love?

Body Friend

- When/how has your body been your best companion?
- In what loving ways have you cared for your body?
- How have you intentionally hurt your body?
- How have you intentionally healed your body?
- What was it like (will it be like) to be in your body when you were (will be) age ten? twenty? forty? eighty?
- What one thing could you do that would most help you love your body?
- Why aren't you doing it?
- Will you?

should expect to be confused by the signals of the body and the social training of the mind. We will make assumptions that are simply wrong. We will interpret things differently in the moment than we do in retrospect. We can use the journal as a place to sort, to get clear before acting, before involving other people. This will still not be a perfect system. No one else is turning you on: you are turning yourself on. *You* are deciding to be open to energy.

There have been times when, lying on the grass in my own front yard, soaking up sun's heat, earth's coolness, the whispering shade of a tree, I have been as erotically attuned as in any sexual experience. This is our planet, our home. We are wired to respond to similar vibrations. When you open to the journey of the body, you open to a love relationship in the body that occurs cell by cell.

With all the revelations about sexual transgressions among the clergy, evangelists, gurus, and others who place themselves in positions of spiritual authority, *we need to take mutual responsibility for maintaining personal boundaries and developing an ethics of energy.*

Spiritual attraction can be a gift of equal exchange between student and teacher as long as it is not exploited or refocused by either the student or teacher. The spiritual body/mind has an intelligence beyond our usual understanding. We get in trouble when we apply ordinary understanding to what is occurring in the body/mind's reality. When we try to make experiences that originate in altered states of reality fit into ordinary reality, we confuse ourselves and act through the ego self, instead of through the spirit self.

The body wants ecstasy. That is how the body knows s/he is alive. Ecstasy comes in abundance—through glowing oceans, through insight, through opening the heart to life and other people. The body/mind challenges us to discern what is really being asked of us as living energy, and then to follow that discernment without allowing ourselves to be waylaid. We need to do what the light instructs us to do. We need to be cautious, stay safe, learn gradually.

Almost every spiritual tradition includes stories of highly developed spiritual leaders who, when they die, are able to simply cross over into light. Dissolving the energy that had held them in human form, they return to the basic element that we all are: light.

10. DREAMS:

SLEEP'S GUIDANCE

One does not dream; one is dreamed. We undergo the
dream; we are the objects.

—*Carl Jung*

Dream reality has long been a fascination for people. We know our bodies are lying in bed, tucked under the covers. The room is usually dark. We know we are not moving. In fact, to ensure we don't hurt ourselves while dreaming, the body enters a light state of paralysis so we can't act out dream actions. Yet, when we wake, we are aware of light, sound, movement, companionship, which have visited us in dreams. Things have happened—even if only in the mind—that elevate or lower our mood, alter expectations, affect relationships. We aren't exactly the same person we were eight hours earlier, and there's nothing we can do about it. There's no control we can exert to prevent ourselves from dreaming again. Whenever we sleep, we submit ourselves to the next spin of the roulette wheel of uncon-

The secret of this countryside
Is in the dream.
It is dreamed
Only once, in childhood or old age.
The dreamer is granted the hawk's clarity,
The bee's faceted eye, the omniscience
Of the owl. The land, and all its
Joy and terror and grace
Appear, and appear as a whole:
There are no troubling parts.

—Jared Carter
"Meditation," from
Work, for the Night Is Coming

Dream Interpretation

There are many forms of dream interpretation and
analysis. This is a self-reliant system you can use in
your own journal.

• When you remember a dream, write or draw the
most significant symbols.
• Record the dream in the present tense, as though
redreaming it.
• Circle the symbols that seem most important (don't
forget, your dream self is a symbol).
• Ask each symbol the following question: "Who are
you and what are you in my dream to tell me?"
• Take a quiet breath.
• Write down the first response that comes to
mind—even if it doesn't make rational sense.
• Go on to the next symbol, or talk with one symbol
until its importance is clear.

scious imagery. In our dreams, we have a relationship to the quest that occurs completely within the mind, and the relationship is interactive. We are both the dreamer and the dreamed.

Everyone dreams, though not everyone remembers their dreams, likes what is dreamed, or knows what to do with these images. In the spiritual journey a kind of bargain is struck: "Okay," says the mind, "you want me to think about certain things. Well, I have things I want you to think about too. Here's my agenda." And up pop dreams. Bizarre and fascinating, energized and symbolic, they rest in the mind's chambers waiting for us to awaken, to grab the journal and write them down.

I remember a dream I had when I was four years old about a bear chasing me, scratching at the screen door. I haven't had this dream since, but that bear is vivid still, and so is the sound of his claws rasping down the membrane of the screen. An image both threatening and exhilarating, full of power. What if I let the bear in? Would it eat me? befriend me? carry me on its great hairy back?

In our dreams we travel the planet and the cosmos, heedless of geographic barriers, of time, species, gender, race. The king becomes a beggar, the beggar a king.

Dreams are a highly symbolic and metaphoric form of communication that requires some learning to understand and integrate into the spiritual journey. In dreams, the usual rules of time, space, gravity, cause and effect don't always apply. *Dreams are a puzzle the mind wants us to solve.*

Some cultures revere dreams as an alternative reality. In ancient Greece, people traveled from all over the known world to dream at the oracle of Delphi and to have their dreams interpreted. In modern, Western culture, dreams have not traditionally been highly regarded except in certain courses of psychological analysis or therapy, though this attitude is changing rapidly. Dreams are a rich source of spiritual guidance that can be independently interpreted by each dreamer.

In journal seminars, the longest class is always the session about dreams. People bring a collection of recorded dreams, and we set

"Who/what are you and what are you in my dream to tell me?"

NEW HOUSE: *I am the new life emerging from the current life, connected, but free of the past.*

BEAR: *I am your imagination, your creativity. I am huge. I get bigger and bigger. I want to play with you. I live at the edge of your life no matter how busy you are.*

WOODS: *I am the world. There are more magical things in the world than you have yet imagined.*

CREATURES/INDIANS: *We are your guiding spirits. If you do not use us, we appear wild and untamed. If you pray, we will carry out the energy of those prayers. When you see us as we really are, then we can reveal our sacred names.*

LOGGER MAN: *I am your male side, the actor who tackles the world. I lead the spirits and am led by them. We are inseparable. It takes all of us to act effectively in the world.*

LETTER: *I am your promise that the man can handle whatever's out there and has your best interests at heart.*

POW-WOW: *I am your turning point. You are being brought to a place where everything happens, where everything can be transformed.*

SISTER: *I am your unawakened self. It is time for me to wake up, not hang back.*

WOMEN WHO ARE MEN: *When you are fully integrated, you can be either/both/all that you are. You are androgynous in spirit. Your physical nature is just something you take on; play with it. No matter how you look, you are not as you seem; you are a soul.*

OLD JEWELRY: *Whatever you have to give up, whatever you barter for this transformation, it will not be anything you miss. You keep what is important; give up old trinkets that no longer have value or whose value you no longer understand.*

INITIATION: *The old women awaken the unaware woman/self. This is a call to come into your feminine power. In the ritual you have to swallow something whole, without choking. You have to open your throat, relax to let this down without*

about interpreting, drawing, sometimes acting them out, and no-body wants to go home. It's such a relief to be able to talk about, share, explore this other world in which we spend a third of our lives. It must mean something: we are "there" nearly as much as we are "here."

The following dream has been interpreted by the dreamer using the simple guidelines presented on page 136. The italicized words and phrases are symbols she chose to interpret by question and answer.

> J. *and I are in a* new house, *or this* house transformed. *Lots of* trees *surround it. There's a huge* bear *in the* woods. *C. and E. drop by. Under the porch there are* loud animal sounds. *We stomp our feet. Out come all these* furry *creatures. Some are* animals; *some are* Indians *dressed in* skins. *There is an* unkempt *but* gentle man *among them, sort of their leader. He is a* logger *in the surrounding* woods. *They go away to cut trees somewhere else. He writes me a beautiful* letter *about the spirit of the wood. All the Indians send me a list of their real names and how to pronounce them.*
>
> B. *and I are taken to a* pow-wow *by a* white teacher. *You bring things you want to trade. I bring old* jewelry, *am bartering with* two women *who delight in telling me they are really men. They want some of the jewelry. There is drumming and lots of crowd noise, then a woman goes into the initiation spot. Chanting reaches a crescendo, stops; there is complete silence. The woman sings, or sputters, is carried into a hidden area by other tribal women. The initiation is something about swallowing without choking . . . B. is here to do this. We keep an eye on the process. The woman seems a little shaken, but fine. I am thinking about J., that as a pipebearer she belongs here. These people would understand her and she would find a good spiritual community.*

To catch your dreams, keep a dream journal, notepad, sketch-pad, or even a small tape recorder by your bedside. Dreams are

clutching, tightening, becoming afraid.
ME: *What do I have to swallow?*
CRONES: *Your true understanding.*
J: *This is not my pow-wow. I will get there by my own route.
The pipe will bring me.*

Dream Work and Games

• Record your dreams in different colored ink, so
you can find them easily.
• Make a list of recurring themes and symbols.
• What meanings do they suggest?
• Write letters to your dreams; develop a
correspondence.

Twilight Imagery:
*I was lying in my bed and all of a sudden I noticed a big
bouquet of lilacs on the dresser and I couldn't figure out how they
got there because lilacs aren't in season.*

Daily Processing:
*I meant to call my brother and see how the new baby is. I got
tired and went to bed without calling so I dreamt about them and
they're all right.*

Entertainment:
*Almost every Saturday, when I sleep two hours later than on
weekdays, I have some kind of movie dream. Something with lots
of plot and action. It doesn't always make sense, it's sort of like
watching several channels of television at once, but it keeps me so
busy dreaming I forget to wake up. And that's its main purpose I
think. My mind has a ball and I don't have to pay for popcorn.*

fragile, not as deeply engrained in the mind as conscious thought. They drift. Wake naturally, if you can, without alarms or radios. Don't shift suddenly from the physical position in which you find yourself. Look for a dream image.

You will tend to have as rich a variety of dreams as you believe yourself capable of having. If you want to know your dreams better, pursue them as you would a friendship. When they "speak" to you, speak back. Treat dreams with respect by writing them down, interpreting them, acknowledging their importance in your life. This is a friendly relationship: both the conscious and unconscious aspects of your mind are working to help you grow.

At times of intense growth, stress, or euphoria, dream recall may be interrupted. You are still dreaming; you're just not being given additional information to respond to when the conscious mind is already full.

The following dream categories may help you think about the kinds of messages your subconscious mind is sending and how to use them to further your spiritual path.

Twilight Imagery is the dreamlike state between waking and sleeping. You aren't really sure whether or not you're dreaming. Images tend to be a crossover blend of waking/dreaming symbolism. For example, you may "see" your bedroom, but a dream symbol appears in it that is not there in waking reality. You may think you said or heard something that's not been spoken.

Daily Processing dreams contain information and symbols from the day: the last television show you watched, bits of the novel you're reading, a snatch of conversation. They have a tendency to remind you to finish or resolve things that got interrupted in waking life.

Entertainment dreams are a form of self-hypnosis that keeps the mind watching inner movies instead of waking up. They are very story-oriented and so full of symbols that the idea of deciphering them may seem overwhelming. Entertainment dreams are a way the unconscious shows off, stringing fantastical events together. They often occur in the first hours of sleep, if you have a tendency to

Problem Solving:

*Sometimes I dream of the house where I grew up and I see myself
and family being there together in the 1960s. Sometimes I'm
playing myself at several different ages, or my brother may be a
kid when he walks out of a room and a grownup when he walks
back in.*

*I think I'm trying to have conversations and clear up actions my
family has never been very good at clearing up. If nothing else, I
learn where I'm still stuck, or see the progress I'm making. I
always pay attention to the dynamics of these dreams—they
have a lot to teach me.*

Power/Victim/Violence:

*I dreamed that I put my beloved show dog out to pee and when
she came back in she'd been cut to ribbons (horrible pun). I was
heartbroken. When I woke up and dialogued with this dream, the
message my dog gave me was that I shouldn't send my prize
possession out for show. After this dream, I'm not so afraid of
blood and guts imagery because I know my mind is just making
sure it has my attention.*

*Sometimes I have end-of-the-world dreams: everything in rubble,
bombs falling, buildings and landscapes on fire, people trying to
band together, get out to someplace safe.*

*The images are horrible, but the dreams have a hopeful quality
too. I think I'm making my peace with the nuclear age, using the
dreams to find my way to think about life and death on a
personal and planetary scale.*

Power Dreaming

• What kinds of power have you refused to accept or
consider in yourself?
• What kinds of power are you getting ready to
claim?

142

be wakeful (bedtime stories from inside your mind), or in the early morning when your mind is trying to convince your body not to wake up.

Problem-Solving dreams are often the result of some mental or spiritual assignment you have given yourself to work on. You may assign yourself dreams very consciously, saying, "I want a dream tonight that will help me better understand _____" or you may find your assignment springing spontaneously out of life events. These dreams often involve interactions with other people with whom you are trying to resolve a problem. They may highlight an issue you have been unaware of or lead to resolution. If you cannot solve a problem with someone any other way, you may dream the resolution. Problem-solving dreams tend to float in time, emphasize the past, or mix time frames. They may be peopled with characters living or dead, currently in your life or not. Time is irrelevant. Space is irrelevant. The probability of the dream solution working in the waking world is irrelevant. All that's relevant is that the mind solve the problem, arrive at a point of resolution and inner peace.

Power/Victim/Violence dreams present the shadows of life. They point out where you are being empowered and where you are feeling victimized. Dreams that contain images of violence, aggression, or other disturbances are often the bearers of the most important messages of the mind. They teach you to look directly and symbolically at whatever you are refusing to learn.

It is a strange phenomenon that as we progress on the spiritual path during the day, our nights may look strangely aberrant. Some people report having intense nightmares during periods when they feel the most connected to spiritual growth.

Nightmares bring the shadowed parts of the self along on the journey. They illustrate what aspects of the self are being excluded in the emerging spiritual self-image. They point out what is in danger of being disowned. *The spiritual journey is integrative, not disintegrative; in dreams, the whole self comes forward for review and acceptance by the mind.*

Disturbing dreams usually have to do with making choices about claiming power or disowning power. Most of the time, power images

It is possible for man to become more whole, for each of us to
make our private journey back to the place of emergence, and find
there the simplest and most real of truths: that we are all at heart
the same, that every body contains every soul and has room for
every act without reference to its quality. There is a deep,
objective awareness of self and universe that is available to us all.

—*Whitey Strieber*
Communion

More Dream Work and Games

• Use dream images and scenes as the basis for
poems and stories.
• Look for dream characters you'd like to get to
know better.
• Make an important dream image real. If you dream
of a magical stone, find a stone that represents that
magic for you. Keep it on your desk, by your journal.

> **Precognitive:**
> *I remember going to third grade, walking up to the new girl in*
> *class, and saying, "Hi, Julie." Nobody could figure out how I*
> *knew her name. Not only that, I knew we were going to be best*
> *friends and we were.*
>
> *I have conversations with people in my sleep before we have them*
> *in reality. If I haven't seen someone in a long time, I anticipate*
> *the visit and have it the night before. Sometimes then we don't get*
> *together because the visit has already "occurred." The energy is*
> *dissipated.*

in the culture are presented as aggressive, violent, or as objectifying of relationships and feelings. Our movie heroes, and now many heroines, are shoot-'em-up experts. They kill the designated enemy of the moment in increasingly graphic depictions of exploding body parts, cars, buildings, planes, and planets. Your conscious mind records these images, and when it wants to talk to you about power, it may pull these images from your visual memory bank.

Don't be afraid of these dreams. They are only forms of energy with no attachment to waking life. They do not become images of good or evil unless you carry them into the world of action. If you dialogue with these images in your journal, you will discover the transforming messages they bring you.

A pilgrim is a person who acknowledges personal power and determines to put it to good use. These dreams are your unused power. So how are you going to channel this energy?

Precognitive dreams are visions of events that haven't yet happened. You are dreaming, literally, ahead of time. That this might be true is astounding to the rational mind, yet it's a nearly universal phenomenon. Western science is reconsidering the nature of time. As we explore space and develop what is currently called "the new physics," different ideas about time emerge and fascinate us. It is *commonplace* for people to dream of events that are going to happen, and for these events to happen in some recognizable form. Precognition may range from trivial details to important family crises or to events that make international news.

If the idea of bending time and precognition is too frightening for your rational mind to accept, you simply won't recall any dreams of this nature, but you may still experience *déjà vu* based on these unrecalled dreams. *Déjà vu* is the eerie sense of having already experienced a moment you've never actually lived through before.

In a spiritual sense, precognitive dreaming invites you to consider the reality of other realities, to question traditional concepts of time and space. *You are not making things happen: you are simply being there while they happen, even if your "life-time" hasn't yet caught up with these events.*

Where does this difference between the past and the future come from? Why do we remember the past and not the future? . . . The laws of science do not distinguish between the past and the future.
                                        —Stephen Hawking
                        A Brief History of Time

Astral:
I was looking for a good friend from college that I'd lost track of. One night in a dream we met in a sort of lighted tunnel, had a good, long talk. We told each other all kinds of things about how our lives had really been in the last 20 years. It was very healing. We obviously still have a lot of affection for each other. I got what I was looking for: a chance to see that he is all right, and to tell him that I'm all right. That's all I wanted. Once we were very important to each other, and there's something about that bond which stays, even though our lives have moved satisfactorily on. I don't doubt any of the information we exchanged by dream—even though I don't remember it clearly. It's mostly an impression of who we are now.

People come and go in life, but they never leave your dreams. Once they're in your subconscious, they are immortal.
                                        —Patricia Hampl

Astral dream travel may be experienced as symbolic or real, depending on what you believe about the astral body and the ability of the mind to unleash itself—for awhile—from the tether of the physical body. Astral dreams may include images of flying, meeting people in a tunnel of light (instead of in a natural environment), seeing things occur from an angle that could not be "from the body," such as looking down, looking up, or telescopic vision.

Whether you believe you really vacate your physical body or not, astral dreaming allows you to carry out important spiritual work in your sleep. It allows problem solving to occur at a soul-deep level of resolution, to check on people and situations dear to you, to maintain relationships in a way you may not be able to maintain them while awake.

In any human life, there are unresolved issues and events, usually involving other people, that we are not able, for one reason or another, to work out in waking life. We may be cut off from our own need for healing, locked in unforgiving attitudes, unaware of our responsibilities, distanced by time, separated by death. Astral dreaming offers us potential connection and healing on the soul level. While our personalities learn to catch up, the soul self continues to strive toward integration and inner peace.

I had such a dream the morning my grandfather died. I was in Switzerland; he was in Montana. We hadn't seen each other in several years. Yet I woke with a distinct impression of his face still in the room, that he'd come to say good-bye and wish me well. At other times I have had healing conversations with people it would be inappropriate for me to contact in any other way; spontaneously, reconciliation has occurred.

Past-Life/Karmic/Reincarnation dreams may occur even if you don't believe in past lives, karma, or reincarnation. These dreams are characterized by life events that you cannot explain, even though in the dream they make sense and seem familiar. During these dreams, "you" may find yourself speaking a language you don't speak, or being someone else in a time and place you both do and don't recognize.

Past Life:

When I was in Israel I dreamed I was walking with my friends there and when I looked down at myself I wasn't wearing western clothes. I wanted to talk to people passing by, but I knew I didn't speak the language. Then a friend said to me, "You can say anything you want, this is another time." I began speaking Arabic, or something that sure sounded like it. There was no sign of anything modern, just this dusty little village.

. . . even if the conscious mind is highly skeptical about the reality of past lives as historical memories, the unconscious is a true believer and is simply waiting to be asked.

—Roger J. Woolger
Other Lives, Other Selves

Spiritual Gift:

A beautiful man came into my room and left a sack of gold in my closet. I knew this man, though I'd never seen him before. I knew he was trying to give me something important and useful. I felt reassured and fell even deeper into sleep. The next morning the gold wasn't literally there, but it was symbolically.

Proceed from the dream outward.

—Carl Jung

Once you accept the possibility of being someone else in some other time and place, these dreams often proceed with more rationality than usual dreams. They are characterized by a sense of story, not the chaotic, action plots of your entertainment dreams, but a sort of *cinema verité*. They are slices of life, only not the life you think you're living now. You may "know" other people, even though they don't look like themselves as you know them now. Gender may be reversed and circumstances mixed differently than in your present life circumstances.

Past-life dreams provide intriguing spiritual gifts, however you want to interpret them. You may use them to explain your affinity for certain people, places, or activities. You may look for themes that seem to carry from one life to the next: what is your soul trying to work out?

Spiritual Gift dreams are offerings from the unconscious that have bearing on what is occurring in your waking life. They are one part of the mind trying to give another part of the mind symbolic insight. If you practice creative visualization or work with an inner guide, these images, characters, and activities may carry over into dreams. These dreams, such as the example at left, often involve a figure of recognized benevolence, an authority literally handing you a gift.

Your dreams are a form of spiritual guidance unique to you. There are many books available on dream meanings, symbols, interpretive techniques. If you read these books, your dreams will begin to talk to you in the language of the symbols you find most interesting. If you don't read any of these books, you and your dreams will develop a language of private interpretation you both understand.

11. INTUITION'S
INNER GUIDANCE

...only when we are silent can we begin to hear the voice that is truly our own—what the Quakers call "the still small voice within."...The source of this voice—which may be without sound, and yet is heard—is called by many different names: the inner guide, guardian angel, spirit guide, the collective unconscious, or just plain intuition. Actually all of us hear the whisperings of this voice every single day of our lives, but many ignore it.

—Rick Fields et al.
Chop Wood, Carry Water

I like the idea that I might stand at my picture window in the morning anticipating that a secret voice will guide me steadfastly through the next twelve hours until I am back in my robe and slippers with the day's duties accomplished. Sometimes these flashes do come, as I gaze out over the suburban yardscape, teacup in hand, half-awake, choosing whether the newspaper or my journal will get my first half hour of waking attention. When I am wise, I choose the journal.

As anyone who's ever followed an impulse knows, our ability to differentiate between flashes of intuition and the rest of the mind's static is certainly not infallible. We head into relationships which appear blessed with potential and which proceed to blow up in our

*We begin life with the world presenting itself to us as it is.
Someone—our parents, teachers, analysts—hypnotizes us to
"see" the world and construe it in the "right" way. These others
label the world, attach names and give voices to the beings and
events in it, so that thereafter, we cannot read the world in any
other language or hear it saying other things to us. The task is to
break the hypnotic spell, so that we become undeaf, unblind and
multilingual, thereby letting the world speak to us in new voices
and write all its possible meanings in the new book of our
existence.*

—Sidney Jourard

Running Tab

* Keep a running tab of intuitive guesses in the
journal.
* Set aside a back page, write down intuitive flashes,
date these notes to yourself.

JOURNAL ENTRIES
3/19 I'm not going to get the job I just applied for.
*3/20 After meeting the project director—not getting this job is a
blessing in disguise.*
*4/22 Our plans for summer vacation will work out, even though
it doesn't look like it right now.*

ME: *Job, why weren't you right for me?*
JOB: *You were right about the director. She's very insecure. You'd
have hated working for her.*
ME: *So what have you got in store for me?*
JOB: *Call Ron. He's got news that will lead to something good.
Listen carefully; it's not what you expect.*

faces a few weeks or months later. We make a U-turn, sure that no squad car is in the vicinity, and suddenly see flashing red lights in the mirror. We dash to the phone sure it's an important call, and someone tries to sell us light bulbs. We are certain the baby's a boy, and it's a girl. We are certain the business deal is a sure thing, and it falls apart during the final negotiations. We often can't seem to get our intuitive bearings. We need to retrain and attune ourselves to recognize and respond appropriately to intuition's guidance.

Intuition is the direct perception of a truth or fact without going first through any reasoning process. You just *know*, and you know that you don't know how or why you know.

We are inhibited in our use of intuition because we have been trained away from our original sense of "knowing" the world. As Jourard says, we have been hypnotized to see the world in prescribed ways. We have been habitually trained to run every thought through our (supposedly) rational minds. Rationalization is not relevant to intuition because intuition does not spring from within the rational mind. It is a gift. Intuition comes *to* us, rather than being generated *by* us. But, because intuition has not been cleared by our rational minds, the intellect tends to reject it. It's a little like being given the ocean and responding, "Because I haven't scooped all this water through my little bucket, I'm not sure it's really water . . ."

The trouble with intuition is it lives on a party line, with lots of voices and impulses and desires crowding around it day and night. While we're praying for some kind of guidance about what to do next with our lives, there's another voice breaking in on the circuit suggesting we go ahead and have a second piece of chocolate cake. It's pretty embarrassing to admit most of what's being said on this internal line, so we throw out the intuition with the impulse half the time.

Fortunately, journal writing provides a way we can practice intuitive skills without social embarrassment. In the margins of my notebook, I often keep a dated list of personal predictions—intuitive flashes coming to me about specific concerns in my life. When I

• Practice listening to and trusting your inner voice.
• Highlight or underline kernels of intuition in the
midst of your ongoing journal writing.
• Look for intuitive phrases:
"I know it's time to . . ."
"I know I need to . . ."
"Because it's right to . . ."
"That's wrong for me because . . ."

> *JOURNAL ENTRY*
> *INT: Finish the novel.*
> *ME: I don't know how the story ends. The characters are getting*
> *away from me.*
> *INT: You will know. Finish the novel.*
> *ME: I have to go to work. I have to keep making a living.*
> *INT: There will be enough money. This is your work. Finish the*
> *novel.*

Affirming Your Intuition

• Design a clear, positive statement of your intuitive
direction.
• Draw a line down the middle of your journal page.
On the left, write the affirmation. On the right, write
the first objection you have to it.
• Rewrite the affirmation. Write the next objection.
• Keep doing this until you run out of objections.
• End by writing the affirmation.

> *JOURNAL ENTRY*
> I choose to successfully finish my novel.
> *You can't, you've been through three drafts and no ending.*
> I choose to successfully finish my novel.
> *Nobody cares about this novel. It's never going to get published.*
> I choose to successfully finish my novel.

read back through the journal months later, I can see where I was accurate and where I was not. If the topic is still of concern, I will often write about it, exploring my own clarity or lack of it. Through such private work, I am learning more and more about the difference between intuition and impulse. I don't know if each of us would experience this difference in exactly the same ways, but the journal provides a place for individual experimenting. The dialogues suggested throughout this chapter are another form of exploration that brings satisfying results to the journal page, and to our lives.

There are five characteristics of intuition that can help us distinguish guidance from impulse.

1. *Intuition is quiet and calm.* It is never pushy, grandiose, obsessive, or manipulative. It does not advise us what other people ought to do, but what *we* ought to do.

    There is an authority to the intuitive message, a dignified "do this, now do this . . ." that does not rely on dramatic renditions, repetition, or pleading. We are either awake and listening, or we are not and the message passes us by. We accept or censor.

2. *Intuition is supportive and directive,* never judgmental, critical, shaming, or blaming. It sees the world as cause and effect.

    One of the clearest hints we have about the difference between spiritual guidance and impulse is whether or not there is emotional weight attached to the statement. A voice that loads its sentences with appeals to the ego, to the personality, to stature in the world, is not coming from intuition. These "worldly" concerns do not apply in the realm of intuition, and are not brought into the bargain.

3. *Intuition is a complete thought, a statement.* Intuition does not lecture, explain, elaborate. The direction is always simple; it is we who throw up the arguments, discussion, reasons why we cannot do what has just been suggested.

    In journal dialogues, like the ones at left, intuition's voice usually states its message, for example, a direction to "finish

John and Helen will never forgive you for using them as the basis
for the couple in the story.
I choose to successfully finish my novel.

*we must . . . learn to dip ourselves in the universe at our gates,
and know it, not from without by comprehension, but from within
by self-mergence.*

—*Evelyn Underhill*
Practical Mysticism

Taking Gifts

Write about one gift you'd take from the universe.
• Why accept this gift and not others?
• What gifts might the universe be trying to give you
that you're not taking?

Test for Benevolence

Ask yourself and write in response:
• Do I feel calm in response to this suggestion, sort
of, "ohh, of course"?
• Do I have the sense I already knew this?
• Do I feel excited and/or inspired?
• Is any fear based on my own doubts rather than on
a real sense that this is "wrong" for me?
• What do I need to do in order to prepare myself to
carry out this directive?
• How closely am I willing to stay in touch with my
intuition?
• What kind of support do I have, may I have?

the book," and the self's voice flails around looking for reasons, permission, ways to accomplish or avoid the task while the intuitive voice simply keeps repeating its request.

4. *Intuition comes to you and through you,* without your feeling as though it is being generated by you. You may experience it distinctly as a relationship with an "other."

Some people find it helpful to imagine a specific source; some find it more helpful to think of intuition as part of the raw energy and intelligence of the universe. There is no right or wrong way to make connection—the connection will work however you imagine it.

Intuition is a continuous stream of information that we filter out except for rare moments of receptivity. To open ourselves to our inner guidance is to come upon a relationship midstream, to walk into the middle of a conversation that has been going on forever, its intimacy long established. "Oh, there you are," you say to your intuition, as though it had been lost.

"Oh, there *you* are," intuition responds.

5. *Intuition is benevolent;* it has our best interests always at heart.

Intuition's messages may not always be easy to carry out; they may challenge and divert us from a path we had intended to follow, but they are not ever misleading. If you are getting direction that is genuinely frightening, to which you have a deep aversion, you will need to dialogue with it and check its source, check your own confusion.

Intuition is a form of spiritual communication. If we believe the sacred is benevolent, intuition should also be regarded as benevolent. The challenge to the rational mind is to accept intuition, despite our noncomprehension at how it arrives at its conclusions, and to use what has not been generated by thought, but given as a gift.

Intuition is evidence that the sacred exists inside us as fully as it exists anywhere else. Intuition is evidence of an interactive re-

JOURNAL ENTRY

Room: Elka comes in her power dress, shaman robes. She hands me a stick of balsa wood, says nothing, smiles solemnly. I know what to do. I know what she means. I have just been given my status: now I am a pilgrim. I am being told I know enough to embark.

Imaginary Room

• Before writing in your journal some days, take a minute and do the following visualization.

Imagine that the space behind your eyes and between your ears is an imaginary room. Design this room to be any way you want it. Stand in the back awhile and absorb its peacefulness. When you are ready, invite a messenger to join you in this place. This messenger has a message for you regarding your spiritual quest/ writing. Look for and receive this message. Thank your messenger. When you are ready, open your eyes and write down your image.

JOURNAL ENTRY

Room: Elka comes again. Stands, turns, offers me her coattail to hang onto. It's a foxtail really. She twists her head around, smiles as if to say—hang on. Hang on—to my writing—to my journey—to the project I am finishing and the one I start. I want to hang on, even though I know she is leading me to some place I cannot yet imagine in my mind. I know her journey is radical. I am tired, but ready. I do not know what to do about all my commitments, but I trust Elka. We test each other . . . are we co-travelers? I feel a gift coming. I take whatever is offered on this path, not to push, not to decide on form. I can only do what Elka directs. Follow. Follow. Follow. She smiles. She offers me the fox's tail. She offers me a place a step behind her lead. I accept with relief.

lationship between the small self and something much larger—the soul, the sacred, a holy light, whatever you want to call it.

Intuition is important to the spiritual traveler because there will be many moments on the quest when it is the only guide we've got. If you do not trust your intuition, if you do not know how to slow way down, go inside and listen; there will be no other sure guidance. The map you are making of your quest is a map of your own intuition concerning what is right for you.

To become more intuitive, slow down, ask, wait, look for a response that meets the above criteria.

Several years ago, while studying with an Indian medicine man, I asked to be shown my totem animal. The animal that came to me was the fox. I have grown more and more appreciative of this symbol for myself. The fox is quick, skillful, well paired. The lesson of the fox for me is to *follow the scent* and not try to get ahead of it. Intuition is the way I make sure I am being led instead of trying to lead.

The fox is a guide who comes often in dreams and meditations, sometimes out in the woods as a special flashing-tailed blessing. You too have special guides, images, energies, that can be personified to help you follow your quest.

There are many methods you can use to define energy and create an image of inner guidance. If you ask for a representation, one will come. Maybe it will come in a dream, in a meditative vision, in a voice or an animal, as an object of nature, a refrain of music. Your role is to ask for a symbol—and then to notice.

In the journal, be thoughtful about what you ask for, and allow interaction between what you think you want to see/be visited by, and what intuition is offering you. The examples on the facing page come from a seminar. Everyone developed a personal image of and a unique relationship to their intuition. Even when people were initially surprised by their images, they realized after working with them for several weeks that they had received exactly what they most needed. These figures and images will change over time. You will have new images to say hello to, and old ones will fade away.

Finding a Guide

- Once you have made your request, notice how it comes.

> I need a friend, not a human friend, but someone wiser, like the parents I wish I'd had. Someone to guide me further in the journey.

- Write about the image you are being given for guidance, and develop a relationship to it.

> I want a guardian angel. When I was little, my grandmother spoke to saints as though they could come to tea. I want an angel who'll come to tea, answer questions, shake her head in warning when I'm about to make the wrong move.

- Describe it.

> I want to stay in touch with my Higher Power. I need to interact with a resource larger than me. Something to call on in crisis.

- Dialogue with it.

> I saw this stately woman, very tall, maybe 6 or 7 feet. I asked her what she was doing here. . . . She said, "I've come to take you the rest of the way."
> I knew immediately all that she meant. I agreed to be taken.

- Draw it.

> I want a guiding hand on my shoulder that steers me right. I promise to move slowly, to be sensitive to the touch. This hand is male, with a powerful ring on his finger, a wizard's hand. I sketched my grandfather's hand and put the ring on it I saw in my mind.

- Dance with it.

> I was driving down the road listening to this exquisite song— something from the Hearts of Space. All of a sudden a man appeared in my mind. He was beautiful, black, dressed in white robes. We danced and danced to this song. My heart just tore open in his arms. Felt safe. I can ask him anything.

We use imagery to translate the immense, unknowable sacred into symbolic terms we can relate to. We pray to a "Thou," not an "it." We have "peopled" the heavens with angels and attributed the earth and sky with familial ties: Brother Sun, Sister Moon, Mother Earth. We look for ways to be in relationship with the energy of the universe.

Such communication is a great comfort. We do not want to make this journey alone, and we cannot make it alone. You know, by now, that Something is there, responsive, seeming to help. Something acknowledges the thank-you spoken at the end of the day and written in your journal entries of blessings. You *are* being guided, and you are learning to follow your guidance.

12. SACRED RITUAL

*When you make the two one, and when you make the
inside like the outside and the outside like the inside, and
the above like the below, and when you make the male
and the female one and the same, so that the male is not
male nor the female female . . . then will you enter the
Kingdom.*

—Gnostic Gospel of Thomas: 25–38

Ritual consists of the external practices of spirituality
that help us become more receptive and aware of the
closeness of our lives to the sacred. Ritual is the act of
sanctifying action—even ordinary action—so that it
has meaning: I can light a candle because I need the light or because
the candle represents the light I need.

Ritual is the way we carry the presence of the sacred. Ritual is
the spark that must not go out. Ten thousand years ago, our fore-
bearers carried the coal of their fire from one shelter to the next.

The dream of the journey comes repeatedly. Over the years the point of departure in the dream varies; I begin in many different places, familiar or foreign to my experience. But once in movement, the journey is always the same. I travel for many days. . . . I travel alone. . . . Beyond the last village lies an open, untracked landscape, the distance so vast and unarticulated that no horizon can be seen. . . .

The tree and the sea announce their identity simultaneously. The earth ends in the sea; the tree grows at the edge. We continue walking toward the great pine and enter the substance of the tree. In the darkness my dog disappears but this does not grieve me. I circle through the multiple concentric rings of the tree, shrinking and aging within each ring. At last the spiraling ends. I arrive at the small dark spot of origination. When I touch this innermost center I realize I am already there. I have been journeying to where I am.

—Meinrad Craighead
The Mother's Songs

Identifying Rituals

In your journal write about the following:
* What rituals do you currently observe as part of your spiritual life?
* Why do you observe them?
* What do they mean to you?
* What connections do they allow you to make?
* What is missing for you in the way of ritual?
* Design a ritual that would meet some of these needs.

Protected in a sack of moss, smoldering, blown on, and treasured, this coal was the source of survival, the gift of heaven. They nurtured it, grass stem by grass stem, until it could bear the weight of kindling, could burst again into flame. When darkness fell, when they needed warmth, they reawakened fire.

Though our lives may seem far removed from these early human origins, you and I also need to carry and nurture an ember of awareness. We need rituals that acknowledge the importance of the quest and the centrality of spirit, which make the outside like the inside and the above like the below.

We may not always feel ourselves centered on spirit, but that is not because spirit shifts: we shift. Our relationship changes, is shaken and strengthened by event and insight. We become clear. We become confused. We need rekindling from time to time. Ritual rekindles us.

When a friend recently turned fifty, she sent her husband out of the house until midnight and called together a group of women friends and colleagues to celebrate. The party started out with the usual trappings, a long buffet of homemade delicacies, drinks that ranged from champagne to spring water. All of us gathered around, not knowing each other, not sure how to connect, just wanting to support our mutual friend. We were middle-class, urban, and suburban women, most of us somewhere approaching middle-age ourselves.

Then Marriá asked us to make a circle. She went around the group and spoke to each of us about our meaning and importance in her life. And each of us responded about her meaning and importance to us. At the end of half an hour, a real group had coalesced from this experience. We understood our bonds and why we were together here. Marria put on music; we danced. We ate more goodies. The music shifted; she put on a record of African jazz. People picked up drums, tambourines, bush pianos, kazoos . . . we joined the music, went into the beat, augmented and riffled the sounds coming out of the stereo. When the record stopped, we did not. We were a tribe now, caught up in our own rhythms, making

No matter how long the meditation, the years of prayer and occult training, the truth comes all at once or does not come at all. Which is not to say that the preparation was meaningless. . . . Not only does it make us strong enough to withstand the lightening when it comes, it also puts us in a position to bring about the lightening.

—Rachel Pollack
78 Degrees of Wisdom, A Book of Tarot

JOURNAL ENTRY

I went to church this morning, took communion, went back to my pew and was kneeling quietly, praying for the week, the world, for comfort for all who suffer. And then EG brought her husband up to the front of the church in his wheelchair, and they came down from the altar to bring him wine and bread. I watched out of the corner of my eye. TG looked just like Lynne looked when she was ill—the puffiness from steroids, the slump of body posture, and I was suddenly struck with a bolt of grief. I cried for Lynne, for the loss of her. I cried for T&E and their loss of each other. I cried for the pain B and I had been talking about yesterday, all the pain in the congregation, known and unknown. . . . The veil fell for a moment and there was no separation between their pain, the world's pain, my pain. We were all one. I entered the oneness of pain. I have been praying for my heart to open, and this is how it comes. This is exactly right, to be vulnerable, flushed free. It doesn't matter whether what flushes me is pain or joy—it too is all one.

Mystery is not meant to be explained, but to be pondered.

—Patricia Hampl

our own noise to the world. Marria danced herself becoming the Crone, the wise woman. The woman who has earned the right to step beyond traditional restrictions, who has come of age.

The moment passed. We settled down. She opened gifts. Timidly, at midnight, her husband came back in the door. We smiled sweetly, appeared to him unchanged, shivered our ways out into the winter's night.

What's fascinating about ritual is that it acts as a gateway to altered states of reality, to our own sense of awe. We become fascinated with what the mind can perceive, what we can experience that goes beyond our Monday-morning assumptions of reality. Spiritual ritual is not about pomp and circumstance; it's an experience of curiosity and reverence, sometimes heart-wrenching, sometimes exuberant. We draw close to mystery, allow ourselves to understand. We are peeled back, opened.

As Pollack says, "the truth comes all at once." Ritual is a blasting open of the ordinary self, being jettisoned into the thrall of the universe, even if only for a moment. We join esoteric reality, sometimes after careful rituals of preparation and sometimes in moments of amazement that we seemingly have not planned. As I mentioned in chapter 2, sometimes something grabs us and we are opened almost without accord.

When we enter a ritual designed to call ourselves toward the sacred, our energy changes. We become more centered, aware of what we are doing. Senses are heightened. Emotions clarified. We are more open to sending and receiving energy than we are in usual moments. We are sensitized to what we are doing, what we are asking for, what we may receive as a result. *Ritual calls us out of the ordinary into the extraordinary; it wakes us from the stupor of usual activities, imbuing them with meaning.* In so doing, it offers us another form of guidance.

The room in my house where I write is ritual space. My office—though cluttered right now with stacks of journals, sheaths of copied pages from other people's journals, piles of books, various chapter drafts, and notes to myself posted everywhere—is still coded with

- Write your prayers in the journal.
- Think out loud to the sacred; look at what you are asking for.
- Write down traditional prayers, the ones you know by rote.
- Look at these words. Think about what they mean; think about what you mean.
- Develop a renewed relationship to whatever forms of prayer you pray.

JOURNAL ENTRY

Dear God, I need help sorting out who you are, whether you exist, whether I have you mixed up with lots of other people and ideas, and whether, if you exist, there is any connection between you and me. When I write "Dear God" it brings forth all my unbelief. The name that people call you has a lifetime's worth of mostly negative associations. Even referring to you as "you" leads me to scoff. How could Something as all-encompassing as they say you are be addressed as "you"? be available for any kind of one-on-one personal exchange? Isn't this a silly idea, a crutch of comfort to get through life?

I have decided lately to act as if you are there and see what happens. I decided I was being presumptuous to think you couldn't exist just because I couldn't imagine you existing. I'm giving the whole situation the benefit of a doubt, and I'm going to keep writing you. I didn't know that, but writing this has led me to think differently than just talking or thinking has done.

Thank you for listening to me, God. Please help me accept that you love me, which people tell me that you do. And if you are there, and if you love me more than I possibly could love, and will help me in any way that I accept your help, then I accept you too and love you too. Amen.

meaning. The heart of the room, which will remain when the clutter is gone, is a code to the rituals I practice. People come and go, notice one thing or another, but they don't know how that rock, this shell, the placement of a candle, the meaning of a small sculpture or painting, ignite this room for me and make it holy space: I know.

There are days I dump paragraphs in my journal, and there are days when writing is a form of prayer. It depends partly on the topic under consideration, but mostly on the attitude I bring to the desk.

On days when I am anxious, separated from my sense of spirit, out of sorts with myself and my life, my eyes rest on objects that remind me of why I am here and what my work really is. It helps. You help too. Part of what connects us is the shared understanding of writing as ritual.

We make journal writing a ritual by bringing everything we can from experience onto the page. We write prayers, write Godalogues, make mandalas and visionary images. We create reflective time, approach writing with patterns similar to those with which we approach the practice of silence.

Writing is magic. Remember the importance of learning to write your own name? The weight of it on the page, the mystery of making your first sentences? Writing is language made tangible, experience saved and savored, life transformed into story. The richness of our writing in the journal is limited only by the time and energy we can carve out for writing and by our own imagination. Some of the exercises in this chapter are designed to blow out the boundaries of our writing routines.

Out of all the rituals I have experimented with in my life, the richest continues to be the act of journal writing. In the course of this relationship, I have expanded the journal far beyond what I once thought it capable of, and also learned to accept the point where writing stops. The journal can point and point and point to the moment of revelation, but in the actual moment there is only revelation.

No matter what tradition you participate in, or what traditions

Writing Mantra

*   If you have been working with a mantra, write it over and over.
*   Let your handwriting go; become automatic.
*   Set the form of your writing free.

Godalogues

These are dialogues between you and the sacred.
*   Address the sacred in whatever manner is comfortable to you.
*   Take a deep breath, let the sacred speak back through your pen.

> JOURNAL ENTRY
>
> ME: *Christina asked me, Will I choose to be the person I am called to be? And if so, what are the implications of that choice. My question to you, God, is—who am I called to be?*
>
> GOD: *Yourself.*
>
> ME: *Oh, come on, that's no answer.*
>
> GOD: *Be yourself today, in this instant.*
>
> ME: *People will go away. Nobody wants to be around someone who's moping.*
>
> GOD: *I didn't tell you to mope. I told you to be yourself. And if you are your true self, even with your anger, sadness, loneliness, you will also have joy and people will love you. Because I made you, if you let yourself out of the shell you've built, people will see what is holy in you. Are you getting this? It's not your light you're hiding—it's mine, and I don't like having my light extinguished. . . .*

you make for yourself, ritual is the way you transubstantiate the raw materials of your life into quest. Just after she turned five, my niece and her mother attended the Christmas Eve pageant with me at the small Episcopal parish that is my worshiping community. Erin hadn't been to a service where communion was offered, though she knew the Christmas story and was eager to see other children acting it out. She came with us to the altar rail, listened solemnly while she was told what the bread signified, took it. Ate. On the way home for holiday dinner I asked her if she liked the service. She got a thoughtful look in her eyes and said, "You know, that bread was delicious."

I laughed with delight. She had gone straight to the heart of Christian mystery; there was nothing in her way. People have for centuries built elaborate liturgical and sacramental rites in order to do what Erin did spontaneously—let herself be fed. The rituals of spiritual and religious traditions are heavy with meaning, not only the meaning we give them, but the weight of long observance. When you participate in a ritual that is Christian, Jewish, Buddhist, Islamic, wiccan, tribal, you attach yourself to generations for whom this ritual has also had significance. You join your observance to theirs. Sometimes, it is like swimming through water: the motion is languid, heavy, yet buoyant.

When you wear a cross or crucifix, a Star of David, a crystal, a medicine bag; when you give up something for Lent, fast on Yom Kippur or Ramadan, mark the phases of the moon, make prayer ties, smudge your house with sage or incense—these are reminders of how you name the sacred. These signs and symbols work because we grant them the power to work, to bond us.

Most of the time, when we knock at the gate of mystery there is only so far we can take the journal along. We cannot write at the same moment we are enthralled. As soon as we write, we become the reporter, the observer, not the initiate.

One way of bridging the gap between the one who is enthralled and the one who writes is to explore practices of writing that take us out of our usual routines. Medieval monks practiced calligraphy,

Make a Writing Altar

- Bring offerings to the place where you write your journal.
- Create space that feels "holy" to you.
- Ritualize how you approach the journal—lay out pens, light a candle, etc.
- Treat your journal as an object of respect.

Making a Mandala

- Collect things: photos, pictures, feathers, sticks, ribbons, etc.
- Find good-sized, sturdy paper—art tablet, tagboard, even light plywood.
- Meditate on images and on the things you have gathered.
- Set aside a block of quiet time and space.
- What fits? Where? Work around whatever artistic weaknesses you think you have.
- Follow the mandala into creation, don't lead it.
- Study it, meditate on it, dialogue with it.
- Allow its meaning to expand and contract.

> *The true mystic is not merely involved in esoteric thoughts or beautiful images of God in heaven. He is totally absorbed in a life movement, a journey in which his essential self—his real self—comes into life with and in God. This "coming to God," as it has been called, is the journey.*
>
> —Marsha Sinetar
> Ordinary People as Monks and Mystics

sometimes devoting their entire lifetimes to one elaborate, illuminated manuscript. Their labor crossed the boundary and became an act of enthrallment. In the Far East, monks drew mandalas, large concentric, geometric circles that represented the cosmos. We can bring this level of meditative ritual into our journals in several ways: by practicing calligraphy, writing mantras, drawing, mandala making.

Mandala is the Sanskrit word for "circle." Sacred circles occur in every spiritual tradition and remind us of the spiral of the spiritual journey. Your journal is a mandala of words. Your life is a mandala of experience. To make a mandala at certain points in our lives lets the subconscious mind illustrate what this particular point of our passage is about. The illustrations of Susan Seddon Boulet which adorn this book are creative mandalas; they illuminate the journey through symbolic visualization.

Some mandalas are small enough to serve as journal covers, some take up half a wall. However you choose to experiment with the enthrallment of writing, allow yourself to break into symbol, into visualization, to bring what cannot be said into the presence of your writing.

April 9, 1970, turned out to be the day I came into consciousness. I carried my journal with me on the pilgrimage of that day, writing in great detail each level of understanding as it occurred to me. There is a moment, the moment of awakening, when the pen is stalled without words. The page is a large ink blot, surrounded by scribbles, as though I was trying to convey the presence of energy itself onto paper. I have no memory of this "writing." A page later the words begin again. This is ritual at work in the journal and in life.

To prepare to use this meditation and others throughout the book, find a quiet place where you will not be interrupted for twenty minutes or so. Ask someone to read the meditation to you or to play back a version of the meditation you have made yourself or have ordered from the back of the book. The points of ellipses (. . .) indicate a significant pause—silence maintained within the text. Pause for as long as you feel comfortable; five to ten seconds can seem a long time in meditation. Double ellipses indicate longer silence.

FINDING AN INNER GUIDE

Close your eyes and relax your body. . . . Take all the time you need to get comfortable. . . . Shift muscles; . . . stretch and relax. . . . Make sure your spine and neck are straight and aligned . . . not held stiffly. There is no stiffness here . . . just comfort, the beginning of calm. . . . There is no hurry now. . . . There is nothing else to do . . . or think about. . . . Just relax. . . . . . .

Notice your breath. . . . Let your breath enter deeply into your body. . . . Let your breath roll into you like soft, heavy clouds that fill you with silence. . . . Inhale slowly . . . deeply. . . . Exhale slowly . . . thoroughly. . . . Let your breath sink in and out. . . . Your breath is a rhythm of calm. . . . Follow your breath. . . . Exhale extraneous thought. . . . Inhale silence. . . .

Take yourself in your mind's eye to a safe and quiet place. . . . There you will see a path. . . . Begin to walk this path. . . . Notice the weather, the temperature, the landscape you are walking through. . . . . . . After a while, you see in the distance an entity walking toward you. . . . . . . The two of you are coming to meet each other. . . . . . . As you get closer . . . notice the feelings in your heart as you anticipate this meeting. . . .

How do you greet each other? . . . What do you say? . . . What does the entity say? . . . What is the entity's name? . . .

. . . What is the message it has brought for you? . . . . . . How will you find each other again? . . . . . .

When you have received your message and are ready, return back down the path. . . . Do you walk together or separately? . . . . . . Follow your breath back to this room. . . . Emerge out of the silence of your body. . . . There is no hurry. . . . Stretch your body. . . . Open your eyes. . . . . . .

Take time to draw or write whatever you want to record from this meeting.

Find images, photographs, paintings, that remind you of this entity and your guidance. Keep them around you as symbols of what you have met upon the path.

IV.
The Four Major Practices

13. LOVE

*As we live we are transmitters of life and when we fail
to transmit life, life fails to flow through us. . . .*
*And if, as we work, we can transmit life into our work,
still more life rushes into us to compensate, to be ready
and we ripple with life through the days. . . .*
*Give and it shall be given unto you is still the truth
about life. But giving life is not so easy. It doesn't mean
handing it out to some mean fool or letting the living
dead eat you up. . . . It means kindling the life force
where it was not, even if it's only in the whiteness of a
washed pocket-handkerchief.*

—D. H. Lawrence
Complete Poems

Spirituality is not an intellectual exercise. It needs to be experienced. Experience comes through the practices of love, forgiveness, trust, and acceptance. Each of these practices is a commitment to opening the heart.

179

. . . Although at times the mind may not be clear, compassion is
always the appropriate response. To have mercy on our
mercilessness. To leave nothing unhealed.

—*Stephen Levine*
Healing into Life and Death

Transmission Awareness

* How do you experience energy received?
* How do you experience energy emitted?
* Write your own stories about times you are
compassionate and understanding.
* Write about times you wish you had been more
understanding.

JOURNAL ENTRY
Lynne called me over to her house to tell me she is dying. I said,
"I know." We hugged and cried and sat down to talk. I cannot
imagine what it is like to be her, to measure out life in hours and
days: an hour not too tired, a day not being nauseated.
Everything I can do for her now is limited to love.
I dance her out of her wheelchair toward the commode. I have
been strong enough to lift her, but not to maneuver successfully
across the room. We twist toward the daybed, her body draped
over mine. I thought love was stronger than this—that I could
lift and hold her just on heart power. We plop safely down to
finish our conversation and wait for another friend to show up
With two able bodies we'll manage to complete the transfer. At
least I didn't drop her, and now, out of her chair, I can enfold
her while we talk. She sits in the circle of my arms and legs,
leans back against my torso.
I tell her, "We don't have to say good-bye because we've never
left anything unsaid. We have the clearest friendship I've ever
known—and who knows what is possible with love. Something
continues after death. We will find it out together, one from each
side." She promises to haunt me and I am glad.

180

That is the mystery at the core of all religious thought: if "God" is love—is pure energy—then to understand energy we need to increase our capacity to give and receive it—as D. H. Lawrence says, to transmit life. We decide event by event and insight by insight whether to open our hearts or close ourselves down. We decide to stretch ourselves to become more than we thought we were a minute ago, or we contract and become less than we hoped. Transmitting life force is a commitment to the particulars, how we respond to the very next stimulus.

> *I was driving downtown on my way to teach a journal seminar, hurrying because I was a little late, didn't want the group to wait. A raggedy man crossed through the traffic stopped at a light. He spotted me in my red car, wove his way toward me, leaned his elbows on the hood, smiled. I met his gaze, smiled back, laughed at his audacity. And that's all he wanted—for someone to see him, to laugh with him a second. He waved and moved on.*

Sometimes we have a tendency to think of spiritual practices as phenomena that occur in the lives of others greater than ourselves, of saints and role models. *Mother Teresa, we say, now there's somebody who makes decisions about life force, who's decided to live with an open heart. That's not my life, not even what I aspire to. I don't want to move to Calcutta.* This line of thought only skirts the issue: you and I *are* making the same decisions, in how we respond to each other, in what attitudes we carry through the day, even in whether or not we kick the cat. Today, right now, as I write and you read, we need to understand the condition of our hearts.

This is why I call these concepts—love, forgiveness, trust, and acceptance—*practices*. They are active and interactive. They require constant commitment to practice them better. We are confronted every minute with choices. And it is necessary that we constantly decide. We should not simply throw ourselves open or closed without regard to our own life maintenance.

It's all about love . . . tell everybody.
—Jeff Buzzetti
AIDS Quilt

How You Love and Talk to Yourself

Inner conversation is the basis of the love relationship
you have with yourself.
•   Write the monologues and dialogues of self-talk
that show your love, or lack of it, for yourself.
•   Is this voice loving? critical?
•   Whose voice is it that loves and chides you?
•   Is there a "sacred" voice you hear within?

Self-Parenting on the Page

Your grown self and your child self need to talk to
each other to heal the rifts of life.
•   To call forth the writing voice of the inner child,
write with the unaccustomed hand. Use a bright
marker or fat pencil. (Your handwriting will be clumsy.
You will use small words to make your point.)
•   Keep your adult self at hand to respond to the
questions and comments of the inner child. Write the
adult's voice with the accustomed hand. Use a regular
pen. (Use language that a child can understand. Be
specific.)

Your grown self, your child self, *and* the sacred need
to talk to each other.
•   Allow an overseeing "sacred" voice to intercede and
teach you how to love yourself better.
•   You are a child of the universe. This is the force
that parents you both.

My partner comes home tired from working with people all day. I'm feeling trapped in the house. "I have to get out of here!" I say. "I can hardly wait to get into my jeans," she says. We look at each other, take the dog to the woods for a long walk, bring in Chinese food.

Spirituality is a commitment to being different in our hearts, minds, and actions. Spiritual practice is the only way we can discover what difference our spirituality makes. Without practice, spirituality is just an intellectual exercise, a puzzle about the universe we find interesting. When we accept these practices, we move from the intellect to the heart and commit ourselves to making active spiritual choices in thought, word, and deed, rather than simply knowing something about the topic.

When Lawrence names us transmitters of life, he is referring to spiritual practice. The most primary of these practices, the one on which the others are built, is love. Though we may not use the same words, transmission and reception of energy is nothing foreign to us. In fact, we count on it. The outward signs of love—the gentle glances, exchange of little gifts and tokens, affectionate touch— are ways we signal each other that this relationship is special, that *we are showing our love*. These signs of love are evident in the ways we treat ourselves, each other, and the sacred. They are important to us because they communicate love in a code of our own designing.

I stop in the middle of the afternoon, take twenty minutes to write in my journal because I need to greet myself on a deeper level. I see my brother's shoulders hunched over the kitchen table and stand behind him, rubbing the muscles because I can't lighten his business load, but I see the pressure he's under. I smudge sage and sweet grass in the house or burn a candle while writing because I want to invite myself open to the sacred.

We know love is not *in* the glance, the gift, the touch; love is the energy *behind* each of these things. Love is these acts imbued

A Blessing a Day

- Remember to record your blessings.
- See chapter seven for a refresher on this exercise.

> *JOURNAL ENTRIES: BLESSINGS*
> *E. was full of love tonight, running up to hug my leg, to snuggle between J. and me on the couch. Love literally radiating out of her and I radiated love back to her. Our soul connection beyond the 3-year-old and her auntie was full open. She'd look at me: Do you see who I am? See Love? Yes, I do. Thank you.*
>
> *A very discouraging day, as far as work goes, but I went shopping and bought beach clothes for our upcoming vacation and this cheered me up. My life is going on. Thank you.*
>
> *P. phoned this afternoon, called me "dearheart"—I needed that added touch. Thank you.*
>
> *We made BLT sandwiches with homegrown tomatoes. The nostalgic taste and conversation was the best part of the day. Thank you.*

A Gift a Day

We not only receive from the world each day, we contribute. Before going to sleep, pause and review the day.

- Write a brief statement, choosing one thing you gave back to the world today that you are willing to acknowledge as your gift.
- End the entry with the words *you're welcome.*

with life force. This is the same life force we studied in the chapter on the body. Not only are we imbued with energy, energy is the nature of the universe itself. This life force has been given many names. The Chinese call it *chi*, the Hindus call it *prāṇa*, the Greeks named it *agapē*. It is the spark within the atom: that which lives, even in those things we do not identify as "living," the beingness of things. Though it's a mouthful to say, the most wholistic term for this energy in English is *unconditional love*, love that is encompassing and ever present. *The physical universe, in its entirety and enormity, is permeated with this energy. And so are you and I.*

Spiritual love is a position of standing with one hand extended into the universe and one hand extended into the world, letting ourselves be a conduit for passing energy. Usually we can't sustain this position more than a few minutes at a time. It's exhausting to be so stepped out of ourselves. We are unaccustomed to it. But a few minutes is enough.

Energy is presence. Thought is form. The good or bad vibrations that we feel in certain places or around certain people come from the energy and thought emanating from them. When we send blessing into the world, we literally create more light. When we send curses into the world, we literally create more darkness.

> *My loving attitude—and lack of it—is immediately obvious in how I drive. I can choose to bless the cars around me, sending forth an imagined beam of light that clears a path for me, or I can curse every driver sharing this stretch of road. My attitude directs the trip, whether I'm scooting along wishing other people safe journeys or cursing every delay and driver who dares weave in the lanes. I've discovered the most amazing relaxation device for freeway driving: going the speed limit.*

Out in public, we have the opportunity to notice and interact with people who are different from ourselves. Perhaps they are richer or poorer, handicapped, a different race or ethnic group, gay, straight, young in a place full of old folks, or old in a place full of

I was the traveling Tarot card reader today, spent an hour with E. laying out what guidance the cards offer her this moon. You're welcome.

S.P. called. I don't mind my own changes being hard, but I hate to watch other people's changes create difficulty. I did what I could to hug her by phone. You're welcome.

Jehovah Witnesses came to the door this afternoon. I know they're only following their convictions, so I told them "God bless you" before I closed the door. Made me sad we couldn't really talk. You're welcome.

Our physical pumping heart is the translating mechanism for consciousness, and the subtle heart is the generative force itself. . . . The heart translates and sends its signals to the brain of a real, underlying conscious response to the world out there.
—Joseph Chilton Pearce
Magical Child

Finding the Loving Child

The soul-child radiates love, is laughing and solemn, at home in the world. Look for him/her in and beyond the journal.
• Write sensuous memories, happy times, moments of unfettered joy.
• Write about nature. Confidence. Excitement.
• Pull out childhood photos, look for that expression—wide open to life.
• Draw, dance, play, dialogue.

young folks. Spiritual practice is the art of taking time to see each other, to let our eyes meet, smile. We discover there is nothing to be afraid of. Spiritual love is what we all hunger after and we notice its presence gratefully.

Spiritual energy brings compassion into the real world. With compassion, we see benevolently our own human condition and the condition of our fellow beings. We drop prejudice. We withhold judgment.

In the journal, we practice love by noting our blessings, many of which are the free offerings of other people, a generosity of spirit. Now, by adding the exercise A Gift a Day, we see how fully we participate in this chain of sustenance. We see how abundant love is and how generous we can afford to be.

> A child is crying in the shopping mall, the mother frantic with nervous anger. The child cries more. The mother is about to hit the child. You walk by, send a thought of love to the child, to the mother. You joke with her, tell her your kids do the same, dispel tension. Talk to this baby—hello, sweetie, what's the matter? Everyone begins to calm down.

Generosity may not have been our original training, but it was our original intent. Babies come into the world as love-dispensing and love-seeking beings. Only the cruel lessons of environment begin to close us down. We may have learned to dole out love, apportion it as though it were our responsibility to decide who gets how much. But in the core of ourselves is that original child/soul who is love personified, sitting gleefully in our hearts. Therefore, the heart is what must guide us—and it does.

Joseph Chilton Pearce, known for his work with natural child development, discusses the heart as having consciousness. Research has revealed that the midbrain, that part of our brains capable of understanding metaphor and symbol—the part of the brain involved in the quest—is connected to the heart by unmediated nerve connections. These connections send the heart information on an instant-by-instant basis. The heart then responds, sending the mid-

The Child of us *has knowledge of the center Ground of religion, philosophy, metaphysics and science—already knowing* all that needs to be known to make it through time. *The Child will lift the willing of us to the High Place and there we reign over our own overcoming.*

—*William Samuel*
The Child Within Us Lives!

What Love Can Do?

- List everything love provides in your life.

JOURNAL ENTRY
Love: makes me see the days differently. Love helps me notice good things happening with other people, with nature, even in my own thoughts. Love fills my eyes with wonder. Love is the way I look at my family. Love is the way I feel reading about sad things in the paper, wishing I could fix pain for others. Love is friendship. Love is the cat on my lap and the dog's head resting on my foot. Love is sitting through Jeremy's hockey games and Becky's ballet recital. Love is making popcorn for us all watching Monday night football. Love is listening to my mother, even when she complains and taking her favorite foods when I visit the nursing home.

brain instructions regarding what response to make to the outside world, to whatever interaction is being requested. Pearce believes we are governed by this "conversation between the heart and mind," and that the heart leads.

If this is so, the rule that applies to the practice of love is, THINK *and do as your heart leads.* Thinking and following the heart is an intuitive action. We practice this action in the same way we practice intuition—working to keep the message clear and ungarbled by our expectations and assumptions about love. Spiritual love is diffuse. It is gentle. It flows into whatever cracks and crevices will accept it.

Spiritual love exercises the connection between the mind and the heart. The reason for exercising this connection is to identify it, use it, and observe what happens. As we grow in our ability to use our hearts, we develop a conversation of wonder in the journal. We are amazed at what love can do and what we can do in the act of love. But also in the course of exercising love we discover and confront our fear. We face the need to drop defenses that have long been with us.

> *Walking in places where I might be afraid, I throw my energy around myself, become a mobile force field. As people come toward me, I look them in the eye, say hello first—sending my message of expectation that we will pass each other with respect.*

Most people learn never to be vulnerable, never to open. Even in the most intimate relationships, they remain guarded, closed, afraid. We treat the heart as though it's a skittery creature, peering out from under a rock, that should never come into the sunlight for fear of predators. The truth is, the heart is a powerful, awe-inspiring force to be reckoned with in the world. When we see this energy fully revealed, when someone stands before us openhearted, we are moved to great calm, not to violence. We want to bask in the heart's light, want to protect and align ourselves with this energy we recognize as also our own.

• List what love is *not* providing, that you wish you
allowed it to.

> *Unlove: I don't know how to let love solve my problems at the*
> *office. I don't know how to let love create better communication*
> *with my father. I don't know if love can help get over the divorce.*
> *I don't know if love will make me feel better about my life when*
> *I'm sixty. I don't know how to let love convince me there's a God*
> *who cares. . . .*

> *Nothing and everything cannot coexist. To believe in one is to*
> *deny the other. Fear is really nothing and love is everything.*
> *Whenever light enters darkness, the darkness is abolished.*
> —Dr. Helen Schucman
> A Course in Miracles

Greeting Fear

• Make a list of current fears—no detail, just an
accounting of everything you're anxious about.

> *JOURNAL ENTRY*
> *1. I don't know if I really want to grow old with F.*
> *2. I'm afraid the kids are going to get into sex and drugs, that I*
> *haven't given them good enough reasons not to.*
> *3. I don't know if we have enough money to keep our lifestyle,*
> *send the kids through college, help keep mom in her home.*
> *4. If one more person needs me, I'll scream.*
> *5. Scream.*
> *6. I still don't know what I want to be when I grow up.*
> *7. Nobody in this family seems to be growing in similar*
> *directions; we scatter from the center all the time until it doesn't*
> *feel like there's any center left.*

For a long time we have been schooled to trust fear more than love. We have been told to watch out, to be self-protective, not to trust, but to stay wary, not talking to strangers. But these instructions discount our ability to follow love's rule: to *think* and do what the heart leads. When we think at the same time as we open the heart, we are connected to a wisdom much greater than the fearful whisperings of our training. We may go into the world— but we take our safety with us. And we let heart power decide when it should be open and when it should be closed. Retreat is easy; we've had plenty of practice in withdrawal. All we have to do is think fear, close down, remove ourselves from intimacy or compassion. We can practice the shielding exercise suggested in the chapter on the body's guidance.

A Course in Miracles postulates that there are really only two thoughts—love and fear—and that these thoughts are mutually exclusive. Love will encompass and calm fear: fear will overwhelm and drive out love. When we are flooded with love, it lifts us into an expansive sense of communion with all life. When we are flooded with fear, it plummets us into isolation from all life.

Love and fear call us into account. If we profess to be on a spiritual journey yet spend most of our time afraid, what journey are we then on? Fear separates us from love, and also from forgiveness, trust, and acceptance. The choice between love and fear is the most basic choice we make.

> There may be more than one entrance, but I know one gate to
> hell: it's in my mind. It is as distinct and boundaried as a room;
> it has a door. Here is where I store the thoughts that separate me
> from love: phantoms of fear, panic, helplessness. Every wrong I've
> ever done remains here, critiqued and recorded. I am judged
> harshly by whatever resides here.

Journal writing about the four practices provides opportunities for us to understand and resolve our fears as well as explore our capacity for love, forgiveness, trust, and acceptance. Most fear has

- If you applied love to each of these fears, what would you do?
- What do you presume the outcomes to be?

> 1. If I applied fresh love to F., maybe I could see him clearly enough to see what I still value about him. We have become so familiar it's hard not to look at each other only through habit and routine.
>
> 2. If I send the kids messages of love and confidence about their ability to make good decisions, it will probably have a better effect than acting like I don't trust them.
>
> 3. I don't know how love can help me with #3. There's probably a way, but I don't know what it could be. I will be thankful for what I have.
>
> 4/5. If I would use genuine love energy instead of obligation, I wouldn't feel so empty. Love is a refilling bucket. Duty, sacrifice, being-a-good-person is an emptying bucket.
>
> 6. I guess I could love my continued explorations.
>
> 7. At supper tonight I'm going to tell every person why and how I value them, how they are important to the family, even if they all say, ohhh mother . . .

- What's keeping you from trusting love as much as you trust your fear?
- Would you be willing to change your mind?

power because it hasn't been challenged. Spiritual practice challenges fear in all its guises. Through writing about fear in exercises presented here and in the chapter on trust, we have the opportunity to become much clearer about the choices we make.

> *The most interesting aspect of this inner damnation is how distinct it is. As I lie in bed waking to the day, I flip through channels of thought as clearly different from each other as radio stations. Before I rise, I choose to proceed along a spiritual and creative path. I will not go to hell. I close that door, choose love. This is where I begin—over and over again.*

14. FORGIVENESS

*Forgiveness is the great "yes." It is a decision in the
sense that you have to will it. You have to choose life.
A person can choose death by not forgiving. So there
is a sense in which you can destroy yourself by not
saying "yes" to the reality that actually exists. That's
the choice, "yes" or "no" to what truly exists.*

—*Thomas Hopko*
Parabola, *vol. XII, no.* 3

Forgiveness is the act of admitting we are like other
people. We are prone to make mistakes that cause
confusion, inflict pain, and miscommunicate our intentions. We are the recipients of these human errors
and the perpetrators. There is no way we can avoid hurting others
or being hurt by others, because this is exactly the nature of our
imperfection. The only choice we have is to reconcile ourselves to
our own flaws and the flaws of other people, or withdraw from the
community. If we choose to withdraw, we withdraw both from our
humanness and our connection to the sacred. That is why Thomas
Hopko calls withdrawal an act of self-destruction. To fully live, we

*When you can forgive both another and yourself . . . you move
from the law of karma (action and reaction) into the law of grace
(resolution)—that effulgent state that transmutes and heals.*

—Brugh Joy
Joy's Way

Forgiveness Inventory Stage One:

People bring many experiences and confused ideas to
the process of forgiveness. You may need to start by
sorting this background in the journal.
*   What do you think forgiveness is?
*   What were you taught about forgiveness?
*   What did religion teach you?
*   Have you ever consciously gone through the
process of forgiving?
*   What worked?
*   Where did you get stuck?
*   What do you know now that you didn't know
then?

*. . . Genuine forgiveness is participation, reunion overcoming the
powers of estrangement. . . . We cannot love unless we have
accepted forgiveness, and the deeper our experience of forgiveness
is, the greater is our love.*

—Paul Tillich
Best Sermons

must choose to enter freely the cycle of interaction in which we will hurt and be hurt, forgive and be forgiven, and move on with love intact. This is what truly exists.

When you will not forgive someone, you fill your life with resentment, paranoia, isolation, righteous indignation, vindictiveness, and false assurance that your perceptions and actions are justified because of the wrong that has been done you. You withhold yourself from human community because you perceive, or at least hope, you are not as imperfect as the rest of us and you don't want to associate too closely with our unforgivable flaws.

When you are unforgiven, your life is filled with recrimination, self-abuse, isolation, fear of further accusation, shame that you have done something considered unforgivable. You withhold yourself from human community because you perceive, or are afraid, that you are more imperfect than the rest of us and that you can never make enough amends to be a fully acceptable member of the human family again.

What results from either of these tracks are two crippled human beings, two crippling experiences, and two states of isolation from the spiritual journey. Both parties are in hell, and the only way out is for reconciliation to occur.

You have to decide: Are you going on a journey to see what love can accomplish, or are you going on a journey to see what revenge, blame, and hostility can accomplish? When looked at in this way the choice seems obvious. It's in the little moments, when a tiny bit of blame seems innocuous, a smidgen of hostility appears justified, and revenge is conjured up as a sweet reward, that you may not consider the consequences. The journey is fragile. What journey are you on?

There can be no love or trust or acceptance, we cannot go further in spiritual practice, unless we are willing to go through the process of forgiveness over and over and over again. Forgiveness is the pivotal point in spiritual growth. Without forgiveness, life doesn't move.

I learned about my need to forgive and be forgiven in the most

Speed-Writing

• Speed-write your anger, your grievances, against another person, an event, any unhealed injury.

• Set a timer for 10–15 minutes and don't let your pen lift from the page.

• When you are done, speed-write again, this time from the voice of the spirit self—what you understand about this situation.

• Set a timer for 10–15 minutes and don't let your pen lift from the page.

Unsent Letters

• Not all acts of reconciliation can, or should, be carried out in person.

• Unsent letters are instruments for reconciling with people long gone from your life, with people who have died or with whom you don't want to make contact.

• Don't censor: say what you need to say.

• Let them "write back"; see the same situation from their point of view.

> JOURNAL ENTRY
>
> Dear Mom and Dad, I am thankful, finally, for all I have learned about myself and life through the struggle of being your son. I wish I could say this to you in person, but I will at least say it to your souls. I feel calm now about our history, and sure that I will not destroy myself because of any lack of healing from our family. This is what kept me bound to you in anger for so many years. I was afraid I was ruined as a person, that I'd never get clear enough to become my own man, to figure out how to take care of myself and find some love in the world. But having reached this confidence, I can look at you with benevolence, a feeling of peace and completion. You have been important teachers in my life. As we age and enter the last stage of our earthly trip, I hope we will be able to find some mutual peace. But in any case, I wish you well.

painful ways imaginable, just as you are learning about your needs. The details are not important; the lessons are essential.

Forgiveness is the absolution of past mistakes, when you cease to feel shame toward yourself or resentment toward others, and you accept, as an act of grace, the possibility of being loved even as you are, even as you have been.

I used to take forgiveness rather lightly, probably intellectually. I was angry at my parents for many years, went through therapy, reached a state of internal understanding and forgiveness toward them and toward my past. I looked back on old relationships, forgave us our confusion, the things we didn't seem to know how to do any better at the time. In the journal, I developed some of the forgiveness exercises presented here and thought I understood the topic pretty well. Then, someone decided not to forgive me. There was no opportunity to discuss reconciliation, only an announcement that we were formally estranged and I was to blame. Suddenly, forgiveness became the central issue of my existence.

Most of what I've learned about forgiveness, most of the healing that has occurred, has occurred in the journal, working deeply with the issues this incident raised about responsibility, intent, good and evil, shame, blame, and the presence of grace. I have come to believe fervently in the imperative need for forgiveness—to accept what truly exists about the human condition, to find the compassion and courage to move on.

You may worry that writing down in the confines of a journal the actions you would like to take is not enough to change your life. Writing *is* action. If, in the course of forgiveness dialogues, unsent letters, entries that allow for anger and grief, you let your heart change, you will find that the heart's power changes the world around you. You become, over time, more compassionate, more willing to forgive as you experience spiritual release.

People rarely set out to harm one another intentionally. Most actions that later require forgiveness are the result of ignorance and confusion rather than malevolence: people *interact* and estrangement results. In the midst of such interactions, *there are always unperceived options for accountability and resolution, which neither person recognizes or*

Respecting Estrangements

As you become aware of various estrangements in your
life, ask yourself in the journal:
- What is the nature of each estrangement?
- Why do you maintain it?
- What purpose is it serving?
- Is there a level at which this estrangement is
appropriate?
- How could you be forgiving and still maintain a
healthy separation?

Forgiving Yourself

- Write down one thing you will forgive yourself for
today.
- Explain why you are willing to forgive yourself,
and what you will do, what action you will take, to
make peace with yourself and allow change.

> To learn respect and reverence for process is what counts; we each
> take our own roads, but it is what one discovers along that road
> that's important, and how one is changed by those discoveries.
> —Judith Guest

Forgiving Others

- Write down one thing you will forgive somebody
else for today.
- Explain why you are willing to forgive them and
what you will do, what action you will take, to make
peace and allow change.

> The only way you can prove you love God is by loving your
> neighbor, and the only way you can love your neighbor in this
> world is by endless forgiveness.
> —Thomas Hopko
> Parabola, vol XII, no. 3

knows how to take advantage of at the time. As a result of our mutual ignorance, there is now pain. What are we going to do? How are we going to learn?

Perhaps these questions have been raised for you through estrangements of family and friends, divorce, death, business problems, bankruptcy, lawsuits, legal issues, ethical dilemmas, spiritual crises—our need to forgive and be forgiven has a hundred variations. The challenge is the same. The purpose of this chapter is to prepare ourselves for reconciliation, to recognize what we need to initiate with others and what we need to be ready to accept from others. And, in situations where reconciliation cannot occur mutually, where we cannot come face-to-face, this chapter helps define ways to experience internal reconciliation and be free.

One summer, many years ago, I worked as coleader of an international youth camp in the West Bank of Israel, only a few years after Israeli occupation. We were the first outsiders invited into this town by the local government. The mayor and some of the teachers wanted to expose their young people to westerners who were not Israelis. So we gathered—about twenty American, German, Dutch, French, and Arab college-age workers—to help rehabilitate a local youth center. On my first day there, the Arab co-leader took me to the houses of all the major sponsors of the project, people who needed to know who I was, and whose support I needed in order to carry out our summer's task. In each house we were offered the strong, sweet coffee of the area. "You must drink it," Besma told me, "or it will give offense." Two months later, on my last day in the town, Besma and I made the rounds again, accepting coffee, saying thanks. "You must leave some in the cup," she said. "It is the proper way to say good-bye."

I have thought often about this ritual for establishing bonds and making orderly withdrawal. There is no equivalent in western culture. Once, after the painful breakup of a love affair, I made the potent coffee, set out two small cups and blank pages at each place at my kitchen table. Sitting at "my" place, I wrote out all the things in my heart I had to say and could not say to my partner. Switching

*Dear God, do you know what they call you? The Almighty.
And I assumed they were right, until the day that Mom and
Jimmy never made it home from a run to the grocery store, left
Dad and me standing at closed coffins. Before I even understood
how permanent death would be, I remember watching my father
slowly crumble, his hands on one large coffin, one small one, grief
hollowing him out until he was as empty as a locust shell. And I
was thinking: how can God do this to my daddy? How can God
watch him suffer this much? And then we went home to the empty
house and over the next months I discovered the irrefutable loss
that is death, and I was thinking: how can God do this to my
family? We are cut in half: two living, two dead. Why can't we
all be on the same side? And I began to hate you, God, for
making such almighty decisions and not asking me, not even
telling me anything about them.*

Forgiving the Sacred

- What haven't you forgiven the sacred for?
- What is preventing you from reconciling with your
image of the sacred?

> *Are you capable of forgiving and loving God even when you
> have found out that He is not perfect, even when He has let you
> down and disappointed you by permitting bad luck and sickness
> and cruelty in His world, and permitting some of those things to
> happen to you?*
>
> —Harold Kushner
> When Bad Things Happen to Good People

Forgiveness Dialogues

- Written dialogues may be the only way we can
carry on conversations of reconciliation.
- Allow the dialogue to follow an intuitive thread of
truth; try not to replay the estrangement.

chairs, I wrote out what I thought he would say to me from "his" place at the table. In this way, I settled our pain and pleasure, gave thanks, parted us evenly in my mind. I left some coffee in each cup.

Forgiveness depends on the attitudes in our own hearts, and is not dependent on the willingness of another to give something to us. Perhaps most of the forgiveness we need to offer and receive will, by necessity and appropriateness, be a private arrangement, a combination of spilled coffee and filled pages. We have the power to say yes to our life conditions, to draw ourselves back into community by cleansing our hearts. And, of course, there is grace, the willingness of the sacred to forgive us, to help us in the cleansing process.

In journal groups, often the first way we look at reconciliation is through an exercise in which we call to mind people with whom we are somehow estranged, whether or not they are currently in our lives. This is easiest through visualization: Imagine yourself sitting in a chair in the middle of an empty stage. Call up, on your right side, everyone you think you may need to forgive. Invite them to approach you, one at a time, talk about (and write down) where you are in the process of forgiveness. If you are able to forgive them, they can move over to your left side. Notice who is on your right and on your left. Look at the agenda you have made for yourself: your forgiveness work.

Use this visualization periodically to see who has moved. You may observe reconciliation operating in your life on a subconscious level, letting you know how your heart has shifted.

Anyone who works a Twelve-Step program is well acquainted with the practice of making amends. Forgiveness is the basis for much of Twelve-Step work. If you need a solid program that emphasizes accountability and reconciliation, look in your community for an Anonymous group that addresses your situation or background.

Lack of forgiveness destroys the peace in our hearts. All it takes is a thought, a name, a reminder of past experience or relationship

X: I really loved you and you scared the shit out of me. I was trying to be the perfect wife. I was following fairy tales, romance novels. You became this very complex stranger, not the boy I married.

O: I loved you too. And I was in a fairy tale too—the loyal soldier, the proud expectant father. It all blew up in my mind. I didn't have anyplace to hide except to start the drinking. . . .

X: Why did you need to hide? Why couldn't we talk about it?

O: I don't remember anybody ever saying we'd need to talk about this kind of stuff. I didn't have words, still don't have words. . . . It's not your fault. I'm still not sure I want to get better. Can you forgive me the pain I've caused you and the baby?

X: Yes. Can you forgive me the pressure I put on you?

. . . the central act of forgiveness and one that indicates spiritual maturity in every case without exception is the forgiveness of the parents. . . . The reason that we can't forgive is that we don't want to face the rage and pain, to admit what really happened. . . .

One must experience in full the pain of the actual harm that was done. . . . That's the block for most people. It has to be gone through again and again, and layer after layer has to come up.

—Thomas Hopko
Parabola, vol. XII, no. 3

Forgiveness Skills

• Look over the writing you've already done about forgiveness and underline the skills you have developed.

to plunge the mind into reveries of resentment, revenge, justifiable hurt and anger, indignation at being wronged, etc. There is a litany to not forgiving. Each of us knows that litany for ourselves. It may be helpful to write it out, to look at all the venom in one place, look at our recurring themes of injustice. What is it exactly that people do which we find so unforgivable? What have we done that is so unforgivable?

I remember years ago learning the depths of my unforgiveness toward myself through exploring what started out as a casual incident. A coworker called, someone I was friends with, but whom, at the moment, I felt uncomfortable around. I was busy, put her off, said I'd call her back the next afternoon. I didn't know what was disturbing me about our friendship and I wasn't ready to talk about it, so I avoided the call all the next day. The day after that I woke in the grips of shame. A voice in my head was screaming at me about what an awful person I was. I decided to write down the whole rant, to the bitter end, in order to understand better its control over me. The last sentence was ". . . you don't deserve to live if you can't keep your word. . . ."

Even then, I didn't really believe that the death penalty was reasonable punishment for not returning a phone call, but the exercise exposed the shame that lay at the core of my being and taught me that I needed to begin exploring issues of forgiveness—for myself and others.

For many people, the primary persons we need to forgive are our parents. Parents play a pivotal role in spiritual development. They provide our original definitions of what it means to be human and what life conditions we ought to expect. The more limited our parents were in their abilities to model a trustworthy human relationship at work in a welcoming universe, the more sorting it takes to create a loving worldview for ourselves.

However, Hopko stresses that we cannot forgive our parents by discounting what occurred. Forgiveness is not a matter of now declaring, "Oh, the drinking wasn't that bad," or "I guess all kids get knocked around like that." Forgiveness means acknowledging

- Gather these skills together under a headline in your journal.
- Take a look at what you know, what you are learning.

> *Forgiveness calls on the strength to be tender, the strength to be awake, to be impersonal, to be noncombative. It gives back the energy that is being thrown away. . . . It simply seeks center.*
>
> —Colin Berg
> Parabola, vol. XII, no. 3

Good Grief

Grief surfaces over and over in the act of forgiving. Let it.
- Look for it underneath your anger.
- Take 10 minutes a day, as you did in the chapter on disorder, to sit down and grieve.
- Write the grief out of your heart with flow writing.
- If there are no words, draw, dance, walk, pet the dog, ask for a long hug, get a massage.

> *To walk as round beings on a round planet cognizant of being interwoven in a circular web of connection with all beings is to understand forgiveness.*
>
> *. . . from the vantage point of circular relating, forgiveness is simply returning energy: returning and receiving energy until any warp in the circle is healed, balance restored. . . . There is no real effort because forgiveness is the natural flow of life. There is no real loss because the flow is circular; it always returns. There is a sacrifice, a giving back that makes whole, makes holy . . .*
>
> *To remember our roundness is our first great healing, forgiving act.*
>
> —Colin Berg
> Parabola, vol. XII, no. 3

exactly what happened, having the feelings we need to have about real past experience, and in this light of comprehension deciding to let go, to let it be over. We need to stop seeing ourselves as either victims or persecutors, and see ourselves instead as family, living in confusion, doing the best we can at any given moment with what we understand to be our options.

Forgiveness is a skill we learn. Any moment of reconciliation represents years of living, endurance, contemplation, and writing which prepare us to step forward into release. Forgiveness wipes out the artificial differences we maintain between ourselves and others. Forgiveness requires that we explore a situation until we more clearly see how estrangement occurred, including our part in its occurrence. When we forgive and are forgiven, we learn empathy.

Empathy is a very intimate kind of knowledge. *Through mutual forgiveness we come to understand a person we have called our "enemy" at a very intimate level, and they come to understand us intimately.* This is why Jungian analyst Nor Hall says, ". . . the solution for healing is made in the blood of the wound itself." Each party to reconciliation, alone or together, must stand in the wounding, endure the pain and confusion of being there until the solution for healing is revealed.

We've seen couples go through this when relationships have been nearly torn apart, and at the moment when two people could easily have split, they have turned to each other instead and begun the process of rebuilding their love. It takes time and courage, a shared commitment to responsibility and honesty.

You may question for a long time your willingness to be so deeply revealed to those who have caused you pain, or to those whose pain you have caused. No one is more deeply bound to another than two enemies; even lovers have greater freedom.

Sometime in my adolescence, during one of our ongoing battles, I remember my mother shouting at me, "If I can't have your love, I'll take your anger!" I wrote the statement down in my first journal, astounded and puzzled, vaguely aware of its power.

Unforgiving anger is energy thrown out like a rope. It entangles

Dreaming Forgiveness

- Dreams portray reconciliation, especially where this cannot happen personally.
- Look also for dreams that repeat a situation, only the ending is different, the wounding resolved.
- See chapter 10 for dialogue dream work.

> *God comes to give us strength to abide inside ourselves, even with our fear, and to reach outside ourselves to others, to touch them with life, not death.*
>
> *—Ann Belford Ulanov*
> *"The God You Touch," from*
> The Christ and the Bodhisattva

Forgiveness Rituals

- Develop a way of offering thanks for the end of estrangement.
- Write down what this act of forgiveness allows you to set aside.
- Write what it allows you to pick up.
- Create a ritual that signifies this ending/beginning.

anyone who grabs on. *Anger needs to be allowed to transform itself into what it really is: a longing for understanding.* We all want to have our side of the story understood, to have our feelings acknowledged as valid and our pain responded to as important. This is the mutuality that can foster our readiness to forgive and accept forgiveness. We want to be able to reach a settlement that is respectful of both perceptions and of what each believes has occurred. We want to be rebalanced.

Colin Berg talks of forgiveness as the energy of return: return to community, return from isolation. When we allow forgiveness to really work, it becomes an act of grace that both the "victim" and the "perpetrator" experience. These old roles are broken down, dissolved in the process of reconciliation. Both people feel the pain, and both people have the opportunity to free themselves of the bond of pain between them. It is true that I have hurt others, but they cannot heal their hurt by refusing to forgive me, any more than I can heal the pain of being hurt by refusing to forgive them— or refusing to forgive life for its occurrences. We seem to expect these days that we should be able to avoid being hurt and that somebody or something ought to be punished, to be assigned the blame, whenever hurt occurs, even in cases that we used to call accidents.

During an ice storm a neighbor skidded off the street, plowed her car through my hedge, and rolled to a halt in the middle of my yard. When I went out to see that she was all right, her first words to me were, "Please, I don't want to get into a legal fight about this." I reassured her that we would find a neighborly way to work it out. The only way we can be free is to give up exchanging moments of prosecution and victimization. Life is too short and too precious to spend it trying to come out innocent. We need to go about our business, replant the hedge.

15. TRUST

God, take me by Your hand. I shall follow You dutifully, and not resist too much. I shall evade none of the tempest life has in store for me. I shall try to face it all as best as I can. . . . I shall never again assume, in my innocence, that any peace that comes my way will be eternal. I shall accept all the inevitable tumult and struggle. . . . I shall follow wherever Your hand leads me and shall try not to be afraid. I shall try to spread some of my warmth, of my genuine love for others, wherever I go. . . . I don't want to be anything special, I only want to try to be true to that in men which seeks to fulfill its promise.

—Etty Hillesum
An Interrupted Life

I had a great-aunt who, no matter what the situation, would always tell me to "trust the Lord." I never much liked this aunt. You couldn't have a real conversation with her. If something good happened she praised the

God doesn't promise to fix things; he just promises not to go away.

—Deborah Keenan

JOURNAL ENTRY
I used to trust God much differently than I do now. I used to trust him to "take care of me"—I mean, keep me from getting too badly knocked around by life. Then in 18 months, I didn't get into law school, Tom and I split, my father died, I lost my job. My whole view of life was knocked out from under me. I didn't trust God anymore.
Then I had this thought: perhaps God isn't in my life to protect me, but to teach me.
That made me pretty mad too because I thought God had agreed to my terms.
Now, I'm deciding getting taught isn't so bad. Maybe that's what I actually need more than anything I thought I needed. I'm coming around to see trust a new way, but sometimes I want my naivete back.

The Evolution of Trust

• What kinds of things have you believed in and trusted?
• What was "trusting" these things supposed to protect you from?
• What are you being asked to trust instead?
• Write a paragraph about how you viewed trust at ages 10, 20, 30, now.

A hero is someone who has given his or her life to something bigger than oneself.

—Joseph Campbell
The Power of Myth

Lord for it, and if something bad happened she trusted the Lord to fix it. And somehow the person living through these experiences seemed to disappear in the equation. In light of how I think about things now, it occurs to me that this habitual response was a way of avoiding the applications of spiritual practice we'll be discussing in the next set of chapters. The way she used trust, she didn't have to do anything else; it all became "the Lord's" problem.

People like my old aunt give trust a bad name. They use it to squelch dialogue and avoid doubt, questioning, or thinking. As part of my journey, I have had to rebuild a concept of trust that can include these things; build a sense of trust that emerges in the middle of my dialogue with life, in the middle of my doubts, fears, questions, and offers me another chance to choose to have faith in the hubbub, not to deaden my sense of reality.

Trust is the decision to keep seeing the deeper path of life and committing ourselves to it, in active partnership with guidance. *Trust is interaction. We* are doing what we can do, *spirit* is doing what it can do, and our lives are the amalgam of these energies.

This whole book is about trust: what to trust, how to trust, when to trust, whom to trust. And trust, even more than practices of love and forgiveness, is likely to bring to mind all our fears and excuses. To commit ourselves to trusting the journey, trusting that our lives are being upheld in some way beyond our comprehension, means that we are in a dialogue of thought and action between our personal desires and the universe's desires for us. This is still, for most of us, a radical change in life posture; that it's one that every pilgrim must eventually reckon with doesn't make it any easier.

The choice to trust is like hanging on a trapeze at the moment you need to let go and swing over to the next trapeze. You need timing. You need the faith to make the leap. You need to tolerate a few seconds of free-fall. You need to be ready to grasp the waiting bar. There will probably not be spotlights or drumrolls, no gasps and applause. Switching from a self-led quest to a quest that follows trust most often occurs in the dark, alone, at the moment we finally say, "Okay, I surrender." We have finally worn ourselves down to

Everything is chance, or nothing is chance. If I believed the first,
I would be unable to live on, but I am not yet fully convinced of
the second.

. . . I feel like a small battlefield in which the problems, or some of
the problems, of our time are being fought out. All one can hope
to do is keep oneself humbly available, to allow oneself to be a
battlefield. After all, the problems must be accommodated, have
somewhere to struggle and come to rest and we, poor little
humans, must put our inner space at their service and not run away.

—Etty Hillesum
An Interrupted Life

Sisiutl, he smells fear and it makes him hungry, and he sets out
after people. . . .

What you have to do is stare him down. Just face him, that's
all. First you find something to believe in, something you Know
isn't ever going to let you down, and then, when Sisiutl comes
after you, you just hang on to what you Know, and you stare
back at him.

. . . Closer and closer he's gonna come, aiming for your mouth, so
he can suck out your breath. Closer'n'closer until . . . he's gotta
turn both'a his heads toward you . . . and when he does . . . left
head is gonna see right head . . . right head is gonna see
left . . . "Who sees the other half of self, sees Truth."
And that's all old Sisiutl has ever really wanted.

—Cam Hubert (Anne Cameron), Dreamweaver

Touching Dragons

• What are your fears? List them. Write a paragraph
describing the fear in detail. (It won't be as scary on
paper as in your mind.)
• What is the purpose of each fear?
• How is the fearful fantasy trying to "help" you?
• What is it designed to prevent you from doing?
• What among these anxieties can you do anything
about?
• What specifically can you do? Will you do it?

the point where the ego gives up and we decide to trust what is beyond ourselves, beyond our individual abilities, perceptions, rules, limitations—even beyond understanding.

We have been warned the journey would come to this moment of relinquishment. Teaching stories recount the tests along the path. The hero with a thousand faces does not attain the prize of wisdom without forfeiting his life—his old life—in exchange for the person the journey makes of him. The person the journey makes of us is one who transcends the ego. Not permanently, for that would not be human, but one who travels in the "I" beyond the "i."

The naked pilgrim wanders the journal without facade. There is no status, no wealth, no knowledge, no worldly power that can help us face the fear of our journeys. *Trust is the only way to release our lives from fear.* And trust is not a permanently granted position; it's a choice, made constantly, over and over again.

In *The Way of the Shaman*, Michael Harner speaks of certain Indian tribes, where the shaman gives a seeker a stick of balsa wood as she sets out on the vision quest. The shaman warns that after a few days she will begin to see visions. Some visions will be beautiful. Others will be terrifying. The seeker will be approached by her personal dragons, her worst fears. This is when she will need the stick. Because no matter how awful the dragons appear to be, if she steps forward and touches each one with the stick, they will disappear and she will be free. But if she runs from even one dragon, it will follow her and drive her mad.

Balsa is a tropical American tree of extremely light wood; the wood used to make airplane models, kite ribs, life preservers. There can be no pretense of safety in the shaman's instructions. He does not say "fight" the dragon, only to "touch" it—to test our fear with trust.

Of course there are two types of fear: imagined and real. All the trust in the world doesn't relieve us of the necessity to recognize and use fear as a healthy warning system. The fight or flight response is wired into our physical and psychological beings, and we need it. Fear is the emotion that puts us on guard, prepares us to deal

Even though I walk through the valley of the shadow of death, I will fear no evil; for thou art with me; thy rod and thy staff, they comfort me.

—Psalms 23:4

Dealing with Real Fears

•   Make a commitment to cope with and respond to realistic anxiety, and then follow through.
•   If you're worried about burglars because your lock is broken, get the lock fixed.
•   List what you have the power to fix or change. Underline these commitments so you can quickly find them and take care of them.
•   Fantasies remain fearful when you only watch the vision to its most horrible point and stop—like shutting your eyes at a movie.
•   Keep writing until you have completed the vision, including *how you would cope* with whatever you imagine.

What has happened here? The unbonded male rapes. . . . The only state [the men] could comprehend was a mirroring of their own isolation and terror. They pleaded with her to be terrified and reflect a madness they could understand. It was impossible, though, for them to act out their roles once she had accepted her death. She was then invulnerable, for how can you threaten a person who is already, in effect, dead? Anxiety arises from avoidance of the fact of our death. . . . She had inadvertently surrendered to the common ground between them, a continuum of possibility. . . . For that brief space of time, they were bonded, their wounds also healed, and they wept.

—Joseph Chilton Pearce
Magical Child

with threatening circumstances. Anyone who walks through the roughest part of town at midnight and doesn't feel fear is not "trusting the Lord," they're just in plain denial. That you or I may decide to deal with high levels of threat by placing ourselves in a spiritual frame of mind is not the same as denying that the fear—or threat— is there.

In a remarkable story at the end of *Magical Child*, Joseph Chilton Pearce relates a woman's experience being snatched at knife-point by two high-strung young hoodlums who push her into their car and begin driving her around New York City, telling her they are going to take her into the woods of New Jersey, rape and kill her. At first she is terrified, but she passes through her terror to a state of calm where she is suddenly able to accept her death completely, and to trust in the rightful outcome of events. The young men press her to tell them what she's feeling as they repeat their intention to kill her. Now that she has no fear of her own, she becomes fascinated by their fear. Accepting their determination to do what they have set out to do, she gently questions them in almost maternal fashion. She becomes filled with compassion. At one point, she even takes the young man's face in her hands and tells him, "It's all right. You don't have to be afraid."

They cannot carry out their grisly task. They fall weeping upon her until she calmly suggests it's time they take her home. When they let her out at the first subway station, she asks them to lend her money for the token, which they do. Then she turns her back on them, walks away.

Trust is an interactive practice. Trust requires that we process information on both the instinctual and spiritual levels. We need to know when fear is real and when it is a product of the mind. We need to be able to transcend fear, to discover the potential trust offers, even in the most dire circumstances imaginable.

The practice of trust requires that we perceive ourselves as more than the ego. The ego cannot comprehend spiritual trust because it doesn't make instinctual sense not to be afraid. When the woman in the story accepts death, she transcends her ego. The woman is

Fear is the mind killer. Fear is the little death that brings total obliteration. I will face my fear. I will permit it to pass over me and through me. And when it has gone past, I will turn the inner eye to see its path. Where fear has gone there will be nothing. Only I will remain.

—Frank Herbert
Dune

Dealing with Fantasy Fears

- Writing helps distinguish between fantasy and reality.
- Writing helps calm you down.
- Dialogue with fear, with the details of a specific fantasy.

God has not brought you all this way to make a fool of you or his plans for you.

—Joy Houghton

Contacting Your Trust

- Dialogue with trust and ask for help sorting through your fear to trust again.

It is now half-past seven in the morning. I have clipped my toenails, drunk a mug of genuine Van Houten's cocoa and had some bread and honey, all with what you might call abandon. I opened the Bible at random but it gave me no answers this morning. Just as well, because there were no questions, just enormous faith and gratitude that life should be so beautiful, and that makes this an historic moment, that and not the fact that S. and I are on our way to the Gestapo this morning.

—Etty Hillesum
An Interrupted Life

genuinely in a place where "she" cannot be harmed, where the "self" she suddenly knows to be most real, cannot be hurt or killed.

Once we choose to concur with the reality that the body/ego will die, our individual, physical well-being is no longer of paramount importance in our lives. Once the woman accepted her death, she entered a state of compassion and curiosity. In this case, her compassion and curiosity were directed at the two attackers, but it is also often directed at ourselves, at the details of our lives, and this is what makes trust a working partner in life maintenance.

One day, dialoguing in the journal, I asked a spirit voice what other attitude would be appropriate if I was not so afraid. The answer was "curiosity." I could be curious. I could be curious about my fear, about the current state of affairs in my life, about my own emotional reactions, about my options, even about pain.

Shortly after her surgery and terminal diagnosis, my friend Lynne proclaimed, "I am learning so much, I wouldn't trade this experience for anything—even knowing the outcome." Of course, I thought, all that's happening is that she's dying—and so am I. She's been given a time frame and situation that liberate her to devote herself fully to her curiosity about life. Our difference is that I don't have such a time frame, or I'm not yet aware of it.

What the process of dying seems to teach many people is how to transcend ego and identify with the spiritual self. This is the recipe for trust. The hard part is to do this without the aid of dramatic circumstances, to wake up on a Monday morning and *choose*. To trust especially at times when nothing *seems* to be happening that gives us reason to trust; we are in a state of neither obvious support nor testing.

I have featured Etty Hillesum's amazing diary, *An Interrupted Life*, throughout this chapter because her writing models the decision to trust. In 1941, Etty Hillesum was a Jewish graduate student and tutor living in Amsterdam at the edge of academic circles around the university. When the Nazis invaded, she recorded the slow, systematic constriction of her life and her growing awareness of what was happening to all the Jews being deported to "work camps"

Clustering Trust

• Using the cluster or mapping technique, free-
associate thoughts on trust, on sustenance, on leaps of
faith.

> *When you play the unlimited game with life, eventually you have*
> *to agree to be played. Only when you severely limit your sense*
> *of life game can you continue to believe you're handling it on*
> *your own.*
>
> —Rebecca Hill

Life Contract

• Write a statement expressing your contract with
life.

> *I find life beautiful and I feel free. The sky within me is as wide*
> *as the one stretching above my head. I believe in God and I*
> *believe in man and I say so without embarrassment. Life is hard,*
> *but that is no bad thing. If one starts by taking one's own*
> *importance seriously, the rest follows. It is not morbid*
> *individualism to work on oneself. True peace will come only when*
> *every individual finds peace within himself; when we have all*
> *vanquished and transformed our hatred for our fellow human*
> *beings of whatever race—even into love one day, although*
> *perhaps that is asking too much. It is, however, the only solution.*
> *I am a happy person and I hold life dear indeed, in this year of*
> *Our Lord, 1942 the umpteenth year of the war.*
>
> —Etty Hillesum
> An Interrupted Life

farther east in Europe. In 1942, she volunteered to work at Westerbork deportation center, where she provided support and services to scattered, disoriented, and despairing families, until her own deportation to Auschwitz in September 1943, where she died two months later.

Fear is generated by trying to impose order or control over things we do not have control over. Life is in control, but not in *our* control. In the grip of fear we try to *make* things happen, or *prevent* things from happening, instead of watching events unfold and determining what empowerment exists for us in any situation. Etty couldn't stop the Nazis, but she made honorable, powerful choices in the face of apparent powerlessness. She triumphed with her trust. She also died—but her words and insights prevail.

But . . . but . . . but . . . an argument ensues in our minds: As long as I'm in this body, there are things I need to do to take care of myself, right? Right.

Trust is not either/or. This polarity is where we all get stuck. This polarized thought process is why it often takes something dramatic—World War II or knifepoint encounters or cancer—to jar us loose enough to go beyond the polarity. Both/and: trust and act. Act on your own behalf within the framework of trust. To do this takes honest appraisal of our talents, options, priorities.

In the journal we draw a map of interaction. You may want to do this literally, using the clustering technique from chapter 6, writing your contract with life, as Etty did in the quote that opens this chapter, and working through layers of fear to see the trust emerging from beneath. It's there. We all have trust. We would be lying paralyzed under the covers if we didn't. Spiritual maturity is a matter of growing that trust, seeing ourselves and our needs as belonging to both spirit and ego.

The day my agent called to say I'd sold this book, we had the worst rainstorm in a hundred years in Minneapolis. I was standing in eight inches of water, carting soaked belongings out of the lower level of my new house. My personal catastrophe didn't create a very auspicious beginning for a book on the spiritual journey, and the

Trust Lost, Trust Found

• Write about a time you lost your trust.
• Write about a time you found your trust.

Sustenance

Ruminate on two questions:

1. How are you being sustained?
2. Have you ever felt sustenance has left you?

• When you are afraid, list all the ways you are being sustained.
• List every reason you have to trust your life path.

> *JOURNAL ENTRY*
> *I have been angry again at the delay in my work—ego angry—that something I cannot control seems bent on slowing down and altering my plans. Now, I am calmed again, shifted out of ego. I find this litany is running through my mind:*
> *X: Do you believe that the lessons you are learning through this delay are useful and worthy insights?*
> *ME: Yes. Absolutely.*
> *X: Are you willing to let the delay continue to teach you whatever lessons are next?*
> *ME: Yes. Absolutely.*
> *X: Are you willing to turn over to God the management of your life, this project and its later success?*
> *ME: Yes. Absolutely.*
> *X: Then live by these convictions. Be a woman of your word and not a woman of your worry.*
> *ME: I think I just married my trust.*

flooding has made me nervous in heavy storms. When rain comes, I can pray for it to stop, or I can keep my eye on the creek and pray for strength to cope well with whatever life is handing me next. The water has never risen as high again, though I've sat through the night watching spectacular flashes of lightning, letting my chest echo with thunder, journal writing about my level of trust.

The fork in the spiritual road is always before us. Something happens: *do we trust it or fear it? And even if we fear it for awhile, will we trust it anyway?*

When I am up in the middle of the night writing, I am looking for the line that is not either/or. I can't just decide it once and cease to think about trust further. As long as I am inter/actively conducting my life, I will have to decide and decide and decide to choose between trust and fear. Although we get to be better trapeze artists, the trapeze never goes away. But there is a net: somewhere the soul knows we can't fall out of the universe no matter how loudly the ego is screaming before we grasp the next handle to hold onto.

So how do you grow trust? First you notice: you get very curious about all the ways trust is helping you sustain yourself that you might be taking for granted. Look in the shadowy parts of your life, there's sustenance there too. Second, ask yourself if genuine sustenance has ever been taken away from you. The answer is no, it hasn't. Not even in deepest despair. Third, look at what you pray for. Are you trying to stop the weather or looking for strength to cope? Sustenance is the prayer that can and will be answered. Fourth, trust is a track record. No one is asking you to trust based on no experience, no sustenance, no relationship. Trust's gift to us—our life sustenance—has already shown itself trustworthy; it is you and I who vascillate, who run off with our fear.

When Etty wrote her contract, she said she would not assume again in her innocence that any *peace* would be eternal, and it was through this insight that she was able to commit herself to trust. Trust is not a promise that good will automatically come, but that something good is somehow already present. *For in* trusting *the sacred is there: it* is *there.*

16. ACCEPTANCE

Sooner or later a choice will have to be made: to con-
tinue on a willful . . . path in which one tries to secure
autonomy and self-determination, or to embark on a
spiritual path in which one seeks ever-greater willing-
ness to become part of the fundamental processes of life
in self-surrender.

—Gerald May
Will and Spirit

Self-surrender is a concept somewhat foreign to the
western mind, and yet, as a longing that lies deep
within the heart, it may be hauntingly familiar. We
know we're not the biggest kids on the cosmic block,
and any time we want to remind ourselves of that, all we have to
do is go outside and look up. Look into the limitless immensity of
the Milky Way and call it "home."

Acceptance is the practice of being at home, within ourselves,
our lives, and the universe. Being at home means that we claim our

JOURNAL ENTRY

X: Am I going to be all right? I feel like everything is going to hell.

O: It will be all right.

X: Am I going crazy? What's the matter with me?

O: You are changing. Remember the meeting with C.? Remember how that went?

X: Yes, but I don't know how I did that.

O: You didn't do anything, you just stepped aside, thought about her instead of yourself. You loved. You told the truth.

X: I'm afraid! And when I do it your way I only get lost and confused.

O: Hear me: Your old way will fail you every time. You can no longer go that way. It will not work. Do you wish to fail again?

X: NO!

O: Then surrender to the will of Spirit. Surrender. Do as you are directed. You will have what you wish and more. It's up to you. Try to control, put your needs, your money, first, and you will fail every time. This is not punishment. You are being guided. You must submit to this guidance, not because you are being overpowered. You are being given the grace of God. This is the greatest gift. Allow it to happen. You will swim in the river of life and all will be as if by magic. You have only one task: submit to the will of God. Allow Spirit to guide you and lead you and you will never fail again.

Meditations

- Sit silently with your journal close at hand.
- Breathe slowly in and out, say to yourself, "Accepting . . ." What comes to mind?
- Say to yourself, "Surrendering . . ."
- Write or draw the images or impressions you experience around each word.

place in the order of things and willingly submit to this order.

I have an exercise I often use at the beginning of seminars to introduce people to different topics of consideration for journal writing. The last question of this exercise is: Is the universe friendly? I hope people will think about their assumptions of support or lack of support in how they see themselves making their way through life. Most people answer yes, they perceive the universe as benign, or at least as neutral to our existence. All goes well until I ask: Okay, if the universe is friendly, why are you fighting it?

With very few exceptions, we do fight the universe, fight the sacred. We misunderstand and avoid the issue of surrender and acceptance and what it could mean to cooperate with life. To see life as an ally rather than a worthy combatant. In a dog-eat-dog worldview, even our language for living is aggressive, militaristic; it supposes a victor and loser in every situation. *Surrender, acceptance,* are foreign words indeed.

Most human beings are ambiverts: we spend much of our time stuck halfway between our desire for self-determination and our desire for something/someone to relieve us of self-determination. We insist on making all our own decisions even though we end up running our lives with insufficient information and small flashes of tardy wisdom. We lie awake nights hoping we are doing the right thing, at home, at work, in our relationships, in our goals. We pray that things will turn out the way we want, and that we won't be the cause if everything gets screwed up.

There are stressful times in everyone's life when the idea of surrender sounds enticing. For a while we hope that a new relationship, a new business deal, a new belief, a new adventure might relieve us of this constant pressure to be accountable. But just let somebody, like contemplative psychologist Gerald May, come along and use the word *surrender,* and the hackles of self-determination go right up. Nobody is going to tell *us* what to do. The desire to set aside accountability is not what's meant by spiritual surrender.

What true spiritual leaders are asking of us in the concept of

May it be happy before me.
May it be happy behind me.
May it be happy below me.
May it be happy above me.
With happiness all around me, may I walk.
It is finished in beauty.
It is finished in beauty.

—*Navajo prayer*

Spiritual growth is not made in reaction against, for all striving against imposed restrictions is imaginary. Spiritual growth is accomplished by inclination toward. We grow like the sunflower, following the light.

—*Joy Houghton*

Happy Surrender

• Write about a time you stopped struggling and everything turned out fine.
• Dialogue with this incident. What spiritual dynamics were at work?

Worrying is a form of atheism. I don't understand people who call themselves Christian or Buddhist or Moslem or whatever and worry. Because you cannot believe in a power greater than yourself and worry. It does not compute.

—*Oprah Winfrey*

Order and Gratitude

• List everything in your life that might be in order.
• On some significant day, like New Year's or your birthday, write out everything you are grateful for in the past year.

acceptance and surrender is one thing only: to accept our unity with all life, and surrender our fantasy of separation. "As the atom, so the universe," said Gandhi. The smallest piece *is* the whole, and the whole is contained in the smallest fragment of itself.

Imagine that instead of being your whole body, you are one single cell within that body. A tiny bit of protoplasm residing in a nice, suburban neighborhood near the elbow. Even as a single cell, you have a place, a purpose, a job to perform, a lifespan, and—in this analogy—you even have consciousness. But how ridiculous that cell by the elbow appears when you imagine it declaring its self-determination, declaring that it's going to "do it my way" without regard for the rest of the body and what the rest of the body is doing.

If, like the sacred, you could look down on this strong, self-determined little cell, with all of its grand schemes and individual plans, you might feel inclined to point out that it is not alone. It is attached to this huge, living organism, and that because of this connection, its plans cannot be carried out in a vacuum. The little cell is in place and must deal with its place. It must accept and surrender to certain life circumstances *before* it can act to get its heart's desire. For acceptance and surrender are the beginning of positive life action—not the end.

Even from a human standpoint, we expect each of our cells to do what they are designed to do. The brain cell should be a brain. The stomach cell should be a stomach. This is order. This is what we expect in an orderly universe. But we do not easily submit our consciousness to this orderliness. We are willful. We decide we cannot trust this order to run something as important as our lives— even though we trust it to run the entire cosmos—and so are constantly looking for ways to take over and establish little strong-holds of anarchy. It doesn't work. But we try. And we try because we aren't sure what the alternative is.

The alternative to our egotistical anarchy is to surrender the fantasy of doing our lives ourselves, each of us alone with our load of stamina and good or bad luck, and decide to align ourselves with

1. *I am grateful for all the strides toward peace, justice and ecology that have occurred around the world.*

2. *I am grateful for the leaders of countries who allow the world to enter this period of swift transformation.*

3. *I am grateful to be alive and healthy.*

4. *I am grateful for my family, their liveliness and health.*

5. *I am grateful for what I am learning on my journey.*

6. *I am grateful for the support of friends. . . .*

I thank You God for most this amazing
day: for the leaping greenly spirits of trees
and a blue true dream of sky; and for everything
which is natural which is infinite which is yes

—*e.e. cummings*
100 Selected Poems

The Big Question

• Ask the universe: "Okay, what do you want me to do?"
• Keep a dated record of responses, the first sentences that flash into your mind. Don't censor.

JOURNAL ENTRY

•*I want you to keep quiet.*

•*I want you to listen.*

•*I want you to listen harder.*

•*I want you to follow instructions.*

•*I want you to keep writing.*

•*I want you to listen carefully when X talks, he's trying to tell you something important.*

•*I want you to go for your dream.*

•*I want you to make a difference to the world that you were here. Etc.*

large life forces. The cell says, "Okay, I admit I'm part of the body." The human being says, "Okay, I admit I'm part of the species, the world, the universe." We decide to come home.

Coming home is a kind of ecstasy. It occurs in layers—whatever layers we are ready for next. Years ago, after a particularly healing therapy session, I drove into the countryside, pulled over to the side of the road, and ran into a pasture shouting, "I belong here. I belong here." Another time, standing in my living room listening to music, I found myself weeping with relief, filled with a deep sense that I was going to be all right. And one October afternoon, I was sitting with my journal in a woods near my house, watching my dog try to dig her way to China and writing, "I wish I could kiss God back for the way I feel right now!"

We become, in these moments, life's companion and life becomes our companion, and there is no separation. We accept. We surrender not to anything contrived or manipulative or coercive: we offer as a gift our little piece of self to life and ask the universe, "Okay, now what do you want me to do?"

"Mastery," says May, "must yield to mystery." Mystery is not such a bad thing. Imagine again that little cell, struggling and struggling to be all that it can be, unaware that by lifting its gaze and shifting its focus from "I-ness" to "we-ness" it could tap into the whole resources of the body. It could belong to a living organism powerful and capable beyond its wildest one-cell dreams.

How? How? HOW? is the big question regarding acceptance and surrender. This is a spiritual practice that almost totally bypasses the intellect. Even when we become clear enough to begin to understand and value what the concepts mean, we still don't know *how* to "get" there. It's frustrating. The journal exercises, the experiences you acknowledge and write about, the ways you make yourself accessible to wisdom, all help, but there is a great deal of waiting involved and working through obstacles, and overall it seems a most irrational process.

Acceptance is the practice of a sacred act: we are choosing to move the ego aside and let the sacred, the soul/self, assume center.

*To the emptied, waiting, disidentified ego, keenly aware of its
poverty and its dependence, something special happens. Someone
comes. Psychologically, we describe this as the subjective
character of the human ego being taken over by a greater subject.
Jung calls it the break-in of the Self upon the ego, moving the ego
over, away from the center of things. One's psychic universe is
thus radically rearranged so that the unconscious can now get in.
Consciousness is opened for good. . . . The sense of I-ness, of
which the ego is a part, also opens onto the unknown and lives
comfortably with it. We know the unknown is there and can
touch us at any time and we accept that is the way things are.*

—Ann Belford Ulanov
Parabola, vol. XII, no. 3

*The mystery of sacramental life is not that we can hold onto
these holy, life-giving moments, these mountaintop experiences
forever—but rather that we are changed by them, and the world
becomes a different place for us—a safer, more loving, more
remarkable place. We undergo transfiguration, and our lives are
molded and re-created by the power of God's love.*

—Todd Smelser

Blessing Obstacles

* When you hit an obstacle, write out everything
good it is offering you.
* Bless it. Love it. Send it light.

Tabula Rasa

* Write to yourself, as though explaining to the
inner child an event s/he has never seen before, has no
preconceptions about. Tell him/her what is happening
in your life now.

In chapter 5, I talked about the evolution of the self, and this is the point of arrival: the need to accept that we share occupancy inside ourselves with the sacred. The quote at left from Ann Belford Ulanov's work is the clearest explanation of this moment I've found. She goes on to make clear that the integration that occurs is not the death of the ego. The ego remains strong, well defined, active in helping carry forward our life work. It is just not experienced any longer as the center of the self. The center of the self is what is now co-occupied. Who'd have thought, starting out, that it would come to this—our relationship to the sacred is that of roommates.

No matter how deeply we choose this, we don't seem able to make it happen by ourselves. We wait. We prepare. We love, forgive, trust. We work through stages of grief: denial, rage, despair, bargaining. We empty out and fill up. We have ecstatic flashes of unity. We say we want more. We say: Okay, I accept, I surrender. And nothing happens. We are dependent upon something coming *to* us, helping us move. And then one day we are on the other side of our waiting. The ego is still there but shifts into the passenger seat. We are conscious of a deeper spiritual consciousness and we don't know how we got here. It's still a mystery. Even we, even in the journal, will not understand all the aspects of our voyage. And that's how it is. And it's all right.

I will tell you what I know; you must tell yourself what you know. And then we live with our hearts' mysteries.

This book was originally scheduled for publication in January 1990 but was delayed due to other projects that superseded it at the publisher. This was not good news to me. I had to rearrange my work schedule for a year. I lost national seminar business. Without knowing what constraints she was really under, I hoped to make my editor change her mind. I stormed and raged in the journal, tried to be composed on the phone. I began to write with great intensity looking for what lessons might be learned. It occurred to me that I was being taught something transformational without being put in a life-threatening situation, and it would behoove me to pay attention. This exploration tore apart the last vestiges of my

Dear Little One, our heart is breaking open. It is breaking out of a shell. Like a caterpillar becoming a butterfly. The caterpillar is locked in a cocoon, wound up tight in her old life, old thoughts and feelings. She doesn't know what is happening. She is afraid she is dying. She thinks she is breaking into pieces. She is being transformed. She is not going to be a caterpillar anymore, but she doesn't know how to be a butterfly. She's not really sure butterflies exist. She's just read about them. When she was little, she longed to be a butterfly, though she didn't know what it would take. This is her dream coming true. And she thinks she is dying. This is our dream coming true too. This is growing into the soul. The cater/ego is afraid. The cater/ego thinks the cocoon is a trap. The cater/ego spins round and round. She cries, rages, grieves—nothing works! she says. Nothing stops the transformation. We will all be all right.

I learned to recognize real beauty through the depth of pain. The fox by the roadside is beautiful: my father is dying. Both are true. Both are beautiful. I accept.

—Kathie Anderson

Speed-Writing While Waiting at the Gate

•   Set the timer for 20 minutes. Don't stop writing, even if you just scribble until the next word comes.
•   Speed-write about denial, rage, depression, bargaining, acceptance.
•   Speed-write about everything you're waiting for.
•   Speed-write about the mysteries of life you still haven't solved.

Between endings and beginnings there is a blank time where nothing is supposed to happen. It's frustrating, fearful, but it's supposed to be this way. Like a tree in winter, on the outside there is nothing going on, but inside is hidden growth. This growth

ego-based contract with the world. It destroyed the relationship I was intending to have with this book and to my career—and these have been healthy destructions. I roamed in and out of despair. I thought God must be toying with me. I was afraid everything I said in the book wasn't true. My feelings were exaggerated beyond the situation itself—always a sign that we are trying to break free of unconscious material.

Active seeking and waiting for acceptance is the bottom of the spiral, as deep into the journey as we go. In Latin, the word *seducere*, the base for our word "seduction," means to lead aside. We have been in a spiral of *seducere*, spiraling inward. This is where we wait until acceptance comes. This is where we wait until we figure how to let go. It is most often a hellish and frightening experience. Sometimes we are stuck here for months, excruciatingly aware of our position and our inability to move away from it, or beyond it. The potential for being on the other side is both tantalizingly clear and totally mysterious. We experience tremendous doubt. We wonder why nobody else seems to be going through this and how come we can't seem to stop going through it.

We are standing in our own death, without dying. We are choosing to cease to be who we have been and to become what the journey makes of us. We go through whatever motions the days require to keep our lives in order, and sometimes we lose even this level of maintenance. This waiting is deeper than despair, but we are more in awe than we are afraid. We are connected to something more powerful than ourselves, and we can't let go. Like a person with hands on a high-voltage wire, the mind has forgotten the commands to the muscles that would release us. We are stuck to the current of the universe, like it or not.

During this time I kept dreaming of gates. In my mind they were all closed. I wrote dialogues with them, I drew them, I drew keys to unlock them. I stormed. I waited. The only way I knew the final lesson of the delay had occurred was when I was able to sustain more than a few days of inner peace. With a sort of surprise, I became aware I wasn't fighting anymore. I wasn't trying to control

explodes in spring. Spring can't happen without the blank time.
We need winter and so it is forced upon us if we do not choose.

—Peter McDonald

JOURNAL ENTRY

How I got here: I got here through the gate. I got here through
the winter of my lethargy and the autumn of my discontent. I got
here by opening my heart, by opening my body, my spine, my
third eye. I got here by noticing that fear is finally irrelevant to
journey. I got here by stepping forward when afraid instead of
stepping back. I got here by risk, by blessing, by synchronicity. I
got here by not giving up. I got here by choice, by choosing, by
determination, and by grace. Especially by grace. I got here
through sustenance, being kept alive, being taught. I have been
working and I have been worked upon. Moved. Fashioned by
forces unseen and imperceptible. I have been grown and I am
finally willing to relax, admit, and let those unseen forces do more
of the work. Maybe there are angels. I got here by way of
everyone who ever loved me and everyone who ever hated me—by
way of everyone I ever loved or hated. People are life shapers to
each other, and sometimes shapers of darkness. We offer each
other love, provide each other hurt, confusion, and through the
light and shadow of our presence—we learn.

I have been lifted up in the middle of my life, given a great
shaking and set down in the exact same spot. Everything is new,
unexplored, changed. Everything is the same.

And that is how I got here, and it is a Tuesday evening and
the sun is setting in Aquarius and will rise in Pisces, turning the
signs and the seasons. And everything is new. New. New.

- Where are you?
- How did you get here?
- Where are you going?

anything. My mind had done a complete turn, from frustration and anger at having my goals thwarted, to immense gratitude for what the delay had taught me. I began to see what the book still needed. I began to think of my editor as having—wittingly or unwittingly—played an important spiritual role.

When the production schedule opened, I began the final rewrite. Things moved with synchronicity again. My sense of sustenance returned. Still I waited at the gate. I was typing. I had no time to be introspective about anything except the current chapter. I was getting ready to fly to Florida to offer three days of seminars. I got up at 5:00 A.M., packed, made an early plane, hung suspended a few hours over the miles of my country. I looked out the window at the clouds; in the distance I thought I saw a gate. It was open. It was behind me. I turned around. Saw my old self. I am who I am. I waved good-bye. In the next spiritual-writing seminar, I wrote the journal entry that faces this page. That's all I know. I didn't give up. It is a mystery, even—especially—to me, to whom it happened. I spun with the spiral until it spit me out.

In Latin, the word *educere,* the base for our word "education," means to lead out. On the other side of the gate, we spiral out and upward. We take action very differently in the world. We experience our interactive relationship with the sacred from the inside out. We have taken our place.

Meditation

To prepare to use this meditation and others throughout the book, find a quiet place where you will not be interrupted for twenty minutes or so. Ask someone to read the meditation to you or to play back a version of the meditation you have made yourself or ordered from the back of the book. The points of ellipses (. . .) indicate a significant pause—silence maintained within the text. Pause for as long as you feel comfortable; five to ten seconds can seem a long time in meditation. Double ellipses indicate longer silence.

FORGIVING YOURSELF AND OTHERS

Close your eyes and relax your body. . . . Take all the time you need to get comfortable. . . . Shift muscles . . . stretch and relax. . . . Make sure your spine and neck are straight and aligned . . . not held stiffly; there is no stiffness here . . . just comfort, the beginning of calm. . . . There is no hurry now. . . . There is nothing else to do . . . or think about. . . . Just relax. . . .

Notice your breath. . . . Let your breath enter deeply into your body. . . . Let your breath roll into you like soft, heavy clouds that fill you with silence. . . . Inhale slowly . . . deeply. . . . Exhale slowly . . . thoroughly. . . . Let your breath sink in and out. . . . Your breath is a rhythm of calm. . . . Follow your breath. . . . Exhale extraneous thought. . . . Inhale silence. . . . . . .

Imagine yourself sitting comfortably on a throne in a safe place. . . . This throne is not elevated yet it provides all the support and safety you need. . . . As you are ready, one at a time, invite any person whom you need to forgive, to come before you. . . . As they approach, bless them with a holy light. . . . Tell them you wish to speak to the light within them. . . . Open your heart and speak from the light within yourself. . . . Greet one another. . . . Greet the light. . . . Tell this person how you have felt estranged and why. . . . Tell this person you are ready to forgive him or

238

her. . . . Tell them what you have learned from your time of un-forgiveness. . . . Thank them for being the instrument through which you learned this lesson. . . . Ask them if they are ready to forgive you. . . . Speak to their light. . . . Listen and speak from your own light. . . . . . . When you are ready, invite them to go in peace. . . . . . .

Still seated on your throne, when you are ready, invite any person who has been unwilling to forgive you to come before you. . . . As they approach, bless them with a holy light. . . . Tell them you wish them to speak from the light within them. . . . Tell them you will listen from the light within you. . . . Greet one another. . . . Greet the light. . . . Ask this person to state his or her grievance with you. . . . Listen to them with your heart. . . . Acknowledge your responsibility. . . . Accept the part of this confusion that is yours. . . . Forgive them. . . . Ask if they are ready to forgive you. . . . Speak to their light. . . . Speak and listen from your own light. . . . When you are ready, invite them to go in peace. . . . . . .

Now, invite yourself to stand before you. . . . Bless yourself with a holy light. . . . See the holy light in both your hearts. . . . Greet one another. . . . What have you not forgiven yourself for? . . . Speak your peace to each other. . . . Make peace. . . . What has your lack of forgiveness taught you? . . . Thank yourself for these lessons. . . . Forgive yourself. . . . Speak and listen from your light. . . . When you are ready, invite yourself to go in peace. . . . . . .

When you are through forgiving and being forgiven, thank the light. . . . You may come here anytime. . . . You are always welcome in the light. . . . . . . Slowly . . . gently . . . follow your breath back to this room. . . . Emerge out of the silence of your body. . . . There is no hurry. . . . Stretch your body. . . . Open your eyes. . . .

Take some time to draw, or write, whatever you want to record from your vision.

V.
Applying the Four
Practices

17. PAYING ATTENTION

Your daily life is nothing else but an expression of your spiritual condition.

—Thaddeus Golas
The Lazy Man's Guide to Enlightenment

In this section we begin the return to the world from the heart of the quest. So far, the quest may have been a philosophical journey, but at this point, the action of the quest awaits us. And after all that we've been through, we need a new framework for taking action integral to spiritual learning. This framework can be explored and developed through discipline, responsibility, envisioning, and empowerment. These are words we have heard for a long time. Now comes the challenge of defining and living them.

The ability to name our activities and their significance is the bedrock for applying the four practices in our lives. *Discipline is the act of paying attention, and following attention with appropriate action. Dis-*

Until one is committed there is hesitancy, the chance to draw back, always ineffectiveness. Concerning all acts of initiative (and creation) there is one elemental truth, the ignorance of which kills countless ideas and splendid plans: that the moment one definitely commits oneself, then Providence moves too. All sorts of things occur to help one that would never otherwise have occurred. A whole stream of events issues from the decision raising in one's favour all manner of unforeseen incidents and meetings and material assistance which no man could have dreamt would come his way.

—Goethe

- What are *you* committed to?

A Peaceful, Happy Nature

- Write down five things you do with a peaceful, happy attitude.
- Write down five things you do that you dislike doing.
- What makes you happy doing the first list?
- What makes you unhappy doing the second list?

The discipline of the writer is to learn to be still and listen to what his subject has to tell him.

—Rachel Carson

cipline first requires that we discover *how* to pay attention, and then decide exactly *what* our attention leads us to do. This is not how most of us were raised to think about discipline.

In western culture, discipline has been incorrectly defined and incorrectly applied. In western thinking, we are taught to expect that discipline will be imposed from the outside: by parents, teachers, drill sergeants, bosses, one's peer group, the clergy. Generally speaking, "good people" are those who *comply* with whatever externally imposed discipline is appropriate to the setting, and "bad people" are those who *rebel* against externally imposed discipline. Compliance and rebellion may become habitual responses, but they do not teach us discipline.

There are times in everyone's life when our minds are so scattered we seem barely able to finish a thought. Everything distracts us with equal intensity. A pile of laundry can turn us away from the book we were reading, the phone ringing can turn us away from the laundry, and the children coming in wanting a snack gets us to the kitchen where we end up reading yesterday's mail. In the workplace, though the distractions are different, our behavior patterns can be similarly ineffectual. The papers on our desks are scattered without priority, the phone acts as a lifeline and time waster, we seem to be spending a lot of time in the hallway or restrooms, circling like dogs who won't lie down. *Without discipline, we are adrift.* In such times, we are pulled about by stimuli, sometimes not even aware of our loss of control. When we do not understand and apply discipline, we can only wait for some catastrophe to occur that is big enough to interrupt the cycle, or for some authority to come along who is strong enough to exert external control. If this sounds reminiscent of childhood, it is. To wander without discipline traps us in immaturity.

Spiritual discipline is a process of claiming our own authority, deciding to train ourselves, to align our lives with purpose. We practice spiritual discipline by developing a new relationship to everything: a relationship based on focus and choice rather than on compliance or rebellion.

If the universe did once begin with a big Bang, something exploding in the void, shooting into zillions of fragments, my mind is still very much patterned on that process—exploding off in many directions, distractions, leaping around in past and future, forgetting the present entirely, or treating it as though it were irrelevant, when in reality, it is all that is. All that I have as my own. I do not possess either the past or the future, where I seem to spend so much of my time. In other words, I have been nowhere, because there is nowhere but here/now. And when I am not present to myself, to the events and interactions of this very instant, then whoever is acting/responding to the events and interactions of the present has precious little support and no wisdom. Because wisdom comes from presence. Wisdom comes from experiencing experience.

Vipassana Writing

• To track your busy mind, sit quietly with your journal. Watch your breath.

• When you are breathing and not thinking, mark *B* on the page; then leave a blank.

• When your mind begins to wander, write down your thought. Catch yourself. Note that you are thinking.

• When you choose to go back to the breath, mark *B* again on the page. Leave a blank.

Meditation is working with our speed, our restlessness, our constant busyness. Meditation provides space or ground in which restlessness might function, might have room to be restless, might relax by being restless. If we do not interfere with restlessness, then restlessness becomes part of the space. . . . Mindfulness is the process of relating with individual situations directly, precisely, definitely. . . . Mindfulness is like a microscope; it is neither an offensive nor a defensive weapon in relation to the germs we observe through it. The function of the microscope is just to clearly present what is there.

—Chögyam Trungpa
The Myth of Freedom

In the middle of writing this book, I participated in a two-day, silent Buddhist retreat to study Vipassana meditation. I wanted some guidance for developing my self-styled meditation practice and I thought that getting out of my life and into a setting where nothing occurred except meditation would be a good way to deepen my silence. I took several books, my journal, and my little blessing-a-day notebook.

A friend and I drove to a Catholic convent about an hour south of the city. The nuns there, as in many such institutions that used to be religious schools, now offer their space and services for seminars. It was dusk, a windy Friday in March. Ellen and I had been talking all the way down in the car, sharing the areas in both of our lives where we were struggling and confused, unsure of direction, feeling out of spiritual synchronicity. We unpacked in adjoining rooms, went for a simple vegetarian supper, a first look and last conversation with our fellow participants. Twenty-five women and men from four states had gathered with an instructor from Massachusetts. After a few minutes making small talk, I was glad for the upcoming silence, the chance to let go of sociability and the need to tell one's story. Just before the meeting began, Ellen turned and wished me, "May you receive what is intended." It was an appropriate blessing.

At seven-thirty, we convened in the meditation room, which would be the focus of the weekend, were given instructions in group and individual conduct, basic principles of Vipassana, and except for the teacher's voice, silence settled in. Please don't read, she said, or write. Trust yourself to stay with your experience. I put my books and journals away.

The discipline consisted of forty-five minutes of sitting meditation, followed by forty-five minutes of walking meditation. There were no great expectations—at least on the teacher's part—just that we would follow the breath, note when we were doing anything else, and choose to return to the breath. Sitting. Walking. Sitting. Walking. Sitting. Walking. Eating. Sitting. Walking. All day.

In my mind, I was busy discovering the lack of focus to which

Defining Discipline

• Write out a childhood definition of discipline, one that you were taught.

> *Discipline is doing what my mother wants me to do, when she wants me to do it.*

• Write out a behavior model definition of discipline you've applied in your own life.

> *Discipline is going off sweets and alcohol and losing ten pounds. Feeling so good about it I go out to supper, have wine, pasta, and a gooey dessert.*

• Write out a new spiritual definition of discipline.

> *Discipline is writing and thinking and meditating until my priorities are really clear and then doing whatever is required and not letting anything separate me from the joy of my own accomplishments.*

> *Buddhism promises nothing. It teaches us to be what we are where we are, constantly, and it teaches us to relate to our living situations accordingly. . . . I am sorry not to be presenting any glamorous and beautiful promises. Wisdom happens to be a domestic affair. Buddha saw the world as it is and that was his enlightenment. "Buddha" means "awake," being awake, completely awake—that seems to be his message to us. He offered us a path of being awake, a path with eight points, and he called it the eightfold path. . . . Right view, right intention, right speech, right morality (or right discipline), right livelihood, right effort, right mindfulness, right samadhi (right absorption).*

> —Chögyam Trungpa
> The Myth of Freedom

I had become accustomed. My thoughts skipped over the past and future, as though they desired to be anywhere except cloistered with me in half-lotus position. I practiced noting my diversions and returning to center focus. Breathing. Thinking. Breathing. Planning. Breathing. Fantasizing. Breathing. Listening. Breathing. Pain. Breathing. Breathing. Breathing. I didn't know it right away, but I was discovering the first aspect of discipline: paying attention and choosing what to pay attention to.

Vipassana means insight meditation. It is the practice of seeing things as they are, just in this moment, being directly connected to experience, giving the moment full attention. I began to notice that I was separate from all these excursions of the mind and separate too from my body, from my discomfort, my restlessness, even my doubt. The sense of who "I" might be at any given instant was impermanent and shifting. Meditation became a lesson in total acceptance: not berating or badgering the mind in any way, just noting, and returning. "I" was always somewhere and I could choose where to be. I began to understand: *spiritual discipline is a choice made at a thought-by-thought level, on a moment-by-moment basis.*

Traditionally we haven't known how to think about discipline at this level; we have viewed it as a form of behavior modification. According to the behavior model, a well-disciplined person develops certain goals about the day's performance, the project at hand, the use of their time, and uses these goals to make decisions about action. If I take two hours for lunch, it will interfere with getting to the health club later. If I eat this French bread, it will cost me two exchanges from supper. If I finish this project, I can go for a walk. The carrot is always hanging before us, but it's not internalized at a level where our actual thoughts participate in clarifying and attaining these goals.

The behavior-modification model leads, over and over again, to the defeat and misunderstanding of discipline. Say, for example, you decide to write in your journal half an hour every morning. If you don't write you are disappointed in yourself; if you do write; you are momentarily satisfied. Your self-estimation rises and falls.

How I get things done seems almost by accident, or in a great rush of panic at the end. I don't know how to work on something at a steady pace, with a sense of daily accomplishment. My mother used to accuse me of this—finding me dreaming over my homework. That she turns out to be right is almost more than I can bear. But she didn't know how to get things done either. She wandered from project to project all the time without any system that I could see.

I read somewhere that if you are the child of two fat parents, you have an 80 percent chance of being fat yourself. Well, I'm the child of disorganized parents, and I have inherited their disorganization. I am organizationally impaired. And I want to change, but I don't know how to start. Well, I do start, but I don't know how to continue. When somebody says the word discipline, I freak inside. I don't have any idea what they're talking about and I'm afraid they know I'm just nodding my head without comprehension.

I don't look chaotic. My house is fairly clean. My laundry usually gets done. I get to work close to 9:00. I read books on time management the way some people read books on diets. I set rigid schedules and then break them—like I've gone on a "time diet" and when I've broken it I snack on wasted time for the rest of the day. It's scary to be how I am. It's in my way. For the first time in my life I want discipline more than I want to avoid it, but after all these years I don't know what it is.

The true beginning of wisdom is the desire for discipline and the care of discipline is love.

—The Apocrypha

Lazy Days

• Do you have permission to be lazy from time to time?

• Are you afraid of your laziness? Why? Why not?

Though this cycle *looks* like a sincere attempt at discipline, it's a trap.

You know how to play this game:

Rule 1: Set a rigid or impossible standard that defines your discipline. (*I will write every day for a half hour.*)

Rule 2: Berate yourself for failure far more than you praise yourself for success. (*I'm so tired of every voice having a conflicting opinion about everything I do.*)

Rule 3: Use lapses of Rule 1 to justify giving up entirely. (*I can't have what I want in life because I'm just not disciplined enough to deserve it.*)

Rule 4: Do not learn from experience; simply repeat the cycle more earnestly. (*See what a good person I am, see how hard I'm trying even if I don't succeed.*)

This culturally accepted model guarantees failure most of the time because it doesn't teach us anything about real discipline; it simply proves that willpower and impulse are equally strong and conflicting forces in the mind. The goal is often lost in the power struggle. This we already know, or haven't you ever dieted? put off studying for a test? avoided making calls? shirked one duty or another? Under this model, we often use discipline as an attempt to make ourselves do what is counter to our values or interests. *We use discipline to make ourselves do what we* should, *instead of paying attention to what we* want.

To use discipline successfully, we need to define our goals in relationship to our values, our life purpose, our spiritual imperatives.

Spiritual discipline is maintained by mindfully applying your ability to choose. This allows you to feel empowered, even when you choose not to write, because *the choice* is the discipline, rather than what you're choosing. *Through minuscule acts of choice, spiritual discipline allows for changes in focus and intensity and invites sacred energy to inspire and influence the discipline process.*

Being mindful of the moment slows us down until we can see the process of choice being made. This is different from following impulses, because mindfulness is based on a central focusing act or attention. In Vipassana meditation, the breath is the anchor, the

- Write about a time you were lazy. How did it make you feel?
- What value lessons did you learn from this time?
- What's it like for you just to "let the river go by"?

> *What bars our way is what makes us travel along.*
>
> —Marcus Aurelius

Choice Making

- What are the little choices that influence your day?
- How do you handle them?
- What choices do you want to make differently?
- What choices do you celebrate?

> *The time it takes to make a decision is like approaching the godhead: you have to bow three times to your fear and ambivalence. You can't just do it once. You have to humble yourself until you're ready to meet your destiny—which is action.*
>
> —Rebecca Hill

Decision Making

- Take a relatively simple decision you're making and write out the process you're using to make it.
- Look for compliance and rebellion.
- Look for behavior modification.
- Look for spiritual discipline.
- If you don't like how you're thinking about a certain aspect of the decision, pause and ask yourself:
  How can I change my approach?
  What options haven't I considered?
- If you were advising someone else, what would you say?

place one always returns to as the focus, when the mind has wandered elsewhere. In the middle of a train of thought, I can stop and ask myself, Do I choose to follow this thought or return to the breath? My discipline, for the period of time I'm meditating, is simply to return to breath. And I do. This is what I choose. My life is simplified. I am sitting still. I have only one choice to make: to focus. The mind wanders. I return the attention to breath. Out of this discipline, a lifeline of experience develops, an inner trust in our willingness to make one simplified choice: to breathe. Watch breathing.

Most of us do not meditate for very significant portions of our lives, but the idea of developing a center of focus can be applied to daily routines. I choose to get my body back in shape after several years of too much time at the computer and not enough exercise, despite my dog's best efforts to take me for a long daily walk. I know what I want. I have defined the level of fitness I am willing to work for, what I think is healthy for my age, my lifestyle, etc. I have made choices about what I eat, how I exercise, how I spend my time, how I will integrate this decision into ongoing commitments that have not changed. Choices occur on a daily basis: do I spend a free hour reading or swimming? Does this food item fit with my nutritional decisions?

Once we can see our choices, taking responsibility for them is not such an overwhelming idea. Discipline becomes a minute-by-minute dialogue between opportunity and goal. The mind will busy itself anyway, thinking about something; we might as well train it to think with us, instead of arguing against us. Discipline is a negotiated mental relationship. It bypasses the usual power struggles that seem to occupy so much of our energy. We develop trust in our discipline. We learn to give and take. We are tolerant of each other. The dialogue with discipline on the next page illustrates this point; the conversation is friendly. This is a wonderful relief after years of self-recrimination about one behavior pattern or another.

Through choice we assume more responsibility for our lives than through compliance or rebellion, which can be quickly used to

Discipline Dialogues

• Using standard dialogue techniques, write out dialogues with discipline, especially when you are trying to change models.

> *JOURNAL ENTRY*
>
> *Discipline: I've lost you again, where did you go?*
>
> *ME: I got distracted. And then I got so distracted I forgot I was distracted. Sorry.*
>
> *D: Don't be sorry, just come back.*
>
> *ME: Deep breath. It's amazing how easily I leave my attention— float off. Get into hyperdrive.*
>
> *D: I am always here. I am always available. All you have to do is notice once, and choose to center on whatever will work.*
>
> *ME: Breathing works. I guess because I do it all the time—like thinking—so it's always there to come home to.*
>
> *D: Be aware of your breathing, while you're on the phone, while you're in the middle of a party, when you're talking to the kids, when you're trying to make a point . . .*
>
> *ME: Do I have to do this forever? Can't I ever master it and be done?*
>
> *D: You mean like losing weight and not thinking about your diet anymore?*
>
> *ME: Well, that's a good analogy.*
>
> *D: No, attention is not like dieting. Attention is like breathing— always there.*
>
> *ME: For the rest of my life?*
>
> *D: What's so demanding about breathing for the rest of your life? This is not punishment. This is reward. You are just beginning to discover the rewards. I promise you, they are many.*

blame outside circumstances if a situation goes awry. We may have been afraid of our choices because they were ego-bound or impulsive and learned not to trust ourselves to make good decisions. Others may have told us that the choices we made were not "good."

This far along in the journey, it is no longer appropriate to avoid choice. It is our responsibility to see that our choices are spiritually correct within the framework of our overall life path, that what we do is aligned with higher purpose. This means my commitment to stay in good physical shape is not just vanity, but recognition that I need my body to perform at a certain level of health and stamina to support my work as well as my pleasure.

After two days of retreat and meditation, my mind was less scattered. When I folded the laundry, I folded all of it. When I read the mail, I sat down and read it. When I made myself a cup of tea and cut up an apple, I stopped to taste it. And when I wrote— I wrote.

The journal is often an excellent barometer of our level of discipline or distraction. When you write in the journal, do you finish your thoughts? your entries? Do you let yourself become distracted, interrupted, pulled away? Have you written lately? As they say on the news, "It's ten o'clock, do you know where your journal is?"

At first, mindfulness can be uncomfortable. We may be accustomed to having only half a thought about anything, and the request that we even finish the sentence may make us nervous. Through true discipline, we are calling ourselves to account. We say we have chosen our path. Then our basic commitment is to keep choosing the path as it becomes clear what the path is—this minute, the next minute, the minute after that. We choose the path, even if it doesn't offer immediate escape or gratification. We are following our heart's desire. We are not trapped: we are choosing. And the more complicated the choice, the more we need to use all that we are learning in the journey, so that the discipline is there. Breathing. Sitting. Breathing. Walking. Breathing. Writing. Living.

18. LEARNING TO FOLLOW

To find in ourselves what makes life worth living is risky
business, for it means that once we know we must seek
it. It also means that without it life will be valueless.

—Marsha Sinetar
Ordinary People as Monks and Mystics

Our primary task in life is to discover and define our life purpose and then to accomplish it to the best of our ability. We have a natural impulse to do this. The way we think about life and journey makes our dreams for the future real— a time and place we head for, as surely as we head for home. Purpose is different from meaning. The search for meaning asks the question "What is life all about?" The search for purpose asks "What should *I do?* How can I best be myself? What am I going to give back to the world?"

"Pretty soon I'll be big," says the small child. "When I'm six or seven, I'll know everything!" The future expands and contracts de-

Growing Up

- What did you want to be "when you grew up,"
when you were age five, age ten, age fifteen,
twenty, . . . five years ago?
- How would you answer that question if someone
asked you now?

> TWO JOURNAL ENTRIES
> When I was six years old I wanted to be a doctor because I was
> convinced that my dolls were real children who'd been struck by
> a horrible disease so that they couldn't move. If I got to be a
> doctor, I'd grow up, find the cure for this disease and save the
> dolls of the world. . . . I have become a psychologist because I
> realized that what holds children immobilized in family systems is
> not a physical ailment, but emotional and spiritual binding. I try
> to help people vivify themselves.
>
> When I was ten, I wanted to be an actor. No other boys my age
> had this dream . . . they were all into sports. But this was the era
> of boys on TV. Beaver, Lassie, My Three Sons. . . . When I look
> back on this, I think I wanted a chance to be my own father, to
> have that kind of relationship with a boy stand-in for myself.
> This dream faded in adolescence, when I finally got into sports—
> much to my dad's relief. But it came alive again when I had a
> son of my own and my father was aging. Finally, I figured out
> the core of it and my dad and I began to talk about some of this
> stuff. He never got to be Ward Cleaver, but that isn't what I
> really needed from him by then.

Childhood Heros and Supporters

- Who were your childhood heros/heroines?
- What about their lives did you admire?
- What options for your own life did you take from
these models?

pending on what it is we are trying to think about. We start practicing very early for the lives we want to lead, the lives we think we are capable of leading, the lives we are told by family and society are appropriate and possible. Our earliest sense of capability develops out of this dreaming. We make space for ourselves in the wide open fields of the future. We begin to imagine who we might be and what our purpose is.

The year I was in fifth grade, my mother, who liked to throw theme parties for her children's birthdays, arranged for me to have a party where all my girlfriends and I would come dressed as what we wanted to be when we grew up. I still have the snapshots from that day, black-and-white frames taken with my Brownie camera. These girls, all now middle-aged, presented themselves with appropriate aspirations for 1957: three nurses, two secretaries, a teacher, several mommies. Marilyn, a fellow rebel, showed up in a beret with a cardboard palette and dreams of becoming an artist. I descended the stairs in a pith helmet, khaki shorts, and my father's white shirt—a sort of hybrid between Albert Schweitzer and Margaret Mead. I was carrying a notebook to make field observations. I couldn't have defined exactly what I was seeking, but I was dressed for adventure.

We are responsible for living the best lives we can at every given moment: this is not a burden, it's just how things are. In order to do this, we need to define what "the best possible life" is, according to our personal values. Then we need to sensitize ourselves to the impact that the spiritual journey is having on these aspirations; we need to prepare ourselves to follow.

Spiritual life is contractual. The sacred cannot dialogue with the unresponsive. The sacred always asks, "Who is ready? Who will carry spiritual action into the world?" Then the sacred waits for us to recognize this call, to step forward willingly and assume our purpose.

In my experience, the assumption of purpose is a moment of resonance, a sense of "Oh, this is what I've been leading up to." This recognition happens occasionally when someone enters our

- What real people in your life turned out to be your greatest guides in childhood?
- Write about these people. Write dialogues, unsent letters; thank them for what they gave you.

> *I saw the Lord sitting upon a throne, high and lifted up; and his train filled the temple. Above him stood the seraphim; each had six wings: with two he covered his face, and with two he covered his feet, and with two he flew.*
>
> *And one called to another and said: "Holy, holy, holy is the Lord of hosts; and the whole earth is full of his glory." And the foundations of the thresholds shook at the voice of him who called, and the house was filled with smoke. . . . Then flew one of the seraphim to me, having in his hand a burning coal which he had taken with tongs from the altar. And he touched my mouth, and said: "Behold, this has touched your lips; your guilt is taken away, and your sin forgiven." And I heard the voice of the Lord saying, "Whom shall I send, and who will go for us?" Then I said, "Here I am! Send me." And he said, "Go, and say this to my people."*
>
> —Isaiah 6:1–9

Purpose

There's something unique you have to offer. Nobody can replace you.

- What are you waiting to do?
- What are you ready to do?
- What are you doing right now?
- What do you sense you are "supposed" to do before your life is over?

> *Response is happening all around me. Every day I hear about someone whose life finally "clicks" and off they go. Once they get it, they have to do something about it. For the rest of us, working up to this moment, it's scary and exciting to see it happen in others.*
>
> —Karen McConkey

lives and our first response is recognition, that we have somehow been waiting for them. Recognition also occurs around events, direction, work, and as aspirations that we thought we'd set aside resurface. We realize the contractual question "Who is ready? Who will do this?" must have been asked, because our response wells up with solemnity. We are making a covenant; "Here am I, send me . . ."

I remember as a child reading Bible stories in which God spoke directly to the Old Testament prophets when He needed something done. All of a sudden, there God was, coming as a voice out of the clouds, speaking out of fire, throwing the rainbow over Noah's ark, wrestling with Jacob, appearing in dreams and visions, talking from burning bushes, giving instructions to the trembling ordinary men and women who were about to find their lives transformed by God's commands. In these recorded instances, the sacred and the human established a definite contract. There were clear instructions and no mistaking the presence of power.

I was fascinated by these awesome conversations, wondered if God would ever choose to talk with such directness to me or anyone I knew. Sometimes I stood on the porch watching summer storms, sensing the power unleashed in thunder and lightning. Sometimes I sat quietly on a mountain rock, daring myself to be in the landscape where God seemed to like to talk. Sometimes I wavered hip-deep in the surf, enduring the suction of waves and sand. No God appeared to speak to me in such commanding ways, and yet the receptivity was laid. And somewhere, tucked in your own life story, your receptivity is also laid.

The thing that is so stunning about the quiet influences of inner guidance is that these nudges and messages become just as compelling as the burning bush. If we thought we were saved from commitment to purpose because of lack of drama—we're not.

Our decision to be the kind of people who are willing to respond was settled long ago. You wouldn't be here, reading this page, writing in your journal, thinking about spiritual journey, willing to act upon your values, if you hadn't already said, "Yes, I will, yes."

If a person feels a longing to be at one with the universe, it is as if the universe feels the same longing to be at one with the person. If I sense a great aching in my heart to be in love with God, it seems that God must in some mysterious way share that aching for me.

—Gerald May
Will and Spirit

Self-Belief

• What would you most like to believe about yourself, about your life's journey, that you find the most difficult to believe?

• What would you need to do differently to increase your belief in yourself and your life?

• What conditions are you still trying to set on your willingness to be led?

> JOURNAL ENTRY
>
> *Life these days feels as fragile, and as regular, as breath. I do not take anything for granted—of course that's not true, I take uncountable things for granted, but there is a tear in the fabric of ordinary reality through which surprise gets in. This is perhaps what is called awareness. A hole of light and dark, the yin/yang hole, where the universe intrudes on my usual blindness. G. said the other day that we are blind to the sacred in our lives, that it happens to us and only later do we understand the event or moment or interaction to have been of the sacred path. The sacred in my life is getting larger; that means the ordinary eye cannot predict what is happening, cannot comprehend it in the moment. This is frightening to the ordinary eye, and what I need to remember is that this doesn't mean this is frightening in and of itself. What's happening is sacred, it contains light and dark— not fright. Why should I be afraid of the sacred? If I back away from the holy, this is opposite from the direction where I need to go. I need to stand in the holy and be aware of it—even if I am blind to the fullness of the moment.*

You have been reading, thinking, writing, talking to like-minded people, looking for community and a framework for journey. All this doesn't mean you're confident of direction; you may still be full of questions, even about your own willingness. You may be frightened and ambivalent. But here you are, in the middle of action, or intended action, suddenly aware that as a result of all these influences, you are called to *do* something you thought you had no intention of doing. You may be about to disrupt the patterns of your life and your family's life and make changes that a few years ago were only the vaguest twilight images. You look up from the day's busyness, from the journal's reflection, and realize you are on the brink of risk. A level of risk you would not have anticipated at the beginning, a risk that feels both foreign and familiar, as though you have been heading toward it for a long time, just not able to speak its name out loud.

You are about to raise your hand and volunteer to carry out your purpose. Examples come flooding to mind: G., with two doctorates, left an academic career to develop a multimedia literacy program. J. is applying to the seminary at age fifty. P. is selling his house and sailing around the world alone. J. is giving up a consulting practice to write novels. D. is having another baby at forty. X. and Y. got the kids in college, started second careers, and got divorced. And I *have* to finish this book.

The questions and issues raised in this chapter aren't often articulated on a daily basis. They make us nervous. They remind us that life isn't only passing on a Monday/Tuesday sense, but that we are also traveling a heroic path. Life's mythic reality pushes to the surface and pushes us along with it. We are invited over and over again to deal with the heroic, purposeful elements within ourselves and within our ordinary circumstances. Increasingly, we become aware that we are pulled along by the momentum we created on page one, chapter one, however we said to ourselves, "There comes a journey."

The unavoidable thing is *we are going to become who we are, and we are going to use the energy released by our becoming to give back to the world.*

*This sounds conceptual. I don't have any other language for it
yet. I need to move directly into the hole. Out of my head, out of
my reasoning, out of my ego, anxieties, fantasies of control. I
need to fall into the hole as I have never allowed myself, and be
led through darkness.*

*Nobody can counsel and help you, nobody. There is only one
single way. Go into yourself. Search for the reason that bids you
write; find out whether it is spreading out its roots in the deepest
place of your heart. . . . Delve into yourself for a deep
answer . . . then build your life according to this necessity.*

—Rainer Maria Rilke
Letters to a Young Poet

Dialogue with Optional Lives

* Dialogue with the self that you are.
* Dialogue with the selves you might have become if
you'd made different choices.
* Look for similarities: what is you, no matter what?
* What choices are yours, no matter what their
adaptation?

*To get to the simplicity of a thing, you have to go through the
complexity; and only once you've gone into and through the
complexity can you state the simplicity. What never rings true is
the person who states the simplicity without understanding the
complexity.*

—Susan Slater Blythe

But we don't step easily into enthrallment when it entails changing the circumstances of our outer lives. We go through a stage of bargaining: Okay, I'll do it: *if* it's not too disruptive, *if* the financial risks aren't too great, *if* it doesn't threaten my relationships, *if* I get support from the right circles. There are no *if's*. Will you do it? Yes or no. Or will you, after all this intentional opening, back away, close down, command your quest to die?

Actually, it's too late for hesitance, no matter how real it feels or how long we hang suspended in it. Becoming the authentic self and carrying out purpose is simply what happens to pilgrims—to each of us—as we spiral out of our reflection and back into the world. We are actors, agents of spiritual change. The quest has made us capable.

Spiritual life is contractual. The contract turns out to be that all our insight and exploration is *supposed* to be applied to the world/in the world. So what do we do? There are several steps of exploration we can initiate from our side.

Step 1: Know your values and define your purpose. What you have now in your life is a sign of what you have most valued and how you have made those values real to you. Your highest value may be a solid family life, it may be freedom, financial security, wisdom, or a combination of these things.

Years of compliance, obligations, and social training may overlie our dream of life purpose, but it's still there. And the quest brings it to the surface. People in my classes come upon these original aspirations and versions of themselves with surprise, with clarity, and sometimes with grief. We experience a sense of reunion between the original self and original dreams and what we have done with that self and its dreams. This is a point for dialogue between the self you have become and the self you set out to be, to evaluate and reclaim choices.

Step 2: Face the impasse of your fears. Once you've laid the ground-work, you need to explore the reasons you think you "can't" fully live out your purpose. We have two categories of excuses: obligation and image. We assume we can't fully dedicate ourselves to purpose

There is in us an instinct for newness, for renewal, for a liberation of creative power. We seek to awaken in ourselves a force which really changes our lives from within. And yet the same instinct tells us that this change is a recovery of that which is deepest, most original, most personal in ourselves. To be born again is not to become somebody else, but to become ourselves.

—Thomas Merton

Decision-making Practices

• Write down, "I need to make a decision about _____."
• If this were a simple world, how would this decision go?
• What can you do to bring your decision as close as possible to the ideal?
• Dialogue with various voices in your head, and people in your life, until your path becomes clearer.
• Keep negotiating with assumed obstacles.

As a [person's] real power grows and knowledge widens, ever the way s/he can follow grows narrower: until at last s/he chooses nothing, but does only and wholly what s/he must do.

—Ursula LeGuin
Earthsea Trilogy

This Is Your Life

• Write a story called "My Life and I."
• See yourself as an active character in your life.
• Do you enjoy each other's company?
• Do you trust each other?
• How do you treat each other?
• If your life were a person, what attributes would it have?

Do you agree on your purpose?

266

because our obligations are nonnegotiable and because the people who matter to us won't approve. Unless you have obligations and no peer group, everybody hits this impasse. When we become aware of these assumptions, we are challenged to go forward, or give up, the dream. If we aim steadfastly through the impasse, we face risk. We face the moment when we will no longer control the process. It's terrifying to face this loss of control and to know on some level that we are choosing to let go of control. If we give up on the dream, we go into depression and despair. We feel helpless and ineffectual and hard-pressed to find ways to keep our self-esteem alive. We have to trust that, by the time we have come this far, the journey ahead is shorter than the one behind. We have to try hard not to turn back.

Step 3: Devote the time and energy necessary to follow your purpose. We were brought up to revere and respond to duty. We have been schooled to carry on the family business or family traditions or cultural expectations. We are now driven by a need to honor spiritual awakening. This inner calling presents us with a much deeper sense of purpose than the one many of us envisioned when starting our adult lives.

And we do not consider ourselves free. We have partners and children and aging parents and our own aging to contend with. We have economic responsibilities and realities—some of which we planned, some of which just happened. We are in debt. We have mortgages and credit cards and a standard of living. We have attachments to extended family, to friends, to our community. And even if we did just close the door and drive off into the sunset, where would we go? This inner calling isn't about place. It isn't even about a group, a defined community. It's much more amorphous than that, and more personal.

Nevertheless, we need to make time for exploring purpose. The next chapter presents a plan for this exploration. There comes a point when, no matter what, we need to proceed. We need to make the contract and then let go of trying to control it.

Step 4: Let the sacred lead. When the spiritual imperative takes over,

Manifesto of The Mad Farmer Liberation Front:

Love the quick profit, the annual raise, vacation with pay. Want more of everything ready made. Be afraid to know your neighbors and to die. And you will have a window in your head. Not even your future will be a mystery anymore. Your mind will be punched in a card and shut away in a little drawer. When they want you to buy something they will call you. When they want you to die for profit they will let you know.

So, friends, every day do something that won't compute. Love the Lord. Love the world. Work for nothing. Take all that you have and be poor. Love someone who doesn't deserve it. . . . Give your approval to all you cannot understand. Praise ignorance, for what man has not encountered he has not destroyed. Ask the questions that have no answers. Invest in the millennium. Plant sequoias. Say that your main crop is the forest that you did not plant, and that you will not live to harvest. . . . Put your faith in the two inches of humus that will build under the trees every thousand years. Listen to carrion—put your ear close, and hear the faint chattering of the songs that are to come. Expect the end of the world. Laugh. Laughter is immeasurable. Be joyful, though you have considered all the facts. . . . Go with love into the fields. Lie easy in the shade. Rest your head in her lap. Swear allegiances to what is nighest your thoughts. As soon as the generals and politicos can predict the motions of your mind, lose it. Leave a sign to mark the trail, the way you didn't go.

Be like the fox who makes more tracks than necessary, some in the wrong direction. Practice resurrection.

—The Whole Earth Catalogue

268

we become true students of our own life process. This moment is both exhilarating and frightening, risky and inspiring. We are a part of a collective energy much larger than ourselves. We begin to sense the impact of our contribution as it ripples out beyond the borders of our individual lives.

This potential for impact is what Professor John Brantner called "the hinge of history," a time when the direction of entire cultures can go either way. Things loosen up. Individuals are pulled into the opening energy and our actions exaggerated, for good or ill. We see this all around us, even in bastardized forms of celebrity, and somehow sense that the decisions we make as single individuals and what we feel called to do have a weightiness that surprises us. We sense a responsibility inherent in our actions that we might not choose but that we cannot avoid. We are actors in the hinge. We play our parts.

This imperative enters our lives in unexpected forms. In the mid-1960s, Dr. Helen Schucman, a psychologist and educator at Columbia University in New York, began hearing a voice in her head. It kept telling her, "This is a course in miracles, please take notes." She thought she was going insane. Finally, a colleague suggested she do as the voice requested and see what happened. Her note-taking became the fifteen-hundred-page manuscript *A Course in Miracles*, which so many people consider one of the most significant spiritual documents of modern times. At one point Dr. Schucman asked the voice, "Why Me?"

The voice replied simply, "Because you'll do it." And so will you, and so will I, whatever it becomes our purpose to do.

19. DREAMING,
LONGING, ACTING

If one advances confidently in the direction of his dreams
and endeavors to live the life which he has imagined, he
will meet with a success unexpected in common hours.

> *—Henry David Thoreau*
> Walden

Before we can do something significant with our lives, we have to do three things: imagine it clearly so we know what we want; be willing to want it very, very much; and take action that moves us toward attainment. The more complicated our life purpose turns out to be, the more we are in need of focused vision, focused longing, and focused action. In this chapter we move through these three steps.

Since I am a writer working around other writers, it is our visions,

There are no idle thoughts. All thinking produces form at some level.

—*Dr. Helen Schucman*
A Course in Miracles

Here-and-Now Statement

• Write an entry that begins "Where I am now in my life is _____."

The inner eye of vision can see what isn't yet there, can reach beyond present circumstances, and can see what, up to that point, has never been there. It truly is an incredible human faculty that is able to see beyond the present and the past, and from the unknown conceive something not hitherto in existence.

—*Robert Fritz*
The Path of Least Resistance

Fantasy Statement

• What are all the paths you can imagine taking from this point onward?
• Travel some of these paths in writing, spin them out on paper.
• Dialogue with the self in these settings.
• Ask yourself how you got here.
• Ask yourself what it's like to be doing these things.

longings, and actions with which I am most familiar. What I have seen of the writing process in myself, colleagues, and students can be translated and applied to your vision, though it is writers' stories I will mostly tell here.

Visioning

Everything we ever accomplish or acquire begins with an idea, a dream, a vision. We are dependent on imagery as the beam that guides us. We want to know when we have "gotten somewhere," and the only way to know this is to create a clear image of a destination, a tangible goal, a measurable result. This is true, whether we want to find the right red sweater, build our dream house, finish a project, or run for president. Thinking about purpose in the last chapter should have stirred this visioning capacity. In the process of making a commitment to discover our purpose, we need to dream. We need to make images, try on various fantasies, explore.

When we first begin to create a vision, we may not see it clearly. Vision starts with a vague sense of something desired, something missing, a hole we want to fill. We start clarifying our vision by becoming aware of our fantasies and secret dreams. When you drive down the highway, when you stare out the window, when you put yourself to sleep by running fantasies starring yourself, what specifically are you imagining? What is the vision you are creating? Out of all this mental entertainment (what I sometimes call "self-amuse"), what are the most important images to you? Which ones indicate that this idea is worth pursuing?

Years ago I began journal writing out of just such a vague sense of something wanted, something missing. In my twenties, I began to teach journal writing out of a similarly vague sense. This time I wanted community, I wanted to deepen my understanding of writing, to learn more about what I had spontaneously undertaken.

Even after *One to One* was published, I didn't understand how to envision a future for myself based on what I had already created

The Crowning Moment

- Think of a dream, a goal, a purpose you have.
- How will you know when it is accomplished?
- Write or draw this crowning moment in your journal.
- Begin expanding on this image until it feels fully complete and real.

> JOURNAL ENTRY
>
> *I am almost to the finish line, ahead of the pack. There are some men ahead of me, I can't tell if any women have made it in yet. I think I'm the first. There are younger women behind me, but they can't catch up. My husband and the children are yelling and cheering on the sidelines. I don't even pretend to be embarrassed, I deserve this. Suddenly everyone is shouting out my time, I'm first, I'm first. I won the marathon! I fall into Jim's arms and he lifts me up over his head. I'm hot and sweaty and screaming, and the kids are pouring water and Gatorade down my front and I don't care. I'm just exhilarated. And there's a picture of us in the paper just like that—a big family hug.*

A-Year-Ahead Entries

- Write a journal entry dated one year into the future.
- Write in detail what you want to have occurring in your life.
- Choose a time to do this regularly, on your birthday or January 1.

This is a good exercise for the whole family to do.

The meditation at the end of this section will help you build a five-year vision.

> *The mind loves to not know completely. Situations that are not familiar tune the system. To get smarter, do the unfamiliar.*
>
> —Magaly Rodriguez Mossman

in my past. I coauthored two more books that don't seem to have much to do with my life's writing purpose, except that they are needed books and I gained experience writing them. I didn't understand that I could *make a vision and follow it*, and neither did most of my friends. We marveled at those who seemed driven by clear purpose, and didn't know how to create it in ourselves.

Dreaminess is a trait we may associate with artistic types, but daydreaming is not the same as visioning. I tell writing students that the beginning of a story is like the threshold of a doorway: You want the reader to feel confident enough in the imagined world so that s/he will step into the story's reality without hesitating. Visioning is the same kind of threshold. We need to create a reality so real to us that we will step into it with a sense that everything we need is present. Visions have size and shape. Visions are sense-based, tangible, populated. They portray the moment destination is reached, the goal attained, the result measured.

Through writing forward-dated journal entries, we practice the most rudimentary power of visioning: admitting what we think, or hope, will happen. By pausing to write about what we might be doing one year, three years, five years from now, we gain an immediate sense of the patterns that frame our direction consciously and subconsciously. Such writing is often the first glimpse we have of the solidity of our choices: If we envision certain events, begin certain actions and stick with them, there will be certain outcomes. Writing the possible future helps us understand *what* desire and *what* action need to occur in order to support the vision. We may surprise ourselves: "I'm not alone—I've found someone." "I'm in business for myself." "I have a baby . . . I didn't know I had plans for a baby!" "We're divorced." "This phase of my life, that I'm so caught up in, is over and I'm onto something else."

Former class participants often tell me that even if they didn't reread their forward-dated entry until actual time had elapsed, that about fifty percent of what they'd envisioned occurred. Envisioning is the mind's way of laying out a grid, and it *will* follow it. It does all the time, whether or not we have consciously set the course.

• List everything in your life that you like and want
to keep:

> *What I have in my life that I want to maintain:*
> *—my partner*
> *—my good friends*
> *—my freedom*
> *—good health*
> *—meaningful work.*

• List everything in your life that you'd like to
change:

> *What I have in my life that I want to change:*
> *—stress level*
> *—lack of trust and general anxieties*
> *—overwhelming office details*
> *—erratic cash flow*
> *—undefined working hours that eat up the week.*

• From these two lists, make a list of choices that
focus on your vision and move in the direction of that
vision.

• Phrase these choices positively. Talk about your
own action: you cannot coerce action for others. For
example, don't write:

> *I choose not to fight with my son,*

but write the phrase:

> *I choose to develop a relationship of mutual respect with my son.*

• Create five to ten choices to work with at any
given time.

• Focus on end result, not on how you're going to
achieve it.

Most of us have been taught to be practical rather than ideal-istic—especially if our dreams and desires are not deemed success oriented. If your greatest dream is to head your own company and be a millionaire, you are probably getting lots of cultural support. If your dream is to create a perfect bonsai, to invent something ecologically useful, to work with children, you may not be getting cultural support. You may be told—or are telling yourself—that it's time for you to be content going to work like everyone else.

We need to learn to act *as if* we could have our dream. *As if* we can have what we most desire. For acting as if we *cannot* have it prevents us from even knowing what we really want. We create excuses. We go after something we consider more practical, more acceptable, less disruptive, that will earn us a living. We have all made such compromises, often without even being aware of it. We have lowered our goals, or turned them aside, and we are left with our alternatives because that is all we can envision ourselves as having. *We have what we consider possible, because life is a constant flow of opportunities and options and we respond only to those that fall into our perceived scope of possibility.*

Years ago an artist told me about growing up in a small Min-nesota town where nobody else she knew had the same kinds of aspirations she did. After high school she went to beauty school because it was the most creative option she could think of to keep herself connected to her real dream. It took her years to broaden her perspective, to get the education and training and support she needed, and to go after her artistic vision—but she did it.

It's our responsibility to tell ourselves the truth, to know what our dreams are. To do that, we first need the vision, and then we need to be willing to feel the depth of our longing and not deny it exists.

Longing

As I write this chapter, the faces of several friends come to mind, each in midlife, thirty-five to fifty; a man whose job is being dis-

Current Choices:

1. I choose to create a life of balance between work and play.

2. I choose to earn at least $X a month and to stabilize my cash flow.

3. I choose to develop meaningful work that supports my life goals.

4. I choose to find a peaceful place to live by trees and water.

5. I choose to vacation one month a year.

Testing Your Choices for Desire

• Ask yourself: "If I could have this immediately, would I take it?"

(This framework for making choices is adapted from the work of Robert Fritz in his book *The Path of Least Resistance*.)

> *It is common to assume that the unknown is unknowable, or at least unknowable by normal means. It is our inexperience and ignorance that can make the creative process seem as if it is an outcome of magical operations, the same kind of inexperience and ignorance a jungle tribe may have about modern aviation. But, in fact, creating is a skill that can be learned and developed. Like any skill, you learn by practice and hands-on experience. You can learn to create by creating.*
>
> —Robert Fritz
> The Path of Least Resistance

Willingness to Long For

• In the journal, admit what you most long for.
• What does it feel like to commit these longings to paper?
• Imagine admitting them to others: what are you afraid of?

    —ridicule?

278

solved from under him; a woman who still wants to go to medical school; another woman who's reclaiming a career dream from high school, which has no apparent relationship to the career she's already developed. Each of these friends is faced with the need to look carefully at the issue of longing. What will they long for and what will they commit themselves to doing as a result of letting loose the passion within them? Our passion for the dream is the fuel that carries us from vision to attainment. *We will be afraid of letting loose our passion as long as we are afraid of going after what we envision.*

There is a comforting thought as we sort our way through longing: *We do not choose a vision, we are not given a longing, unless we are also given the ability to fulfill it.* We may be confused about what we long for versus what others want us to long for; we may choose not to fulfill our longing, but the ability was not what was missing— *raw talent accompanies raw desire.* We may lose the timing, fear failure, fear success, fear being stopped by disaster or accident—but the talent is there if the longing is genuine.

We often act as though disaster or accident is the primary inhibitor, that it's somehow "dangerous" to go after our visions, but most of the time this is a way to avoid other fears. Timing is crucial to some dreams and requires that some people develop incredible confidence at a very young age. A fifty-year-old has missed his chance to be a child prodigy. Fears of failure cause us to give up in the early stages, to decide, when *necessary* obstacles occur, that we were not meant to have our dream, that the universe is signaling us that we are on a wrong track, that we should settle for what others are telling us, or we are telling ourselves, is the more comfortable, usual route. We can view success as a threat, invest so heavily in a particular project that we won't allow achievement, won't move out of the struggle that has become a kind of status quo.

I have been teaching writing for a long time. Occasionally, I work with students who have a natural talent for words but for whom writing is a pleasant pastime; they don't long for it. I envy them sometimes, when my own longing is dragging me about. Other students have a less-developed skill but a much higher degree of

Even a thought, even a possibility, can shatter and transform us.
—Nietzsche

Write Your Vision Fully

* See, hear, taste, touch, and smell your vision.
* Revise your vision as goals clarify or change.
* Put a copy up on the wall.
* Read it out loud to yourself daily.
* Let your vision be an evolving reality you interact
with as you grow.

To be exceptional means to be outside the norm, to be unusual, to be alone. We don't often think of it that way, but when we start longing for something, we become the exception. We have to choose between wanting to belong and willingness to follow the lonely, individual path of the dream. . . .
I needed to be convinced that my desire to write was based on talent to write, which is a gift from God, as is all talent. And once I acknowledged the spiritual source of the talent, I saw that the imperative to do something and the ability to do it are really the same. The longing, the ability, and the opportunities are all the same. They are all spiritual. They are the way God acts. Our job is to choose to have faith in this triumvirate instead of having faith in neuroses, doubt and anxiety.
—Joy Houghton

desire and determination. They work to improve, sentence by sentence, paragraph by paragraph. They will not be stopped. They ride their longing, and are ridden by it. They are in love with their necessity to write. They see publication, they imagine readership, they long for their story to be told and assume responsibility for telling it. They do not like failure, rejection slips, critique, more than anyone else, but they view these things as a necessary part of the creative process, and so must you and I.

As I write this, my friend Joy has just turned fifty years old. She's been an artist, a goldsmith, a printmaker, a therapist, a financial adviser, a business consultant. . . . Three years ago, she finally admitted to herself that she'd always wanted to be a writer. She set about developing her skills and writing the first draft of a story. She learned from this process and began the second draft. She studied informally with writing friends who critiqued and helped her. She read the kinds of books she admired and hoped to emulate. She fell into longing with the process, let herself want it more than she'd ever wanted anything, even though she had no guarantee that her desire would be sufficient to produce the book she had in mind. She began the third draft. She anguished over her process. She grieved that she hadn't known how to envision and admit her desire twenty-five years ago. She did not give up. The book is succeeding. She has carefully thought out the process and endured the long preparation period before she could show her dream to the right agent, the right editor, the right producer. She is succeeding because she dared to define, dared to long for, and dared to take correct action.

Longing is not just for artists or for people who want to excel in some grand, public way; longing is the necessary fuel for all our dreams. Longing makes the difference between resentment and empowerment. Most of the time, it is not others who prevent us from attaining our dream, but ourselves, our unwillingness to want something so much or our confusion about how to transform longing effectively to action. We need to use our longing in productive ways.

For many people reality is an acquired taste.

—Robert Fritz
The Path of Least Resistance

Current Reality

• Make an objective list of the circumstances in your
life.

> *Current reality is, I'm making just enough money to get by month
> by month.*
> *Current reality is that I want to open this business before the end
> of the year.*
> *Current reality is I don't know how I'm going to accomplish this
> goal.*
> *Current reality is that I make the commitment anyway.*

• Make an objective statement of the emotional
feelings you have about your circumstances—without
getting into the feelings.

> *Current reality is that I'm scared. Current reality is that I'm mad
> at myself for not knowing the things it's so obvious I need to
> know. Current reality is that I'm also excited, that I finally have
> a vision that fits me.*

Creative Tension

• Make an image in your mind of creative tension (a
tightrope, a stretched rubber band, a cat's cradle);
meditate on this image.
• Dialogue with this image.
• Ask it what it has to teach you.
• What old beliefs about tension will you have to
give up to work with it creatively?

Acting

In a seminar called "The Art of Creative Completion," Gerald Allan and I led participants through the five-year vision included at the end of this section. What the vision gives people are two clearly defined points in time and circumstance: where you are today and where you intend to be five years from today. The meditation creates an immediate sense of gap. That gap is filled with stepping-stones of action—how we move from here to there. *We can have all the passion in the world, and not attain our dream unless we decide to act, and think carefully about what actions to take.*

There are steps to action but no formula. Actions are created by an amalgam of your dream and the circumstances available for making that dream a reality.

First, you need to know where you are, clearly, without hedging, so that you have a firm reality to push off from. This is what Robert Fritz calls "current reality." The journal becomes the repository of current reality as well as the repository of vision. You can see and compare where you are and where you want to go.

Second, you need to envision a lifeline between these points. It needs to be tense, like a tightrope, something you can walk along. The necessity for tension requires that we develop a different attitude about tension: this is *creative tension*. Creative tension is what creates the path. When we lose tension, we wander without focus. We have to decide over and over again to stay close to the tension, to walk the wire. The journal becomes the repository for redefining and learning to work with tension, to see it as our partner, not an enemy.

Third, you need to consider all possibilities for action, and question how these possibilities relate to the tension. For example, the young woman who cleans for us has successfully run a cleaning service for several years. She has used this business to put herself through college, develop business skills, stabilize her income, and make the transition from college to adult life. But cleaning other people's houses is not her heart's desire. She wants to open a flower

We have just moved into a house we started envisioning five years ago. As we got closer to being able to afford to move, we spent the last year making it more and more real in our minds. We lay awake nights and told each other the layout of this house, how each room looked, what the view was like, the atmosphere and what we wanted to feel like living here.

I imagined inviting people for dinner and showing them the rooms. K. drew architectural sketches. We went to the realtor and banker, decided to take on this commitment. We put the old house on the market. We envisioned new owners walking through and falling in love with our little house. The first couple who saw it bought it. Then we were free to go looking and we recognized this house immediately from our mind's eye. This house is our vision realized. People say it takes a while to feel at home in a new place, but we have already been living here a long time. I am already "at home."

Embracing the Opposite

•   What parts of yourself have you not been using that you need to use to reach your goal?
•   Why have you disowned these aspects of who you are, and how will you integrate yourself with them?
•   If you let the opposites inside you exert their power, what do you think would happen?

(When this is a positive fantasy, you are ready to proceed.)

shop with arbors growing inside and exquisite, unusual flowers. She wants to bring pleasure to people in an uncertain world, something whimsical and wistful and romantic. To be the shop where people stop when they really want to show their hearts to others. And she is faced with choices: people ask her to clean yet another house, they suggest she combine cleaning and flowers, they offer to back a version of the business that is not her dream.

Over and over again, she must choose to stay clear in her vision. At the same time, she needs to keep learning, to adopt the business skills that will allow her dream to work, to find out how the marketplace functions, to accept advice that is truly helpful and balance her strengths and weaknesses.

The world does not conform to our dreams. We need to make use of how the world is. Only from the position of being fully in the world can we influence it and give it our gift. My young friend has a gentle heart. She wants to love the world through flowers. But this is only a pipe dream until she is willing to love the pragmatic, business, financial, realistic aspects of her dream and herself as much as she loves the beauty.

Success is a bonding of pragmatism and faith. This bonding is a learning process. It necessitates giving credence to the pragmatic as well as the spiritual. We, who read books like this, may tend to value the spiritual at the expense of the pragmatic. The world is not either/or. The businessman with contempt for intuition needs to befriend that place inside himself he cannot explain. And the writer with contempt for the commercial applications of her craft needs to embrace the market.

> *Spirituality is a matter of balance. We envision, we long for, we act, and through this process we take our place and our power in the world.*

20. BECOMING
PERSONS OF POWER

*Men and women of integrity
and simplicity of heart, loving
to follow righteousness, are by
the secret touches of a holy
Light guided to God.*

—Robert Barclay

Life is relationship: *we are empowered and empowering all the time.*
Empowerment means to give others what they need,
and to allow others to give us what we need. When
this exchange is lighthearted, we don't pause to call it
anything. Only when it's serious, heavy, challenging, do we stop
to name it.

It is pleasurable to feel you have something of value to offer; it
is pleasurable to receive something of value. Empowerment is the
act of giving and receiving, exchanging the basic life commodities
of energy and attention. We give each other encouragement, praise,

We are light going through a prism. The light is always there, but only we can act as its prism, concentrate and filter it. We make of the light of the cosmos, a rainbow with a mouth and arms.

—Jarrett Smith

Mutual Exchanges

• Write three examples of how someone dared to respond to your requests for empowerment.
• Write three examples of how you helped empower someone else by your response.
• What gave you the courage, the confidence, to say or do what you did?

Little Voice of the Heart

• Look for messages from the heart that come through in the middle of other writings.
• Ask this voice for messages, for dialogue.
• Be still. Listen softly.
• Thank this voice when it speaks to you.
• Ask for guidance.
• Write down your heart's instructions.
• Do as you are guided.

• When you override your guidance, do so honestly. Take the risk fair and square.
• Admit in the journal what you are choosing to do instead, and why. What desire do you hope to fulfill? What do you wish to learn?

support, delight in each other's presence, lessons from each other's points of view.

You know who your empowerers are—they're the folks you call on to feel better, when you need a little cheering up, when you want someone to tell you you're doing fine, *and* when you need someone to help you tune in to your truth, when you need someone to halt you in your tracks a few minutes and help you think about what you really need to do. You have your list, and you are on other people's lists. Empowerment is mutual.

A friend calls. She says her job is ending. She's afraid and almost broke. We're tempted to pacify her, to reassure her with platitudes, but a little voice inside our chest urges us to tell her: "You were bored. You've said for years you wanted out, but you didn't get out. Now life is taking care of it. Do what you know you long to do. If you didn't have the ability, you wouldn't want it . . . so do it. Figure it out. Talk to lots of people about your dream. They'll help you if you believe." This may not be the sympathy she thought she called to get, but it's the empowerment she needs.

Then something happens to one of us: we, who have been telling everyone to go for their dream, wake up one day and aren't sure about our own dreams. We're discouraged. Delays and obstacles seem insurmountable. We get on the phone or go out to lunch; and this friend, or another, listens to their small voice and tells us, "You've overcome obstacles before. These aren't necessarily problems, they're challenges, they're part of the process. Tell me an intermediate goal you can define and reach. Name three blessings so far this week that support your dream. Read to me from your journal; tell me your vision again. You can do this. Nothing's the matter. Just don't give up."

Exchanges of empowerment give us what we need—*and no more.* In both of these examples, the empowerer doesn't overstep the bounds and try to do for the other person what that person needs to do for him/herself. Empowerment does not rip off someone else's challenges and do them ourselves because it makes us feel noble or powerful to "help"; empowerment isn't a means of busily avoiding

Dear Larry, I've decided to live. Not that I have much choice, but I think I've been trying to show my love for you by joining you. I can't see you. I don't understand what death really is, though I believe it is something. These past months that you've been gone to death, I have been dead in the middle of life—not feeling anything, not doing much of anything. I'm getting ready to come alive—slowly, like a plant waking up after a long, harsh winter. I see a tiny, green shoot here and there in myself, trying not to get frosted out. What I want you to be sure of is that even if my heart comes alive again, I will still love you all the rest of my life. Please become my angel and watch over me as I struggle to move on. And please be there to greet me, when I step into the light. Your loving wife . . ."

REMEMBER to use a variety of journal techniques you've already learned. Many of them are directly empowering.

JOURNAL ENTRY

FRIEND: "It looks to me like you're way stressed out and not sticking to your plans for finding a job that doesn't require this kind of time commitment of you while you're still trying to raise toddlers."

X VOICE: "Shut up! Who asked you?"

HEART VOICE: "I asked her. I asked her to tell you for me because my whisper doesn't seem to be getting through, and neither do the whispers of the kids."

X VOICE: "The kids are fine."

FRIEND: "The kids are coping; you aren't coping."

X VOICE: "You're right. I'm not doing what I said I would do. I forgot. Do you know what I mean—life gets so distracting, I simply forgot?"

HEART VOICE: "Your friend just took a risk here, do you think you'd like to thank her?"

X VOICE: "Thanks, Judy. One of the ways I count on you to be my friend is to dare to tell me this stuff. I know I'm not always easy to talk to, but I get over my gruffness in a few minutes."

the harder challenges of our own lives; empowerment is saying and doing what we know *in our hearts* is right—and not letting the mind's rationalizations goof up the fair exchange of power. And empowerment is listening carefully to the other person's needs and responses, and respecting them.

In the journal, empowerment is evidenced by the presence of dialogue, by writing down the messages of the little voice of the heart, heeding what is being said to us, and interacting with these nudges of guidance. The little voice encourages us to do what we know we need to do. To stay connected to our empowerment, we need to validate the rightness of what is being said—in what we write, and how we respond.

I watched a woman going through bereavement. At first, in her grief, she deadened herself, emotionally joined her husband in that dark passage. When the little voice would speak to her, she didn't want to listen. She didn't want to go on, didn't want to open up to new life. One by one, as the time seemed appropriate, her friends encouraged her to come alive, to stop feeling guilty for the newness, for the opportunities, for having more life to live. As a result of what they said to her, she eventually decided to live again.

Sometimes, if we're avoiding the truth, when someone else says it, we experience a flush of embarrassment at the exposure. Empowerment requires the willingness to confront and be confronted, to support and be supported, to encourage and be encouraged. This is not always the most socially comfortable or easiest exchange. Our discomfort is what empowerment costs—and it's no big price. It's only a moment's discomfort.

I have learned to use this flash of embarrassment as a signal that what's being said is probably right on target. The little voice in my heart is saying, "Hear, hear, that's what I've been trying to tell you too!" and the voice of my resistance is saying, "Don't pay attention. Tell them to back off and mind their own business!" I try to keep my mouth shut long enough to sort out my response a little. Sometimes a brief journal dialogue makes the dynamics very clear.

The exchange of empowerment is quick and clear-witted. Its

God is not static. God is in constant creation, constantly being created.

We are not static, either. We are in constant creation.

—Cil Braun

JOURNAL ENTRY

I always thought that by the time I began to experience spiritual power, I'd feel ready for it, and I don't. I see myself becoming a "powerful person" in the eyes of other people around me. People look to me for guidance. They assume I have information. They call me on the phone and intercept me in the hallways. How did I get to be the expert? I don't feel like an expert inside. The past few years have been hell. I've been fighting for my life—literally and figuratively. I lost my job. I got cancer. I don't know how long my health will hold, whether I'll live to see the children raised. Every dream I've ever had is up in the air. And this is the moment when others suddenly think I have power? Ten years ago I would have reveled in this deference. Now, it puzzles me. I don't know how to respond. I'm looking for someone more powerful than I am who can help me figure out where I am in my life, and all these other people are looking to me to be that person for them. This is a very strange situation to find myself in. Maybe this is what William Blake (?—it's been a long time since high-school English!) meant by the "chain of being."

What Is Being Asked

There will be moments in your quest when you feel overwhelmed, as though too much is being asked of you.

* Why do you think the sacred thinks you can handle this?
* What are you capable of now that you believed you were not capable of before?
* How has this contract with the sacred come about?

clarity comes from its source in love and concern. Empowerment is offered in a flash of insight, a phrase of encouragement, a shot of belief from within or without. We are not trying to make others do something *our* way, only to help them find *their* way.

We give empowerment to ourselves as well. It is the gyroscope inside us, righting our course and righting it again. Empowerment within comes from the little voice of our own heart, and from our willingness to interpret events positively, to keep realigning ourselves with our visions, with our acceptance, with our relationship to the sacred.

When we take up the spiritual quest, we invite creative forces to interact with us and to impact our lives in ways we cannot predict and will not control. We find ourselves in a relationship with power, needing to become a person of power, not ego power, but spiritual power.

Spiritual empowerment is evidenced in our lives by our willingness to tell ourselves the truth, to listen to truth when it's told to us, and to dispense truth as lovingly as possible when we feel compelled to talk from the heart.

When things happen that look disastrous, empowerment allows us to see them as a stage of life that's over and to look for the next challenge that will advance us toward our dream. When we fight against what is, it drains power. As soon as we accept what is, we are empowered to figure out how to move forward.

Empowerment is attunement. We are guided toward this attunement in the journal through dialogue, through dream and meditation messages, through the emergence of probing questions that appear suddenly on the page and focus otherwise meandering writing. We may have the sense of being constantly prepared for something, and not know what the preparations are for until much later. We live with a sense of unfolding destiny, not for fame, but for response to the times in which we live. We look beyond the journal for a model of personal power with which we feel comfortable.

We are always scouting for exemplary behavior. We want to see the finest of human qualities displayed so that we might learn

Renewing Your Contract

• Take ten minutes right now. Write a fresh contract with your life.
• Look at some of the earlier contracts you've written.
• How is your understanding of your contract with the journey changing?

> *In many ways, constancy is an illusion. . . . Of any stopping place in life, it is good to ask whether it will be a good place from which to go on as well as a good place to remain.*
> —*Mary Catherine Bateson*
> Composing a Life

• What do you want from the sacred?
• What do you believe the sacred wants from you?

> *Mystics tell us that when God draws near and acts directly on the soul, the soul is pulled loose from all it has loved in place of God. . . .*
> —*Ann Belford Ulanov*
> Parabola, *vol. XII, no. 3*

Naming Guides

• Identify your guides who are real people.
• Identify your guides who are dream figures.
• Identify guides from literature, movies, fantasy.
• Dialogue with these figures. Talk to them about power: how they handle power, how they advise you to handle power.

from them and learn how to find these qualities in ourselves when we need them.

When I was thirteen, fourteen years old, I read all the biographies I could get out of the library, especially biographies of women. Most of what I know about the lives of Marie Curie, Eleanor Roosevelt, Margaret Mead, Katharine Hepburn, Ingrid Bergman—women of my mother's generation and older—comes from that period of exploration. I was in search of permission to define my own life, to discover how a person could make her own rules and what the consequences were. Whoever we admire mirrors what we want to learn. We test out our readiness against the standards of behavior we see in the role models we choose. Could we be as courageous? Could we take such a clear stand? Could we make this or that sacrifice? How would we handle such success? such failure? such tragedy?

As a result of choosing and watching our models, and listening to our heart's voice, we can teach ourselves to behave as we desire. By choosing every day, even in small ways, to do what we know is right—acts that always require some level of risk—we develop those qualities of greatness we admire, and we become role models ourselves.

As we make these choices, we incur loss. But we find that what we loose is either inconsequential or already gone—smoke and fantasy. We experience grief as part of empowerment because it teaches us to notice more and more clearly what *is* inconsequential and what is substantial in all our choices. When asked what he would save if his house were on fire, an artist replied, "The fire."

When we do what we know in our hearts is right, we are rewarded by the responses of those around us who immediately recognize the rightness of action. We find ourselves in community with those who perceive from the heart. We submit to the omnipotence of the universal heart.

The farther we dare go on our quest, the more spiritual power is available to us, and the more reciprocally we are available to be used by power. *As we are choosing, we are also being chosen.*

I live my life in growing orbits
which move out over the things of the world.
. . . I am circling around God, around the ancient tower,
and I have been circling for a thousand years,
And I still don't know if I'm a falcon,
or a storm,
or a great song.

—*Rainer Maria Rilke*
Selected Poems

In a recent speech I said that the process of writing this book had taught me the necessity of "volunteering to lose control" over many aspects of my life that I had previously assumed required my attempts to maintain control. A questioner asked if I meant that I lost one kind of control, to replace it with another? No. I tried that and it didn't work. Over and over I had to replace control with faith.

To become a person of power is to become a person of faith. To become a person of power is to choose the heart over the head, and experience the heart as the great receiver and transmitter of right insight, right thought, right action. To become a person of power is to listen before we act—to follow the sacred touches that guide us.

For the little voice turns out to be the voice of the sacred, and through practicing empowerment, we let the little voice become the big voice, let it step out front and guide us home from within.

Meditation

To prepare to use this meditation and others throughout the book, find a quiet place where you will not be interrupted for twenty minutes or so. Ask someone to read the meditation to you or to play back a version of the meditation you have made yourself or have ordered from the back of the book. The points of ellipses (. . .) indicate a significant pause—silence maintained within the text. Pause for as long as you feel comfortable; five to ten seconds can seem a long time in meditation. Double ellipses indicate longer silence.

CREATING A FIVE-YEAR VISION

Close your eyes and relax your body. . . . Take all the time you need to get comfortable. . . . Shift muscles . . . stretch and relax. . . . Make sure your spine and neck are straight and aligned . . . not held stiffly. There is no stiffness here . . . just comfort, the beginning of calm. . . . There is no hurry now. . . . There is nothing else to do . . . or think about. . . . Just relax. . . . . . .

Notice your breath. . . . Let your breath enter deeply into your body. . . . Let your breath roll into you like soft, heavy clouds that fill you with silence. . . . Inhale slowly . . . deeply. . . . Exhale slowly . . . thoroughly. . . . Let your breath sink in and out. . . . Your breath is a rhythm of calm. . . . Follow your breath. . . . Exhale all extraneous thought. . . . Inhale silence. . . .

In your mind's eye, go to a room that is comfortable and relaxing. . . . Settle into a favorite chair or some large pillows. . . . When you are ready, pull down a blank screen in front of you. . . . You are going to create a vision of your life five years from today. . . . You are looking for what you have done with your dreams . . . your purpose . . . your power . . . in the next five years. You are looking at the future you intend to create. . . .

First look in a mirror and see yourself. . . . How do you look? . . . What are you wearing? . . . How have you changed from how you look today? . . . . . .

Now look around you. What is the place you are in? . . . What environment have you created for yourself? . . .   . . . Walk through this space. . . . Take your time. . . . Notice the colors, sounds, smells, textures of your environment. . . .   . . . Who is with you here? . . .   . . . Find your working space. . . . What is it like? . . . What have you created around yourself in the space where you create? . . .   . . .

What are you working on, five years from today? . . .   . . . What has happened to your dreams and projects now? . . .   . . .

The telephone rings. It is a call for you. . . . Who is it and what do they want? . . .   . . .

A reporter comes by to interview you. The reporter asks the following questions. What do you reply?

- What is your greatest success or achievement? . . .   . . .
- What has been the greatest crisis you overcame to get here? . . .   . . .
- What's the best advice someone ever gave you? . . .   . . .
- What's the best advice you ever gave someone else? . . .   . . .
- What's the most exciting part of your life right now? . . .   . . .
- What role has your spiritual journey played in who you are and what you have accomplished? . . .   . . .
- What's your next goal or project? . . .   . . .

When you are finished talking with the reporter, walk again through your environment. Choose one thing to bring back with you, one symbol that will guide you from here to your vision. . . .   . . .

When you are ready, return to the room with the movie screen. . . . Follow your breath back to this room. . . . Emerge out of the silence of your body. . . . There is no hurry. . . . Stretch your body. . . . Open your eyes. . . .

Take time to draw or write whatever you want to record from this vision.

VI.
Traveling in the World

21. THE POINT OF RETURN

The completed journey always ends with a return, a home-coming to the ordinary world of conventional reality that was left behind. This world has been transformed, if our journey has been successful, into a new world, seen with fresh eyes. The end of the journey is the beginning of a new, empowered way of life.

—Ralph Metzner
Opening to Inner Light

To say we return implies we've been somewhere else. There are times in all of our lives when the journey pulls us out of our usual routine. We have not been caught up in the busy, workaday world; though, in most cases, we have not been exactly removed from it either. There has been a kind of psychic barrier, a development of purpose or life event that has held us apart. We may have created this withdrawal, as in the case of a friend who is sailing around the world, or had it thrust upon us by circumstance, as in the case of another friend who's been coping with the loss of her husband. For whatever

Only those who dare to let go can dare to re-enter.

—Meister Eckhart

Returning to Questions

- Who are you now that you are not who you thought you were?
- How has the journey changed you?
- What of your old life is coming with you?
- What do you need to allow to drop away?

. . . for a long, long time, my mind didn't work. I could not listen to the news on the radio with understanding. My attention came unglued when I tried to read anything but the lightest froth. My brain spun in endless, painful loops, and I could neither concentrate nor think with any semblance of order. I had always rather enjoyed having a mind, and I missed mine extravagantly. I was out to lunch for three years. . . . One spring afternoon, I was walking back down my lane after getting the mail. . . . The sun was slanting through new leaves, and the air was fragrant with wild cherry blossoms, which my bees were working eagerly. I stopped to watch them, standing in the sunbeam. The world appeared to have been running along quite nicely without my even noticing it. Quietly, gratefully, I discovered that a part of me that had been off somewhere nursing grief and pain had returned. I had come back from lunch.

—Sue Hubbell
A Country Year

reasons, the journey has demanded the major portion of our time and focus. We may be returning from a long project, from writing a thesis, from a year of pregnancy and enthrallment with new parenthood, from a long illness, or caring for someone who's been ill, from bereavement, or even the happy isolation of new love.

It may still be Monday in the middle of our lives, but we are not who we were, and we are not where we were when we began this quest.

As we near the point of return, the world begins forcefully to intrude. Time for introspection, perhaps even the ability to settle into silence, evaporates like fog that's been burned off by the morning sun. Ready or not, we are presented with new tasks. We are propelled back into the mainstream and challenged to bring what we learned in withdrawal into the busiest corners of our lives.

I wrote this book three times. The first draft and the second draft bear almost no resemblance to each other except for chapter titles. After the intense labor expended on the second draft, I had less than twenty-four hours between mailing the manuscript and showing up at a large corporation to start writing sales training manuals. The culture shock was as real as if I'd just flown in from Tibet. I looked like a normal human being, a freelance writer who'd done these kinds of jobs before, but inside I was still on my pilgrimage. The vocabulary switch alone was exhausting. The established patterns of introspective writing were replaced overnight by technical jargon and the pace of business. My point of return began. Fortunately, I had ten months of this before attending to the final editing and rewriting of this book. It took me every minute of those ten months to adjust to life "beyond the book," and develop a way of talking to myself about the changes the journey had brought me.

As we enter the stage of return, the level of transformation we have endured and the consequences of that transformation become real. We have undergone a restructuring of our belief system, our self-concept, and our life purpose. The outer trappings of our lives may still look relatively undisturbed, but internally tremendous change has taken place. We may not be ready, or able, for all of these changes to manifest

• Write one-page biographies about your journey:
Once there was a pilgrim who . . .
• Write in the third person—it helps perspective and
frees creativity
• Allow elements of your story to become symbolic,
metaphoric.
• Write at least a dozen of these entries before
rereading any of them.
• When you do review them, what themes and
insights emerge?

> *JOURNAL ENTRY*
>
> *I am no longer separated from my spiritual life in the way I used
> to be, but I'm separated from almost everything else. Friends call
> me on the telephone: I don't know what to say. I don't want to be
> social in the old ways, yet I yearn for some kind of
> companionship. I don't want to do the same old things and am
> looking for a new dimension of work and responsibility. It's not
> very well defined. I don't even look the same to myself. My face
> is familiar, but there's an expression in it I don't recognize.
> "What's going on?" I ask the person in the mirror. She shrugs
> her shoulders, doesn't know either. I feel more alone than I've ever
> felt in my life. Nobody knows me: I don't even know me. Is this
> really where I was headed?*

Explaining Return to Your Family

If you have a mate, return can be a tenuous transition.
• Stay in communication.
• Create guidelines:
What do you want to explain?
What response do you want?
What kind of support are you asking for?
• Reread some of your recent entries before talking to
your partner to get as clear and articulate as possible.

themselves on a daily basis. We want to hold steady while we practice looking at the world from the perspective of a new self.

It's as though we become Rip van Winkle. We are a mystery to ourselves, walking around the kitchen muttering, "How did I get here? Where is here? Whose hand is this? Whose face?" You look in a mirror and you see a familiar stranger looking back.

This can be an extremely disorienting time, even more disorienting than other parts of the journey have been. If we've been on a real journey—and we have—where are the postcards, the souvenirs, the tan lines? We are accustomed to having labels and anecdotes to dispense whenever someone asks who we are, what we do, what we have been up to lately. In the period of return, we have no handy labels. We have lost the ability to speak coherently about experience because we have traveled off the edge of any expectation we had, upon setting out, for what the journey would mean, would do, or where it would land us.

Because of this loss of articulation, return is, by necessity, a time of deep and private inner sorting. No one else can fully appreciate or understand the disorientation. You are saying good-bye and hello, recoupling your self with your life to see what fits. Your journal may be the only confidante you have.

Writing during the point of return helps us get our bearings, but don't be discouraged if your journal writing is vague and fuzzy, full of large words that seem finally to capture what's happening to you as you write the entry, and look like meaningless gibberish the next time you open the book. Return presents us with a second quest: the search for the words to articulate our experience.

When my friend Lynne died, the closest I could come to articulating my return from caring for her in her final illness was to write that I knew we were going through a similar transformation that had, for the time being, different ends. Her transformation was complete: she died. Mine was, and still is, much harder to understand or talk about.

This is a normal part of the journey. The old self-concept has broken down, and a new one is taking its place, which is harder to

- Be brief.
- Choose your moment carefully, when both of you have time and energy to share.

He who has faith cannot talk about it. He who has no faith should not talk about it.

—*Franz Kafka*

Dialogues of Return

- Write dialogues between yourself as you were starting the quest, and as you are now.
- Write dialogues between your old beliefs and new beliefs.
- Write dialogues between the ego and the soul/self.
- Look for continuity.
- Build bridges that help you see the journey over a span of time. Perspective can't be forced, but it can be encouraged.

Affirmation of Return

Affirm for yourself: *I choose to succeed in the world and in the spirit at the same time . . .*
- What does this mean to you?
- What would you do to manifest this affirmation on a daily basis?
- What would change at work?
- What would change at home?
- What would change in your mind?

discuss and share with the world: *You are coming into your soul.* And that is exactly what is required because your life is changed and only your soul can adequately respond to the capabilities the journey has created in you. It is not the stuff of annual holiday letters to college buddies and far-flung aunts and uncles.

Return presents us with the need to reassess a number of things about our lives: everything from lifestyle to relationships to direction. I took a lot of clothes to the resale shop because I couldn't stand the colors I'd been wearing. I changed my hair. I changed my eating and exercise habits. I changed the type of meditation I practiced. I let some old friendships go, as clearly as I could, and found myself not sure how to make new ones. There were vacuums in my life, things that had faded away during the time I'd been "gone," and details I'd picked up I didn't even know where. I found a worshiping community that felt like home and went back to church.

I remember standing in my kitchen talking to a friend on the phone, crying and saying, "I've crossed a line in my life and I don't know anything about life on this side of the line—not who I am, not what I will do for meaningful work, not who will be with me. I have some desires about who and what I hope will come along, but no surety whatsoever." That's the way return is: we have no surety whatsoever, except for the faith in the journey we have developed along the way.

No one seems quite sure what this point is, only that it spontaneously occurs. We are not able, forever, to stay at the deepest points of journey. We are destined to wake up one day and find ourselves plunged back into the ordinariness of things.

Fortunately, as journal writers with a long habit of thinking to ourselves on the page, we have a kind of lifeline to our own writing, which helps us keep our bearings.

What we are in need of is story—a new story that integrates spiritual experience and our lives. Many books on spiritual journey talk about this point of return, but few speak of it in any other terms than metaphor and symbolism: "seeing the world with new

After one arrives at the summit, after going through the total transformation of being . . . there is yet one more step to the completion of that journey: the return to the valley below, to the everyday world. Who it is that returns is not who began the climb in the first place. The being that comes back is quietness itself, is compassion and wisdom, is the truth of the ages. Whatever humble or elevated position that being holds within the community, he or she becomes a light for others on the way, a statement of the freedom that comes from having touched the top of the mountain.

—Ram Dass
Journey of Awakening

JOURNAL ENTRY

On the slopes of Mount Kilimanjaro: Mountain. Goddess. God. Woman. Mother . . . At the summit your forehead is barren. Rocks are all that live. Blinding light. Snow and sun keep me from seeing your beauty. I cannot see your eye of wisdom. I am blinded. The hills in the distance look soft and lush, bathed in beauty. An eternity of sky intervenes. I climb your surface traversing your steps, difficult mouth and nose . . . openings I climb around and over, not in, not seeing or imaging your passageways. What keeps me on the surface path, so afraid that I do not notice the openings around my feet? I cannot stay at the summit. You are too bright. Too dazzling. You take my breath away. You blind my eyes. Your magnificence is too much for me, too intense to see, to touch, to feel.

I have to come down. There is the lushness of life in the rain forest, the promise and temptation of enlightenment at the top— discovered to be barren, yet filled with austere wisdom. Life is to be lived in the middle, colorful places. Go beneath the surface, the obvious path, and experience richness and beauty in your human womb of existence.

310

eyes," "descending from the mountaintop to the valley below," "re-entering the village of life." We seem unable, at least at first, to tell the truth straight out. At first, we're too close to it yet to know what it is, and then, as we do begin to see it, it sounds absurd, even to our own ears. And there's the little matter of survival and credibility. People who come down from mountaintops and tell the waiting community they've been having a lovely chat with God haven't always received the kindest of welcomes. We do need to tell our experience, but return is the point when we are learning *how* to tell. So, we practice telling the fable of our journey, allowing elements to first appear in metaphor and symbolism of our own and slowly teach ourselves to speak a language of transformation that we are willing to communicate.

For eventually that is what return becomes—communication. Those who travel to the edge of experience are charged to bring back wisdom, leadership, and action to the community. In traditional hero myths, the hero is driven to leave by the awareness that his/her secular culture is dying and is in desperate need of spiritual rejuvenation. The hero takes on the quest to learn what this rejuvenation might be. Inherent in such quest from the beginning is the willingness and commitment to return and teach, return and lead, return and contribute.

Our secular culture *is* destroying the planet. People *are* crying out for guidance, you and I among them. But this is no longer the age of the singular hero who will travel our hardships for us—this is the age when the ordinary person takes up the voyage, takes up the obligations of return, becomes a person of power.

22. FINDING YOUR PEOPLE

*Life has taught us that love does not consist of gazing
at each other, but in looking outward together in the
same direction. There is no comradeship except through
union in the same high effort.*

—*Antoine de Saint Exupéry*
Wind, Sand and Stars

We lose a lot of people on the spiritual quest, and we find a lot of people. Through the work in the forgiveness chapter, we have practiced saying good-bye as clearly as we can. Just as we have no ritual for leavetaking, so we also have no ritual for greeting. We have not been taught, or encouraged, to make relationships based on clear contracts. Even in relationships that are not romantic, a romanticized expectation seems to apply: Good friendships are just supposed to

Friendly Inventory

* Write a definition of the word *friend*.
* List all your current friends.
* Write a brief history of your friendship and how it has evolved.
* Why are you still friends?
* What kinds of things do you get from them?
* What kinds of things do you give?
* Are there changes you want to make in each friendship?
* What (if anything) still seems to be missing in your friendship group?
* What are you looking for?

JOURNAL ENTRY

I thought I had lots of friends until L. died. Somehow her death seemed to suck my sense of friendship away with it. As I grieved I realized her death was symbolic of the end of a kind of friendship—the great, good palship of growing ourselves up together. We went through therapy at the same time, railed at our families together, lovers, work, all the early life crises. Now I can't replace her because I can't replace that time in my life or my comfort with our old intimacy. So, here I am trying to sort out who is left, and who is out there I haven't met yet. And I feel so shy. Want to be careful. Want to arrive fresh, without trailing the whole long, messy story of my journey like a tattered blanket behind me.

. . . rejoice in your growth, in which you naturally can take no one with you, and be kind to those who remain behind, and be sure and calm before them and do not torment them with your doubts and do not frighten them with your confidence or joy . . .

—Rainer Maria Rilke
Letters to a Young Poet

happen. Good business relationships, partnerships, committee memberships, are all supposed to develop spontaneously. All relationships have a contract, a number of contracts. When looking for people who can provide meaningful companionship in our life of return, we need to draw up a clear contract, so that more time and energy can be spent on communication, play, and work.

Finding your people means exploring in your journal what you are looking for, and then clearly proceeding into the world to find other living, breathing, evolving human beings who are interested in traveling in similar directions.

We learn to make relationships in progression. As children, we size up other kids on the playground, bring over a toy and find out, in a few minutes, whether or not the chemistry works. In adolescence, we make friends by shared interest and activity, by shared secrets and values, and the common stance of rebellion we have adopted toward the adult world. There is a long period of adult life when friends are based on stages of growth. We make friends who have similar jobs, dating patterns, who may be married or not, who have children the same age, common career goals and leisure interests. If we go through therapy or crisis we find friendships where we can spend intense hours talking about problems, insights, breakthroughs, where we can develop histories of shared confidentiality and successful problem solving.

For months in the early stages of return, I felt as though all my life experience relating to other people no longer applied. I had one close friend left from the days of mutual crisis support. We had a long trust record but were no longer tracking each other's crises as the basis of friendship. I was part of a close circle of women writers who talked about our lives and work. I had a group of fairly new friends and acquaintances, people I'd come to know in the midst of my spiritual withdrawal, seekers who liked to take walks or lean over the lunch table and share views of the cosmos, though we didn't always know much about each other's daily lives. I remained close to my partner and to my brother's family. I worked with students and kept up basic networking with professional col-

Family Inventory

- Define the word *family.*
- According to your definition, who is really in your family?
- How can you help your family relationships accommodate all your spiritual journeys?
- What family obligations do you choose to carry forward into this phase of life?
- What kinds of things do you get from your family? What kinds of things do you give?

> *If the family were a container, it would be a nest, an enduring nest, loosely woven, expansive, and open.*
>
> *If the family were a fruit, it would be an orange, a circle of sections, held together but separable—each segment distinct.*
>
> *If the family were a boat, it would be a canoe that makes no progress unless everyone paddles.*
>
> *If the family were a sport, it would be baseball: a long, slow, nonviolent game that is never over until the last out.*
>
> *If the family were a building, it would be an old but solid structure that contains human history, and appeals to those who see the carved moldings under all the plaster, the wide plank floors under the linoleum, the possibilities.*
>
> *—Letty Cottin Pogrebin*

leagues. If I looked the same to others, I certainly didn't feel the same. I felt like a stranger in a strange land, bringing a set of social customs with me that were totally outside my awareness—so that I didn't know how I looked from the outside and didn't understand my responses from the inside. It wasn't very comfortable, but it gave me time to think. My thinking is still in process.

I decided that while I treasured the relationships that survived from these other periods of my life, that when making new relationships I couldn't go back and use old techniques for greeting. I couldn't remember, anymore, how my old best friend and I got to be best friends. I couldn't remember how I made friends in college. I couldn't imagine telling my life history to someone as a way of saying hello. All these forms of greeting, which had once felt so appropriate, now felt as antiquated as grabbing a box of crayons and walking across the kindergarten room. But I didn't know what new forms of greeting might be appropriate.

I'm not alone in this social puzzlement. Many people are emerging from introspection with the desire for different kinds of relationships and aren't sure how to make connections based on autonomy and spiritual journey. We're going to have to invent new ways of greeting and new customs for maintaining relationships that support us wherever we go.

To begin getting my social footing again, I made a list of what I intend to bring to new relationships. These are my commitments as I worked them out in the journal:

1. I will maintain appropriate boundaries. I will recognize and honor the boundaries of others.
2. I will take responsibility for my own journey, my own personal issues. I will make and accept amends as we go without drama.
3. I offer and accept compassion and support without trying to improve, fix, solve, or critique.
4. I take responsibility for my own energy and how I interpret it. I will not manipulate my energy or make assumptions that I don't check out.

Basic Contracts

- What do you want to bring to your relationships, old and new?
- What do you want others to bring?

JOURNAL ENTRY

Thank God for my friend, D. After three hours of tea and conversation, a walk around her city block, I feel so blessed. We seem not to have gathered a messy history around us, in spite of knowing each other through 15 years which have certainly been messy periods for us in other ways. That we love and respect each other is without question, and almost without notice, so calm are the waters between us.

Maybe that is part of the reason people project needs and expectations onto so many of the other people they love: it creates drama, and there's a certain deliciousness to drama, a heightened awareness that seems worth the accompanying pain.

But I'm at a time in my life where I will trade turbulence for calm. All my closest friendships are based on our ability to greet each other in the eye of the storm. For none of our lives are calm. We are speeding through midlife in what seems to be a 20-year roller-coaster ride. I want to go to my friends for a few hours of sanity, to talk and listen, to have my life held in someone else's mind, to hold theirs, to provide some kind of helpful commentary, to signal love. . . . When I couldn't get to sleep last night, I decided to spend my last moments awake calling to mind the faces of everyone I love, thanking them for being in my life and asking God to bless them. It was a wonderful way to end the day.

You be perfectly you, let me be perfectly me: uniquely and mutually flawed. And together we can discover what it is to be human, and what two humans might be capable of being together.

—Joy Houghton

5. I am only interested in equal relationships where empowerment is mutual. We both teach the other: we both learn.

Out of this sorting, over several months' time, I began to ask the questions that show up as journal exercises throughout this chapter. Over and over people tell me they are looking for closer friends, for a partner, for clearer communication at work, at home, at church. We seem mystified about how to go about this. The mystery is: Why won't we be direct? Why are these taboos so ingrained it doesn't occur to us to think contractually about our relationships with each other at the beginning? We know, in retrospect, when relationships go wrong, that it was the contract that was broken, changed, avoided. After a while, if we reflect on it, we can often see what the contract was: "You didn't take care of me, even though I kept taking care of you." "I was going to be your special friend, and then you met Jane and I got jealous." "You were supposed to be willing to put family money into the venture if the start-up capital wasn't sufficient." "I joined this organization to get attention and I'm not getting enough . . ." And so it goes. Maybe the reason we don't make clear contracts at the beginning of relationships is that we become ashamed when they don't work out. However, each of these contracts, if they had been negotiated clearly, would have greatly increased the probability of the relationship's working. It's all a matter of where and how you're willing to take your risks: up front, or at the end.

My list is just my own. You, in your journal, can devise a list that feels appropriate to you and what you're ready to offer. This will neither make you a perfect human being nor lead to finding perfect human beings, at least it hasn't worked that way for me. Carrying such a list in mind may even make your mistakes more glaring, exposed, embarrassing when there is such an obvious shortfall between intention and reality. But overall, I believe directness helps. It rebalances the social world. It introduces autonomy into relationships where we might not have thought to ask for it, or assume it. By this point in our journeys, no leaders are left. There

*. . . humanity is truly at an evolutionary choice point: we know
in our hearts that we are either going to have to grow up very
fast, change ourselves in radical ways, or we will destroy
ourselves and perhaps the entire planetary ecosystem as well. We
have a desperate need for greater awareness of our own inner
dynamics and processes if we are going to survive the twentieth-
century global crisis.*

—Ralph Metzner
Opening to Inner Light

• Whom are you looking for?

*I need two new people in my life, a playmate and a mentor. I
want to find someone who has a healthy sense of fun, with whom
I can pick up the playful parts of my life again. I want to find
someone who understands the part of the business world I'm in
and can help me make some wise career decisions.*

• Where are they?

*To find my playmate, I'm going to look at the folk dance club,
I'm going to enroll in some of those one-night adult education
courses that have an element of playfulness about them, I'm going
to check out volunteering at the comedy gallery, and I'm just
going to start announcing to groups of people—like at parties I
get invited to—what kinds of things sound fun to me and see if
any playmates emerge.*
*To find my mentor, I'm going to start asking everybody, Who is
already good in this business? I'm going to go in and out of
shops and meetings, call the Chamber of Commerce, check out
business leaders in the library, attend an introductory meeting of
organizations I might want to join.*

are teachers who are peers. We have assumed our authority by listening to our inner voice, and that voice must continue to direct us in our social lives.

Directness is also a way to establish compassionate boundaries around relationships that are more limited. I have friends and relatives who aren't likely ever to sit down and negotiate contracts with me, either from my list of what I bring and want or from the list below. I still love these people; I just don't need to have the same kind of relationship with them, or they with me. My ninety-eight-year-old grandmother is proud I write books, even if she's not interested in reading them. That is enough for us. We have long understood the affection between us, and I, at least, understand its limitations. We have a relationship that is respectful of who we are.

Each of our life circumstances is different. The list below and the exercises on the facing pages allow us to look at our lives and determine what we are looking for.

1. WHO ARE YOU LOOKING FOR?

This is a chance to ask yourself who's missing in your life and what qualities you seek. You may value trustworthiness over any other quality. Great. What does that mean? How will you recognize it? What kinds of trustworthiness have you got to offer?

Everything is an equal exchange of energy. This is how the universe works. To be clear in contracting with people, we need to know what the exchange is and be ready and willing to offer an equal exchange. There are no free rides. The private list I developed in my journal is an open definition of what I'm willing to exchange; it needs to be carried out very specifically.

2. WHERE ARE YOU LIKELY TO FIND THEM?

Once you are clear who you are looking for and what you are willing to exchange, where are these people likely to hang out? If you don't know, start asking around. I found my church community because a friend who knew the kind of seeking I've been doing

- How are you going to greet them?

> *With my playmate, I think we can set up some open and fun
> contracts right away. . . . Do you want to go canoeing? Do you
> want to try roller skating? We'll get a sense of the territory pretty
> easily.*
>
> *With my mentor, I want to be just as open, but more laid back
> and mature—this is not a contract between two nine-year-olds.
> And it's not a contract where I want to be relating to a father or
> mother figure either—I want a mentor, not a surrogate parent. So
> I think I need to state clearly what kinds of mentoring I'm
> looking for, and that I'm interested in seeing that she or he gets
> something back from me. And not just flattery. Something real.
> I need to do more writing about this as I do my research. I think
> the research will help me get clearer.*

- Then what are you going to do?

> *With my playmate, we set up a time to go play and see how we
> get along in the actual activity. Like, last year I wanted someone
> to go for walks with, but when I asked Susie, I found out we
> walk at such different speeds, we just laughed and decided we
> weren't the right partners on that front.*
>
> *With my mentor, I want to spend several hours a month getting
> business advice, to see him or her once a month for lunch—my
> treat—and to have him or her available by phone at a level we
> both feel comfortable with. We can let it develop from there. I
> want to negotiate clearly every step of the way, so that this feels
> empowering to both of us.*

asked if I'd like to join him one Sunday. This is a community full of the kinds of people I'm grateful to know. There are social-cause organizations, social services, interest groups, community agencies—get creative and talk to people. Ask them where they get their support. Ask them how they found their own community. Go back and look in chapter 1 for guidelines in starting a journal group. Start, or join, a book club. If you tacked a sign on a bulletin board saying, "I'm reading *Life's Companion: Journal Writing as a Spiritual Quest,* anyone want to join me?" what do you think would happen?

3. HOW ARE YOU GOING TO TALK TO THEM, GREET THEM?

As you find your people, you will need to decide what you say after you say hello. You need to check them out, and you need to offer them the opportunity to check you out. You first—you're the one who's done the journal work, who has the agenda. If your *gentle* directness is responded to well, then you both take the next step, whatever is appropriate to the situation.

Not only does exchange need to be equal, it needs to be compatible. If one of you is looking for a lover and one is looking for a friend and another is looking for a volunteer to work in the soup kitchen, some contracting and negotiating better occur quickly so communication stays clear. Make sure you are listening as clearly for their contracts as you are presenting your own.

4. IF YOU AGREE YOU ARE LOOKING FOR EACH OTHER, THEN WHAT?

A relationship is made up of things people do together. We have friends we talk with, friends we go to the movies with, friends we march for worthy causes with, friends we meditate with, etc. In some friendships we do more than one thing, in some only one. Not only do we contract for general qualities, we contract for activities, for how time is spent together, what level of intimacy is expected.

- How will you support each other's dreams?

> *The purpose of play is to go out and be happy—no matter what else is going on, to lay down cares and have fun for a while. This shouldn't be hard to support in each other, and I don't mind if we become close enough friends to talk about real things while playing. I like that kind of complexity.*
>
> *The purpose of mentoring is to validate the level of expertise someone has developed, and to use it wisely. I can support my mentor's dreams by acknowledging accomplishment and talking about what he or she wants to do next, as well as letting them be genuinely helpful to me.*
>
> *We see God in each other, or not at all.*
>
> *—William Dorn*

Finding Community

- Define the word *community*.
- What is your idea of spiritual community.
- Envision and write about your ideal community?
- What do you do together? What do you provide each other? What are the concerns, beliefs, actions, that bind and motivate you?
- What diversity of people do you want in your community?
- Where do you already have community in your life? How can you add to this?

5. HOW WILL YOU SUPPORT EACH OTHER'S DREAMS AND GOALS?

Whatever ways we end up relating, we need to support each other's dreams, however that's appropriate. There are women I play racquetball with, and most of what we know about each other has to do with the game, but we support the dreams that relate to improving the game. There are friends whose lives I know intimately, and the support we offer each other reflects that level of intimacy.

In finding our people, we are experimenting with new ways of being in the world. There are over five billion people on this planet. How we relate to each other has long been in need of change. We start in the small circle of our lives and slowly expand outward. If directness works with one person, with five people, a committee, a journal group, then maybe it will work with a precinct caucus, a PTA, a city council, an organization. Maybe we can begin demanding that leaders and officials negotiate with us, speak directly, tell the truth, keep commitments, reflect honest values and act on them.

There is part of the journey we cannot do internally and we cannot do alone: we need community. Directness is one way to find and develop it. I wish you well in your finding, and look forward to seeing you somewhere along the way.

23. CHOOSING YOUR STAND

You are only as powerful as that for which you stand. Do you stand for more money in the bank and a bigger house? Do you stand for an attractive mate? Do you stand for imposing your way of thinking upon others? These are the stands of the personality seeking to satisfy its wants. Do you stand for perfection, for the beauty and compassion of each soul? Do you stand for forgiveness and humbleness? These are the stands of the personality that has aligned itself with its soul. This is the position of a truly powerful personality.

—*Gary Zukav*
The Seat of the Soul

I like to vacation on small islands. I love the chance to explore in miniature a piece of land surrounded by sea. There is one mountain, one forest, one village, one valley. It's like having my own personal planet, just the right size to comprehend how interconnected everything is, and how precious. When the rain comes, when the wind blows, when the crops grow or fail, when the fish bite or don't, everything is clearly affected. An island is small, the same size as my compre-

The Earth, its life am I,
The Earth, its feet are my feet,
The Earth, its legs are my legs,
The Earth, its body is my body,
The Earth, its thoughts are my thoughts,
The Earth, its speech is my speech.

—Navajo chant

Thinking in Life-Forms

- If you were not human, what animal would you be?
- What landscape?
- What kind of tree?
- What would you say to yourself if you were a river?
- What kind of weather are you today?
- Draw in the journal, from the point of view of the bottom of the ocean, the heart of a volcano, the center of the earth.

The universe is not made in jest but in solemn incomprehensible earnest. By a power that is unfathomably secret, and holy, and fleet. There is nothing to be done about it, but ignore it or see. And then you walk fearlessly, eating what you must, growing wherever you can.

—Annie Dillard
Pilgrim at Tinker Creek

Dear Gaia

- Write a love letter to the planet.
- If you could give her anything, what would it be?

hension. So I can also see how *my* presence affects everything. The water I use, the flower I pick, the berries I eat, the garbage I create, the people I join, must all be dealt with respectfully. I like the experience of microcosm, but I always feel vulnerable, aware of the fragility of life itself. An island changes me: it changes my heart.

I am an earthling. I love the earth. We cannot trade in the earth, as though it were an old car we are trying to ditch before the expense of major repairs. This planet is our home. And more than that, it is our Self. We are one here. We are molecular structures that have evolved into a wide variety of forms, but that bear the blueprint of our common origin, the cauldron of matter that was our birth. If we love ourselves and honor our journeys, we also need to love the earth and honor her journey.

The point of returning is to *do* something. From the depths of the spiritual spiral, we are drawn back into the world in order to act. That is our calling, what shaman Don Juan called "choosing a path with a heart." *Spiritual growth is not complete until it directs us to spiritual action.*

Generativity, the art of giving back, is our most profound human agenda. Generativity comes from allowing our hearts to open to a cause, to accept a challenge because it seems ours to accept. Whatever other dreams and purpose we have discovered, during the point of return we will also discover a need to give something significant back to the world—to be generative.

There are plenty of causes to choose from. There are plenty of needs to be met. There is an active role waiting for us to step forward. The thing is, to sustain the action, we need to do it because our hearts open up and direct us, not from guilt or shame or obligation. This creates a strange kind of tension in the spiritual traveler.

We are assailed all the time by causes. Every day's mail brings another plea for money. The phone rings and someone wants us to volunteer time and energy, to walk around the block for the heart fund, to write letters for Amnesty International, to help at the homeless shelter, to set out clothes and household items to be picked up by the Goodwill; the list is endless. We often respond

Living in Time

• Write about the five most significant historical
events that have occurred in your lifetime.
• Write about five historical events beyond your
lifetime that intrigue you.
• What do you think about your place in history?
Where do you see yourself fitting in?

JOURNAL ENTRY
*Three workmen are taking down six cottonwoods that have been
crowding the southeast corner of the house and dropping limbs on
the roof. They need to go. Several are rotten, hollowed out by
ants, old age, too many seasons. Yet they are magnificent trees,
seventy feet tall with mammoth trunks and a troop of high
rustlers—graceful, swaying limbs.*
*On the coffee table, this week's Newsweek talks about the
greenhouse effect, the damage of deforestation. I read it
accompanied by the buzz of chain saws as six oxygen producers
come down from the half acre of earth in my care.*
*How quickly these blades work. A wedge cut here, there on the
trunk, controlling its fall exactly between the pine and the
telephone pole. No wonder men go into the forests and do not
stop: it's so powerful an act. What took 10, 20, 50, 100 years
to grow, a man takes down in 5, 10, 20 minutes.*
*We are having a drought. I feel a drive toward activism rising in
me again. I am looking around my insular little life with new
concern. My lawn is parched, my cottonwoods rotting, my pond
polluted. The earth and I are coming to an agonizing
consciousness together through these hot and sunny days: the
malaise of the planet is very deep, deeper than my own malaise. I
must act. I go out to walk among the fallen giants, touch their
severed trunks, thank them. Tell them good-bye.*

to these requests, send off a small donation, sort the clothes, write the letter, but I, at least, know that my heart is not always in these duties. I often do them because I feel it is my obligation to do them. It's part of what I give back for the privilege of having enough money to pay most of my bills and keep a roof over my head. This is necessary maintenance; it is correct response, but it's not generative.

Generativity occurs when the heart leaps up and declares to us: *This is my cause, this is what I take on. I do not want to pass through life without trying to correct and love this particular situation.* For many people wandering around in the point of return, we aren't quite there yet. We haven't found our cause, or we haven't found the heart's connection to it. We are practicing on the small stuff, waiting for the link between heart and action to be made. We are waiting for passion. We believe that something is coming, but we're not sure of the form. A friend recently emerging from a time of spiritual crisis wrote that she is filled with hope and a sense of destiny—but she doesn't know what it is—and neither do I.

We are living in the first epoch of human history where *every* human being is asked to be generative. Where the species as a whole is challenged to make great, evolutionary leaps in our understanding of what we give and what we take. The island of the earth is shrinking. Our interconnectedness is clear on a global scale. What I think we are waiting for is our hope.

In October 1962, when John Kennedy and Nikita Khrushchev were deciding whether or not to blow up the world, I was sixteen years old. This confrontation, known as the Cuban Missile Crisis, is the closest we've ever come to willfully annihilating ourselves— letting two men sit in offices on opposite sides of the world, with their trigger fingers very near a red button. There was a moment during those days of mounting tension, probably just after Kennedy appeared on our small black-and-white television to tell us what was going on and that he hoped we'd all be here in the morning, that I took a metal letter box, filled it with my report card, a picture of my house and family, a few mementos, and my journal, and buried it in the woods behind the backyard. If we did blow ourselves

*Because everything we do and everything we are is in jeopardy,
and because the peril is immediate and unremitting, every person is
the right person to act and every moment is the right moment to
begin.*

—Jonathan Schell

*A global awakening can only happen from a spiritual awakening
that is of global dimensions.*

—Matthew Fox
Original Blessing

Witnessing

- Set aside a place in your journal where you note
world events.
- Include press clippings, photos, commentaries—
whatever seems important to you.
- Write brief responses to headlines.
- Develop rituals that help you build a relationship
with what you record.
- Develop rituals to remind yourself of your "place"
in the world.
- Write letters of condolence, concern, and
celebration to world events.
- Create a way of blessing, or praying for, all living
things.

*It's only when we have nothing else to hold onto that we're
willing to try something very audacious and scary; only when
we're free of the allure, the enticements, the familiar and
comfortable lies of the patriarchy will we be able to alter our
perspective enough, change our feelings enough, gather enough
courage to see and grab the next rope and continue our journey
home.*

—Sonia Johnson
Going Out of Our Minds: The Metaphysics of
Liberation

332

up, I wasn't sure who I expected would find this time capsule—maybe Martians, maybe huge intelligent cockroaches.

The game of nuclear brinkmanship was over in a week. I plunged back into denial, dug up my journal, and lined up a date for the Sadie Hawkins Day dance. But more was buried in that hole than the words and trinkets of my adolescence, and it's taken me many years to retrieve the intangibles I left there—to retrieve my hope.

We generate hope by choosing to follow our hearts into a cause and focusing on a desired outcome. In the journal, we include news of the world. We use differing journal formats to experiment with the relationship between our inner lives and the events of the world constantly happening around us. As the connection to activism occurs, we allow "our cause" to enter our lives, our writing, our time. It is not necessary to choose a life of dramatic sacrifice: *it is necessary that we discover what we will love that is beyond our own concerns, and love it actively.*

To work in the world lovingly means that we are defining what we will be *for*, rather than reacting to what we are against. To be *for* something gives us the perspective to see things close up and to see them in the long perspective. To define what we're *for* also requires specificity—clarifying the piece of the vision we assume as our responsibility. This clarity often starts in the journal and moves outward from there into action.

We start new actions from a stance of naïveté—hearts open, we step confidently forth, hoping for quick success. I remember this surge of hope from my time in the 1960s, when I politically opposed the war in Vietnam. There came into the campus office of Clergy and Laity Concerned, where I worked, a group of photographs of napalmed Vietnamese children. These pictures were so heart-wrenching I was absolutely sure that once the Congress saw them, they would be moved to end the conflict, bring home the young men, make restitution to these children and their families. If I had been in power, that is how I would have responded. But I was not in power, and that is not how they responded. I buried my hope again for a while.

- Keep a list, add clippings, write about the good
things happening that give you hope day by day
- Write about people responding with activist
spirituality.
- Look for role models of action and learn from
them.
- What about these activities attracts you?
- What are these people doing that seems helpful?
- What do they inspire you to do?
- What dreams of contribution do you have?
- What do you love enough to let go of? to sacrifice
for?
- How have you changed your life already?
- What are you preparing yourself to change further?

JOURNAL ENTRY

I am making my stand with the garbage. Every Thursday when I carry the bags down to the end of the driveway, my satisfaction at cleaning out the house is destroyed by my grief for the earth. I see in my mind the mountains and valleys of garbage I help create. I cannot do this anymore!

I recycle all the newspaper, cans, and glass. Still there is too much. It's those plastics, the things they used to put in glass and now make unrecyclable. I walk around the grocery store with a pad of Post-it notes, writing to the manager: I will not buy this product because of its wasteful packaging.

One day I took a box full of my own jars, and paper bags, paid for my groceries, then sat down to free my food from plastic, Styrofoam, and other excesses, explaining to everyone what I was doing. Other shoppers were sympathetic. The manager wanted to know if I was trying to get on the news. I told him, "This is your garbage, I don't want it."

I write manufacturers and boycott poorly packaged products. I go through dumpsters full of cardboard, load up the station wagon and drive to the recycling center. I will not stop!

We need hope, clarity, and heart to keep acting when we run into difficulties. In any cause, complexities that we did not anticipate appear. We may need to be able to self-generate hope for a number of years in order to keep acting steadfastly toward our goals. This is one of the marks of spiritual leadership: hope seems to come from the vision, rather than the immediate circumstances. As Martin Luther King used to say, "Keep your eyes on the prize."

I didn't understand this in my early twenties, and neither did many young people in my generation. Those without the spiritual grounding to regenerate lost hope fairly quickly and became angry, frustrated, sometimes violent. Eventually, many of us withdrew in confusion and began the long process of finding maturity, which has taken most of our available time and resources the past twenty years. But we are emerging again, and we're not spiritual "kids."

There is a crisis point in activism, when because of the complexities our efforts may seem to fail. We need to expect this and be ready to cope with it in a spiritual context. When this occurs, the solution to our discouragement is to become more communal in focus. This is the point we are at now: where many individuals of good-hearted concern are disorganized, discouraged, and in need of a viable, activist community. This doesn't simply mean showing up at meetings; it means trusting others enough to submit our cause to larger purpose.

When we have taken our cause and isolated it as our burden, become ego-bound with it, we have the least hope. We see that we are small, often ineffectual individuals, and the problem remains large and complex. We get overwhelmed. "How am I ever going to make a difference?" we wonder. "I am trying to be for bread and justice, but the world keeps breaking my heart." We don't have to take up our cause alone; in fact, we can't do it alone.

Group process restores hope by joining our action and ideas with other people's actions and ideas. Maybe one original idea for solving a problem simply doesn't work, or needs resources that can't be mustered alone, or that might be improved with input. Suppose the journal writer tackling the plastics in her local grocery store

Think Globally, Act Locally

- What do you think this means?
- What are you willing to let it mean to you?
- In what ways are you already thinking globally?
- Acting locally?

> *Holistic society is coming upon us from a variety of sources that cut across the traditional left-right political axis. Feminism, ecology, ethnicity, and transcendentalism (spiritual renewal) which ostensibly have nothing in common, appear to be converging toward a common goal. . . . Their goal is the recovery of our bodies, our health, our sexuality, our natural environment, our archaic traditions, our unconscious mind, our rootedness in the land, our sense of community and connectedness to one another. What they advocate is the direct attempt to get back from the past what we lost in the past four centuries: the attempt to recover our future.*
>
> —*Morris Berman*
> The Reenchantment of the World

Ethics and Action

- Write about times you refused to do something because it went against your ethics.
- Write about times you've taken a stand, helped others take a stand, and how it made you feel.
- What action are you ready to take?
- Who can act with you?
- What kinds of support are available in your family? among friends? your community?
- What cause do you choose in love and passion for survival?
- How can you do what you need to do with joyfulness?

joined or formed a radical recycling group that had an impact on all the grocery stores in the area, and a letter campaign to the manufacturers and local governments caused a significant chain reaction. And suppose when this woman wears down, when the baby is sick, there is someone else there who can pick up the standard a while. And suppose that every tactic that fails serves as the taking-off point for brainstorming for another tactic. As my friend Jerry Allan says, "Anything worth doing, is worth doing wrong for awhile."

Somewhere out there in the world right now are people who will solve the problems we now only dream are resolvable, and they will not do it alone. They are in need of every one of us—to gather pieces of information that contribute to understanding the whole picture, to practice trial and error, to sustain the pressure and determination that keeps issues in the forefront of our minds. These may be scientists working to discover new plants to feed the world's hungry, cures for diseases, ways to reduce garbage to usable fuel or neutralize radioactive waste. These may be political leaders working to devise more equitable forms of government and distribution of resources. These may be social leaders insisting on reforms from within. These may be spiritual leaders that help us make the quantum leaps necessary to refashion the world.

Every one of us who is willing actively to love the question, contributes something vital to the knowledge that will provide the answer. We don't have to struggle alone. We don't have to be the one out front. We just need to be willing to do our part and take our place. We need to lead when we are able, and follow when we are able. I'm following the words and actions of people ahead of me, and leaving words and actions for people following me. And you leave words and actions for people following you, and they leave words and actions for those who follow them.

We are interconnected human adventurers, five billion Hansels and Gretels. All that is asked of us is that we trust each other enough to take the hand before us and offer a hand to the one behind us. The rest is history—and the future.

24. FAITH IN THE PROCESS

What we call the beginning is often the end
And to make an end is to make a beginning.
The end is where we start from.

—*T. S. Eliot*
Four Quartets

There is no graduation ceremony at the end of this book. We will have to make our own rituals, not for ending, but for the beginnings we make from endings, the places where we start from, over and over again.

There came a journey . . . And we have reached the place we longed for when we began. We have succeeded. We have come to the edge of all we know and all we believe and all we can endure and all we can wonder about, and we have—again and again—found new firmament beneath our feet so that we could take one more step. And this is how we continue: Stepping into the unknown, stepping off the perceptual cliff, to find that there *is* something

*The Great Father is a shepherd chief. I am his and with him I
want not. He throws out to me a rope and the name of the rope is
love, and he draws me to where the grass is green and the water
good. I eat and lie down satisfied. Sometimes my heart is weak
and falls down, but he lifts it up again and draws me onto a
good road. His name is Wonderful. Sometime, it may be soon, it
may be longer, it may be a long, long time, he will draw me into
a place between the mountains. It is dark there, but I will not
draw back. I will not be afraid, for it is there between these
mountains that the Shepherd Chief will meet me and the hunger I
have felt in my heart all through this life will be satisfied . . .*

—*Psalms* 23
translated from Indian sign language

Making Endings and Beginnings

• Write your own creation myth. Meditate. Listen to
music. Lie upon the earth and ask for her story:
Where do you come from?
• Write your own ending myth. Meditate. Listen to
music. Let go of all you need to, and make a ritual of
leave-taking.
• Make your own chant of thankfulness. Sing these
words in the woods, in the car, while mowing the
lawn, tell your pets and teach your children.

there, that the ground will materialize under our feet as soon as we are ready to step on it—and not before. If this is not the usual way to walk around the block, by now we ought to have become accustomed to it, to have faith in the process.

What have we learned?

When we define a purpose as our own, we grow into the task.

When I was six, I desperately wanted a bicycle. In the Sears catalogs that came to the house, I circled the pictures of little red and blue bikes, complete with training wheels. My family didn't have much money at that time; in fact, I'm sure my parents were struggling to keep the rent paid and food on the table. One day a bicycle appeared—and it was not the bike of my dreams. It was huge, for one thing, a twenty-six-incher, fat tires, so heavy that I couldn't leave it on its side in the yard and lift it again on my own. It had rusting chrome fenders, was obviously secondhand. The seat, even in the lowest position, held me high above the pedals. I remember sitting on this useless throne while my father took blocks of wood, several of them on each side, and pounded them in place until I could reach the pedals and push. This was no learner's bike. I would get on and ride, or fall.

The journey is like this. We can underline and circle our hopes and expectations, but our purpose will always be different, will come with its own specifications, its own demands for what we need to learn. Watching my father doing the best he could with what he had, I asked him, "How am I going to ride this bike? It's too big. I'm afraid."

"Your legs will grow," he told me. "And you won't be so afraid once you have learned how to fall."

The questions we have of the journey change radically at points along the way, and yet they are still the basic fuel that drives us onward.

Our questions are always the dividing line between what we know and what we don't know. Now our questions are different from the ones that propelled us at the beginning. We are looking at different issues. Out of our questions, we have developed a dialogue of faith in the process that carries us forward.

Amazements

- Make a list of the things that most amaze you at this point in your journey.
- Do you want answers, or have you fallen in love with your amazement?
- Tell yourself and tell children your own stories about these mysteries.
- Ask them for their stories and help them write them down.

JOURNAL ENTRY

As the sun broke through scattering clouds, Joy and I went fishing at a nearby lake. The light, slanted at the end of the day, turned the tree next to us to light and filled the air with gold dust as it reflected thousands of shiny insect wings. I walked up the road to get a better view. Joy stood in the light, making a halo of herself against the minty twinkling tree and cast out a thread of light upon which the flapping silver fish would dangle until released back into the lake. I saw LIGHT. Everywhere, light. And I understood: the world is made of light, sustained by light, created and held together all in light. And in that moment I knew: I am the tree. I am Joy. I am the line and the fish and the lake. The air is alive and we are all one in the light.

God had illuminated me in both my eyes. By them I behold the splendor of light in the darkness. Through them I can choose the path I am to travel, whether I wish to be sighted or blind by recognizing what guide to call upon by day or by night.

—*Hildegard of Bingen*

When you don't know what to write about next, ask yourself: What's the next question?

I used to be afraid of questions, afraid that the sacred would be angry if I asked them, afraid that I might ask a question that indicated how faithless I was. But through the unending act of journal dialogue, questions have become an intimate conversation with life, with journey, with the sacred. Questions have become my friends, because I know they will bring me into a frame of mind where I can hear response, not the final answer, but the next response I need.

Little by little, in increments we can understand, we receive instructions, guidance, hope, help, support. We keep writing, because writing is an avenue through which the universe may talk with us. We keep talking, because sharing our questions and dreams is the way we tell others what we need, so that they can offer it to us.

Life is a great unending opportunity to see things differently, to keep reframing disaster and discouragement into faith.

There is pain and there is joy. There are hills and there are valleys. We are not always comfortable, but we can ride it out. We grow into our tasks through the act of reframing our discouragement and disasters. Every time we go through this process, we feel innocent and vulnerable, hopeful and unsure, and what we assume to be our weaknesses turn out to be our strengths. We have worked and worked on the blank page until we have become the blank page upon which life works.

And we have learned that we are not alone, and that we have never been alone.

The trade we made, giving up the ego and its fantasies of valiant, lonely struggle, is the opportunity to see ourselves as children of the universe on a great quest, this time with trust in the sacred, with trust in others, with trust in an expanded understanding of who we are.

When I first heard the phrase "life's companion" in my mind I thought it referred to the journal, this bit of a record we carry with us, tucked under our arms. As I began writing, I thought, "Life's companion is our consciousness, the awareness we bring to life

* Describe a time in your life when you felt new, unused, fresh.
* What was the feeling like? Was it frightening? wonderful? a little of both?
* What in your life right now could or does give you this feeling of newness?
* What could you create in your life that would give you this feeling?

Grace happens.

—Peter McDonald

events that teaches us to use them positively." As I wrote more, I thought, "Our life's companion is the sacred in all its forms explored here—the conditions of travel, the four guidances, the four practices." And now, as I stop writing, I believe life's companion is simpler than all this. Our life's companion is simply *help*. Because help will come. Help does come. Help cannot fail to come.

As long as we have help, we can do what we need to do. We are like Don Quixote, each choosing our windmill, and individually and together we go forth into the world to work for our heavenly causes.

The world will be better for this—and so will you and I.

Meditation

To prepare to use this meditation and others throughout the book, find a quiet place where you will not be interrupted for twenty minutes or so. Ask someone to read the meditation to you or to play back a version of the meditation you have made yourself or have ordered from the back of the book. The points of ellipses (. . .) indicate a significant pause—silence maintained within the text. Pause for as long as you feel comfortable; five to ten seconds can seem a long time in meditation. Double ellipses indicate a longer silence.

CHILD OF THE UNIVERSE

Close your eyes and relax your body. . . . Take all the time you need to get comfortable. . . . Shift muscles . . . stretch and relax. . . . Make sure your spine and neck are straight and aligned . . . not held stiffly. There is no stiffness here . . . just comfort, the beginning of calm. . . . There is no hurry now. . . . There is nothing else to do . . . or think about. . . . Just relax. . . . . . .

Notice your breath. . . . Let your breath enter deeply into your body. . . . Let your breath roll into you like soft, heavy clouds that fill you with silence. . . . Inhale slowly . . . deeply. . . . Exhale slowly . . . thoroughly. . . . Let your breath sink in and out. . . . Your breath is a rhythm of calm. . . . Follow your breath. . . . Exhale extraneous thought. . . . Inhale silence. . . .

Be still. . . . . . .

Be your breath. . . . . . .

Use your mind to follow your breath . . . . in . . . out . . . in . . . out. . . .

That is all. . . . . . .

Be your breath. . . . . . .

You were once a child. . . . And the child you were still resides within you. . . . . . . Invite this inner child to sit on your lap . . . . . . to sit with you in your breath. . . .

Place your hand palm up. . . . Invite the child to place its hands in your hands. . . . . . . Feel the child's hands in your hands . . . the fingers warm and trusting . . . nestled in your grown-up hands. . . . . . .

Be your breath. . . .

Be still. . . .

You are grown . . . and you are still a child. . . . You are a child of the universe. . . . Inside you, the Universal Parent resides. . . . Invite this parent, your Guardian/Companion, to sit with you in your breath. . . . . . .

Feel yourself placed in Its palms. . . . Feel the backs of your hands, resting in the larger palms of this universal support. . . . Feel the child's hands resting in your palms. . . . . . . You are sitting in the sacred lap, as surely as the child self sits in your lap. . . . . . .

Be still. . . . . . .

Be your breath. . . . . . .

You are filled with the source of all knowing. . . . You are attuned to your body, and your body is attuned to the universe. . . . . . . This is the light that you came from. . . . . . . This is the light you are traveling toward. . . . . . . Here, in the light, everything is all right. . . . . . .

When you are ready, follow your breath back to this room. . . . Emerge out of the silence of your body. . . . There is no hurry. . . . Stretch your body. . . . Open your eyes. . . . . . .

Take time to draw or write whatever you want to record from this silence.

End Piece

And it won't help any, it won't get us anywhere
   it won't wipe away what has been
   nor hold off what is to be
   if you hear me saying
   —LOVE is a little white bird—
   and the flight of it so fast
   you can't see it
   and you know it's there
   only by the faint whirr of its wings
   and the hush song coming so low to your ears
   you fear it might be silence
   and you listen keen and you listen long
   and you know it's more than silence
   for you get the hush song so lovely
   it hurts and cuts into your heart
   and what you want is to give more than you can get
   and you'd like to write it but it can't be written
   and you'd like to sing it but you don't dare try
   because the little white bird sings it better than you can

so you listen and while you listen you pray
and one day it's as though a great slow wind
had washed you clean and strong inside and out
and the little white bird's hush song
is telling you nothing can harm you,
the days to come can weave in and weave out
and spin their fabrics and designs for you
and nothing can harm you—
unless you change yourself into a thing of harm
nothing can harm you.

. . . .

I give you the little white bird—
and my thanks for your hearing me—
    and my prayers for you,
    my deep silent prayers.

—Carl Sandburg
"Little Word, Little White Bird"

Acknowledgments

A book is just a stack of paper, the outpourings of its author's mind, until it is shown and given access to the world that will bring it to print. So first, I want to thank the people at the beginning and the end of writing who helped me get this book into the world, agents Jonathon and Wendy Lazear, and Toni Burbank, executive editor, Bantam Doubleday Dell, her able assistant Linda Gross, and copy editor Katherine Balch.

I also want to thank the journal writers who have worked with me over the years in many classes, seminars, and lectures where we have thought together about the importance of personal writing. I especially thank those who entrusted me with pages of their private writing and gave me permission to include them here. They allowed this book to speak in many voices—which is as it should be.

I have done my best to thank people along the way and to acknowledge the blessings and lessons that have brought these thoughts together. Beyond this privacy, as the book goes into the hands of its readers, there are several people I want to thank publicly.

Thanks applies most deeply to Joy Houghton, long-time partner and friend, a woman of exceptional mind and insight. We call ourselves "amalgamated cranium," and this is the truest description of who we are and how we serve each other's thinking. This book could not have been done without her; it is partly her. It was my contract to put this journey down on paper, to frame it, write it, but we have thought through much of it together and shared its lessons.

Each draft has had its own support group. First draft, Cil Braun and Gayla Reger walked with me around and around the lakes of Minneapolis and its suburbs while I sorted my way toward prose. Second draft, my groups listened to me, my classes listened to me, Anne Ziff read the draft in Connecticut and offered good commentary. In the final rewriting process, I had additional support from Peter McDonald, Phyllis Bleiweis, Kathy Lewis, and Ellen Dubuque.

There are two groups of women who have supported my life and writing throughout: my writer's group—Judith Guest, Deborah Keenan, Rebecca Hill, Patricia Hampl—whom I want to thank for their friendship, for being there, for educating me about writing in a wonderful process of peer exchange. Deborah Keenan read this manuscript, helped me with quotes, journal writing suggestions, and advised me to "cut out the whacky esoteric phrases." Any such phrasing that has made it into the final text is not her responsibility. I also want to thank my spirituality group—Kathie Anderson, Cil Braun, Ellen Dubuque, Gayla Reger—for sharing insights and experiences from their own quests, and for their willingness to let the conversation drift around to whatever chapter I was working on.

Thank you to Todd Smelser, Susan Moss, and the community of Saint John the Baptist, for welcoming me home.

It is finished in beauty.

Christina Baldwin
Golden Valley, Minnesota
spring 1990

ABOUT THE AUTHOR

Since the mid-1970s, Christina Baldwin has been a leader of the renaissance in personal writing. Her first book, *One to One: Self-Understanding Through Journal Writing* (M. Evans, 1977), has become a national classic, and her seminars have helped thousands of people become journal writers.

Baldwin holds a bachelor's degree in English from Macalaster College, St. Paul, and master's degree in Psychology from Columbia Pacific University, San Rafael, California. She lives in Golden Valley, a suburb of Minneapolis.

Christina Baldwin's workshops offer a communal experience in writing, working, and playing with life transitions. Her primary goal, in both writing and teaching, is to empower readers and participants and to encourage people to apply their power toward social and spiritual change.

If you would like to book Christina Baldwin in your community, receive a schedule of upcoming appearances, or order meditation tapes, she can be reached through P.O. Box 27533, Minneapolis, MN 55427.